"An account of the shifting temporalities, spatialities, and formalities of African cinema by one of the finest scholars of African cultural productions. Kenneth W. Harrow rigorously redefines the contours of world cinema with a brilliant turn to the worldmaking projects of African films, running the gamut from video production to digital film. The resulting book is smartly historicist, formally innovative, and theoretically intelligent. Harrow has produced a field-shaping book."

—**Cajetan Iheka,** *Professor of English, Yale University*

"Harrow's book – original, eccentric, provocative – establishes African cinema from the long 1990s to the present as a singular, powerful alternative to world cinema. Translating from quantum mechanics to critical theory, Harrow brilliantly reframes key issues raised by postcolonial theory, deconstruction, and apparatus theory."

—**Carmelo Garritano,** *Associate Professor of International Affairs and Africana Studies, Texas A&M University*

AFRICAN CINEMA IN A GLOBAL AGE

This book traces the developments in African films that were made from the 1990s to the present within the evolving frame of what came to be called "World Cinema" and, eventually, "Global Cinema."

Kenneth W. Harrow explores how, from the time video and then digital technologies were introduced in the 1990s, and then again, when streaming platforms assumed major roles in producing and distributing film between the 2010s and 2020s, African cinema underwent enormous changes. He highlights how the introduction of the continent's first successful commercial cinema, Nollywood, shifted the focus from *engagé* films, with social or political messages, to entertainment movies, but also auteur cinema. Harrow explores how this transformation liberated African filmmakers and resulted in an incredible, enduring flow of creative, inventive, and thoughtful filmmaking. This book presents a number of those critical films that mark that trajectory, projecting a new sense of African film spaces and temporalities, while also highlighting how African films continue to find independent pathways.

This book will be of interest to students and scholars of African cinema and world cinema, as well as researchers specifically examining African cinemas and their relationship to globalization.

Kenneth W. Harrow is Emeritus Distinguished Professor of English at Michigan State University. His work focuses on African cinema and literature. He is the author of *Thresholds of Change in African Literature* (1993), *Less Than One and Double: A Feminist Reading of African Women's Writing* (2001), *Postcolonial African Cinema: From Political Engagement to Postmodernism* (2007), *Trash! A Study of African Cinema Viewed from Below* (2013), and *Space and Time in African Cinema and Cine-scapes* (2022). He also co-edited, with Carmela Garritano, *A Companion to African Film* (2018).

AFRICAN CINEMA IN A GLOBAL AGE

Kenneth W. Harrow

Routledge
Taylor & Francis Group

NEW YORK AND LONDON

Cover image: suteishi / Getty Images

First published 2024
by Routledge
605 Third Avenue, New York, NY 10158

and by Routledge
4 Park Square, Milton Park, Abingdon, Oxon, OX14 4RN

Routledge is an imprint of the Taylor & Francis Group, an informa business

ISBN: 978-1-032-50252-6 (hbk)
ISBN: 978-1-032-50251-9 (pbk)
ISBN: 978-1-003-39759-5 (ebk)

DOI: 10.4324/9781003397595

Typeset in Sabon
by Apex CoVantage, LLC

For Liz

CONTENTS

FIGURES

ACKNOWLEDGMENTS

Work on this study began somewhere early in the 2010s when the drama of globalization was becoming a central preoccupation. As the workings of neoliberal capitalism became dominant it seemed much of the world of cinema was being reshaped, especially as the powerful platforms of cinema distribution began to expand worldwide. Following that, films were increasingly shaped so as to meet the requirements for a digital economy. What was African cinema to be during this period? Africa was a latecomer to Netflix, but eventually the popularity of DVDs and then the expansion of African networks like Iroko and many others began to change the landscape. Netflix now streams much of Nollywood and other popular African films. In this book, I undertook to attempt to situate African films that were made from the 1990s down to the present within the evolving frame of what came to be called "World Cinema" or, eventually, "Global Cinema."

Thus the study began when some of my students—Olabode Ibironke, Cajetan Iheka, Carmela Garritano, Connor Ryan, and later Amrutha Kanipulli—were researching some of these issues. Their work always inspired me and opened me to the new worlds they were discovering, especially Carmela in Ghana and Connor in Lagos. Once opened, those worlds continued to grow with their work, from which I benefitted enormously.

I must thank Cajetan Iheka especially for continually reminding me, "How is that study of World Cinema coming?" The perceptive reader can see how the early chapters, caught up in attempts to answer that question, shift with the later sections. My goal was to present African films as generally moving in their own direction, somewhat marginally to that global imperative, while at the same time being heavily influenced by Nol-lywood's complete infatuation with it. At the time that I worked on this manuscript I also served as the African Studies Association's programmer for the showing of outstanding African films. That task eventually led to the ASA's board determining to formalize a committee that would award a prize to the best African film of the year, along with runners-up. I was very lucky to share the work of the committee with Marissa Moorman (whose knowledge of Lusophone cinema is nonpareil), and with my generous col-league Tama Hamilton-Wray and the talented filmmaker Jean-Marie Teno, and Samba Gadjigo. We debated film after film for determining the win-ners, and in the process had to view dozens of the most celebrated or talented films of the past two years, each time. The work of the committee continued most recently with Allyson McGuffie and Carmela Garritano who were also incredibly engaged and excited about all the films we had to view for the award. As a result of this work, it was possible for me to view recent films that were still struggling for distribution. I feel the last section is a strong testament to the creative work currently undertaken by African filmmakers in a time when the pressures to shape their work to fit the algorithms of Netflix and Amazon Prime are so compelling. The many filmmakers who shared their work with our committee—dozens of them, and their teams—made it possible for me to study their work and present some of it, hopefully, to this wider audience. I enlisted the help of many people over the years to suggest where I should look for "the best African films" of the year, and must thank Lindiwe Dovey, Lindsey Green-Sims, Steve Thomas, Connor Ryan, Carmela Garritano, Tundi Onikoyi, Sheila Petty, Jonathan Haynes, Julie Papaiouannou, Vlad Dima, Sheila Petty, Akin Adesokan, Noah Tsika, Matt Brown, Moradewun Adejunmobi, Rachel Gabara, Bhakti Shringarpure, Alessandro Jedlowski, Olivier Bar-let, Obododimma Oha, Maryellen Higgins, Frieda Ekotto and especially Melissa Thackway; along with the folks of ArtMattan and Icarus Films who provided many vimeos for us. In truth, it would be impossible to thank all those who contributed suggestions, and provided the desperately needed contacts, that made it possible for us to view the films.

I am very grateful to the support and friendship Manthia Diawara has shown me over the years, and in providing permission to use his wonder-ful film *An Opera of The World*. I am grateful to John Akomfrah for having inspired me for decades by his work, and giving permission to cite lines from his Installation, *Vertigo Sea* (the scene was Water-After-All). I thank Tundi Onikoyi for permission to use chapter four of this study that had previously appeared in his volume *The Cinema of Tunde Kelani: Aes-thetics, Theatricalities and Performance* (Cambridge Scholars Publishers,

2021). Thanks to ASIRI Magazine and the main source "Delcampe.Net" for use of the image of Lagos.

I am grateful for permission to use the image Brooklyn Now: Atlantic Antic Crowd, by Sebastian Blake Howard.

I could not have completed my work on this manuscript with the full support of my wife Liz Harrow, who has been always present through all the zoom calls, the struggles to meet and discuss the films, and then to view the best. She was part of that world of cinema that we both first really encountered in Yaounde in 1977–79. She edited the entire work, enabling me to avoid the infelicities of writing to which I am prone, and giving clarity to the cloudy moments. I hope some of the clouds remain, as they are part of my notion of how to write a scholarly text, and some readers can still continue to scratch their heads as I do.

INTRODUCTION

African Cinema in a Global Age

Kenneth W. Harrow

As Claire Denis was releasing her first major film, *Chocolat* (1988), Nollywood's birth was adumbrated by the appearance of video films from Ghana and Nigeria. The first really successful commercial film that kicked off the Nollywood revolution was *Living in Bondage* (Rapu, Nnuebe, 1992).[1] Denis's film was a semi-autobiographical auteur film, a debut in her powerful African centered films. She had previously worked with major New Wave directors, including, especially, Jacques Rivette and Wim Wenders. Her engagements with African cinema could be understood in postcolonial and diaspora terms as she set her films on the continent and dramatized much of its major conflicts, like the fighting in West Africa that involved child soldiers, the question of independence when French troops still were present on the ground; or simply growing up in late colonial times in Cameroon.[2]

Kenneth Nnuebe's film could not be more different. He breaks the mold of politically committed African cinema that often sought to validate African culture. *Living in Bondage* (1992) can be said to have inaugurated the shift toward a successful commercial turn in African cinema, and with its appeal in the use of the esoteric it radically rewrote modes of African filmmaking (Haynes 2016). Nollywood embraced the popular in all dimensions: pop culture, popular audience appeals, success measured by distribution and financial terms, and the promotion of genre cinema.

As film theaters were closing across the continent in the 1980s and 1990s—not unlike many arthouse and film theatres throughout the world (Lobato 2012)—the video film revolution presented audiences with new home video technologies that lured many away from the old downtown

DOI: 10.4324/9781003397595-1

theatres and the evening-out experience. The palatial theatres that regaled movie-goers everywhere from Dakar, with its Paris theatre, to my home-town Mt. Vernon, with its RKO and Loews theatres, attracting full-house crowds on Friday and Saturday nights, were rat-infested and decrepit by the end of the 20th century. In many parts of Africa young men turned the venues into sites of predation, as many have already attested (Haynes, Larkin, Lobato). The final blow came when the cost of maintaining cel-luloid projectors became prohibitive, and the worn-out equipment began to damage the films themselves. *(Bye Bye Africa*, Haroun 1999). The shift from the cinema of the "fathers" to that of the next generation—sons and increasingly daughters—is treated in a tongue-in-cheek fashion in Bekolo's *Aristotle's Plot* (2000), a film initially intended to celebrate the turn of the millennium for world cinema. The old equipment, the tsotsis who frequent the theatre "African Cinema," and the cop who chases down the thief "Cinema" all echo the parody which involved a "new" age supplanting the "old." FESPACO had not really caught up. It still was dominated by the antiquated mentality that privileged serious engaged films, whose mes-sages had long since lost their impact. In 2017 I attended FESPACO and was surprised not only at the failure to include digital or Nigerian films to any real extent, but even more so at the old-school approaches that Bekolo had so well put down in *Aristotle's Plot*.[3]

Videos dominated until VCDs and DVDs supplanted them; at the same time digital platforms began to emerge and compete. In 1997 Netflix be-gan its business of distributing DVDs, and ten years later shifted the focus to online streaming. African participation was slow to follow. While Africa Magic and other competitors emerged, the former beginning in 2003, Net-flix continued to expand worldwide, including into South Africa in 2015, with Amazon and Canal Plus the following year. Most of the continent is now covered by platforms that stream films, with Netflix the strongest player, though not without major competition.

More than they are bringing commercial films to African audiences; many African directors are now, in 2022, the time of this writing, creating films that satisfy Netflix's algorithms. Many Nollywood and other African films can be viewed online. As the auteur Denis marked something of a looming endpoint to the dominance of FESPACO films, with their serious political engagement that had heavily influenced the work of African and European filmmakers, commercial interests that defined the workings of industries, not auteur cinemas, finally began to prevail.

What kinds of films did Africans or their European collaborators create in these 30 years since that turning point of the long 1990s? My question is not how digitalization of cinema influenced new creative works, but sim-ply, what African cinema became in this digital age, an age we often define as dominated by neoliberal capitalism and globalization—the period I am identifying as the "global age" in this study's title. As cinema began to shift from primarily national cinemas and national industries to worldwide global ones, many of the films "became" somehow, as if by the magic of capitalist power forces, "world cinema" or "global" cinema—terms heavily laden with negative commercial or popular connotations. They were often fated to be viewed by millions of airline passengers, with their limited screens and limited attentions, rather than being closely watched and treasured in arthouse, much less revolutionary, venues. What began with *Living in Bondage* liberated African filmmakers and commercial energies, albeit with a body of trite, stock-in-trade films; but there was also an incredible flow of creative, inventive, moving, and thoughtful films coming from many countries across the continent. This book will present a number of those critical films that mark that trajectory, projecting a new sense of African film spaces and temporalities.

As we move from the long 1990s down to the present (a shifting moment, as I am writing the first version of this preface in late August of 2022), there has been a growing tendency of recent films, and especially "auteur" or independent African films, to be co-produced and co-constructed by crews and production companies that include both African and European or non-Africans. Many are made by directors like Mati Diop, or others whose location in an African space might well be geographically situated in Europe or the United States, "abroad"—or more accurately and truthfully, not really "abroad" any more, not in "diaspora," though still in many ways African. Some directors (Maïmouna Doucouré, *Mignonnes* [2020]) might now be calling themselves "French," while taking as subjects, as in *Mignonnes*, African migrant communities (see also Alice Diop's *Nous* [2021], and Dorothee-Myrien Kellou's *In Mansourah You Separated Us* [2019]). The drama of our times and their lives often turns on immigrant issues, stories, and sensibilities. However, what had once been "Maghrebin" and then "Beur," "Arab-French," or "Muslim-in-France," say—or their equivalent communities elsewhere in Europe or the United States—has changed: we can no longer speak of such cultures, peoples, lives, and dramas as "diaspora," in the old sense of the term. And to pretend that American or French or German identities remain untouched by the newly arriving immigrant peoples, with their lives, languages, and cultures, is to remain ensconced in the denials of rightwing nationalists.

That leaves us asking how to assess the passage from then, the long 1990s and its new digital age, to contemporary films, a generation later; how to mark the trajectory of these films that this study will be exploring, in more or less chronological order.

The key, older question of Johannes Fabian was to ask what was at stake when the outsider looks at the "Other," assuming that *he* is occupying a time and space, a temporality and location, that purports to be modern, when observing Others living in some version of the past. For Fabian this was the great sin of anthropology—and we would say of the liberal arts and social sciences—that sought to maintain the positionality of modernity in the face of those societies and peoples still "in the process of becoming" modern ("en voie de développement"). That is, in Fabian's terms, the "denial of coeval time" that modernity was grounded on, was based upon: "we" are modern, "you" are becoming modern.

The films of the past thirty years fly over the oceans with the immediacy of a jump cut, and instead of imagining a time here and another time there, give us the impression that a mobile phone call from here to there can bring together different locations with immediacy. We could say, with Fabian, that the events in both locations occur simultaneously; that the temporalities of each people in each location are marked, equally, in their own way by participating in the present, thus, as Gikandi (1996, 2011) would have it, jointly forging the features of modernity. For Fabian it was important that there be no "décalage," no cleft in time between here and there.

But he is wrong on that point, at least technically. Disparaging modern physics, he saw in relativity no useful concepts that might mark time or bodies on the macro-scale. If he were completely right, we could not have GPS systems, as they rely on special relativity to measure how time moves more slowly as a moving body increases its speed relative to one situated in an inert location. This phenomenon is called time dilation. Realizing that the location of the moving object depends on the point from which the observation is made—that the point of observation changes the measurement of when and where an event takes place—Einstein early on came to the conclusion that there can be no simultaneity between events when measured or observed from different locations that have different axes of location.

Taking this as a starting point, we can say that if we are to deny non-coeval temporality it isn't because time is objectively the same everywhere, or even that temporalities could be called universal, evenly distributed, or objectively existent apart from those who observe or measure them, but rather are being constructed with each experiment, each observation, each different observer. It isn't that my time is modern and yours is backward or not yet modern, but that I am creating modernity in the act of setting it off from your temporality—and typically by introjecting into my "modernity" the position of "truth" and all the power that accompanies such judgments (as in, "let me show you," "tell you," "help you to be modern"). The problem is not anthropology and its other, or othering, but even more, not knowing how much our very acts of observing are always already marked by orientations, biases along axes that are pre-liminary, prior, pre-conditional.

We could take this speculation on the shakiness of what we had assumed to be objective time—our own measurements of time, our own abilities to measure without interfering in what we were observing—take these basic concepts of relativity and apply them to the changing facets of cinema, notably African cinema, to ask how non-coeval temporalities have shifted their features from their early biases along the axes of modernity to contemporary axes that deny the simultaneity of coeval timed events. That is, to ask what we are doing as we see these films disarticulate the temporalities and spatial locations of what had once represented Africa, Africa abroad, or diaspora. We can then de-privilege Greenwich Mean Time, as William Kentridge does in his Harvard lectures (2014).

Relativity is based on the relation of the observer on the inert platform and the moving cars of a train as it increasingly speeds up and moves away. If the person with the clock were on the train, the station would appear to be moving away, in the opposite direction of that of the train, and the person on the platform would be experiencing time dilation and length compression. And were they to come together 20 years later, it might be the person on the inert platform who would be so many years younger than the one on the train, contrary to the perception of time from the point of view of the one on the train. Time dilation—faster time, slower time—does really work, but only relative to those outside the one time frame, i.e. GPS depends upon the relativity of two points of observation, not just one.

We need to imagine, then, the progression of a series of films from one point in time to another as not ineluctably taking meaning and indicating a direction, the so-called "Arrow of Time" always associated with progress. This is the great threat posed by the denial of coeval time, the primary sin of anthropology, the primary weapon used by modernity. That said, how can we pretend to observe a series of films as if comfortably ensconced in a chronology that would mark their progress on a linear trajectory?

Michelle Wright (2015) is right in identifying this—the Arrow of Time, the direction of progress—as the worst sin of the Enlightenment, and to seek to disrupt it through special relativity. But Carlo Rovelli goes one step further in seeking to establish that time emerges only when particles—or indeed other objects—collide or interact. If we are not limited by thinking that quantum functions only on the micro-sub particle level, then we might consider the collision or coming together of other beings . . . or movies . . . colliding, interacting, and generating time. Time is the product of physical interactions—not something objective and outside all matter, as Newton had thought (Rovelli 2018). It requires an observer to create measurements that purport to explain the causality and temporality that mark the interaction.

This description cannot take place without an observer, so the entire process is best described as that of an "apparatus," with apparatus theory here touching much more than the orientation of an ideology, but the full mechanisms that generate the understanding of the event. In a real sense, the event itself is created by the act of observing it, since it is the observation that puts together parts that all together combine to make up the story, i.e. the experiment and its results. Every film is the same. Its meaning is constructed as it is being observed by us, its causality along with its temporality and space. And as we do this, with full confidence of having understood, we simultaneously occlude our own acts of seeing, observing, making sense of, and constructing the scenes, motives, meanings. We have been trained by life to understand the world in these terms, terms dependent on causality, temporality and its Arrow of Time, of past-present-future existing independent of our material world. This orientation cannot be undone. But when we watch a film, we have the choice of seeing ourselves as observers, and reading ourselves as we read the film texts. We have the choice of doing this with the films I am considering in this study. In the act of seeing them, through the optic I provide as my own readings, we can also read back to the long 1990s relative to the present to ask, repeatedly, is this where non-coeval time can be seen to have been constructed and deconstructed? Where modernity and its locations can be dissembled and reassembled? Where we can disturb enough to return the gaze of the film, and finally recommence, as Hannah Arendt (1958) would have it, as each child starts out in the world? Not with the new eyes of a child, of course, but with something different, caught in our eyes, to make us aware of our vision.

The project intended to spark this approach can be described as having three sections. In the first, I place Denis's *Chocolat* in conjunction with Nnuebe's *Living in Bondage*, both of them points of departure following the late stages that came before. If this resembles a conventional chronology, it will be up to the reader to see a conjunction that makes the logic of Arrow of Time chronology insufficient.

The second section involves a body of six works that move gradually toward the experiences of Africans in places like Brooklyn (e.g. *Mother of George* [2013]), or Belgium, Manhattan, and California. I set the stage for this dispersal of space by examining modernity in the work of Tunde Kelani, especially in *Thunderbolt: Magun* (2001) and *Ti Oluwa Ni Ile* (1993).

What then follows is a trio of films involving the brilliant actor Sotigui Kouyate, including Dominique Loreau's *Les Noms n'habitent nulle part*

(1994), Mahamat-Saleh Haroun's *Sotigui Kouyaté* (1995), and Rachid Bouchareb's *Little Senegal* (2000). Moussa Sene Absa's similarly themed *Ainsi meurent les anges* (2001) works in counterpoint to Anyaene's *Ije* (2010) with iterations of failed departures putting into question the classical immigration stories of struggle and ultimate success.

These films are placed in conjunction with Kelani's own celebration of Yoruba culture as defining the center of his worldview. For Kelani, modernity is the inevitable opportunity and curse, the site of disease and cures, that are always best met with Yoruba understandings, and cultural practices, often emphasizing language, dance, and even curses. The gas stations in *Ti Oluwa Ni Ile* (1993) will be built and sacred woods will be chopped down, but Kelani remains faithful to the belief that we can sustain our lives with practices remembered from the past. All of the five films mentioned above return to similar questions of migration or the transposition of people into foreign cultures, and the need to remember and retain what our parents and grandparents had lived, spoken, and acted out. The section ends with Dosunmu's powerful *Mother of George* (2013). The cinematography by Bradford Young was award winning; the richness of the visual elements matched the complex drama that put into question Kelani's faith in the traditional world, as a couple who are unable to conceive turn to practices that throw into relief how genre roles are strained to the breaking point when Yoruba values clash with western medical practices in Brooklyn.

The last section evokes the dramatic changes accompanying relocations of people, often incurring loss of lives and tragedy, but also openings to new possibilities. The filmmakers of this period have moved considerably away from the early paths of African cinema and its politics of engagement. Instead of a path of national liberation, there is the question of how, in an age dominated by global forces and their accompanying authoritarian states, the humanist imperative could survive. Diawara's *Opera of the World* presents the dramatic features of immigration by juxtaposing the perspectives of major cultural figures in Europe with his own Africa-based performance of an African opera dealing with immigration. Diawara's rich voice-over provides the link between the two worlds. Death haunts his vision as the sight of drowned bodies is punctuated by the singers' laments. Alain Gomis takes us one step further, with his haunting fable *Tey* (2012), with Saul Williams playing the role of Satché who is aware of his impending death, adumbrating the turn toward the unreal we have recently viewed in Mati Diop's zombie film, *Atlantiques* (2019) or the Kenyan Mbithi Masya's film of the spiritual world in the after life, *Kati Kati* (2016).

Portrayals of grandparents discarded by their children haunt this final section. At times the visions of adult children shunting the old aside entail enormously bitter traces, as in the films concerned with showing elders being cursed as witches: Rugano Nyoni's *I Am Not a Witch* (2017) and Maia Lekow and Christopher King's *The Letter* (2019) are two compelling films on this topic. The most unforgettable performance of the old woman embodying the past and her community, facing global destruction of their village and ways, is seen in Lemohang Jeremiah Mosese's *This Is Not a Funeral, It Is a Resurrection* (2019). Mary Twala, on the verge of her own departure from life, plays the role of Mantoa, who seems to bring us to the border between the past, the present, and the future, periods seen as coeval, and again posited against the single dimensions imposed on their lives by modernizing globalization pressures brought by the state.

More fundamentally, these "witches" take us into the world of old age and death to an extent never seen in African film before. We started this study with the child "France" in *Chocolat* and in most of the next generation coming after the sons and daughters of the revolutionary stages of African cinema. But as the "Independences" and their dawning hopes were transposed, the vectors of progressive stories became deflected. The "mother" of George could not provide him with a child, and the identity of the true father had to be hidden. Satché's impending death looms before him and the community, but unlike Soyinka's Eman in *The Strong Breed*, there is no air of a sacrifice any more. As with Agamben's "bare life," there is no more value ascribed to the old; no loss with their passing. For the global economy, their worth lies entirely with the property their heirs expect to receive on their passing.

More recent work shifts temporalities and lifetimes into arenas never portrayed with the first generations of African cineastes. At times this generation of films posits the greatest challenge to temporalities unhampered by the Arrow of Time, i.e., to find in age and death moments not properly described as marked by degeneration, decay, and rot. Even rot and death become Other when the Arrow of Time is temporarily dethroned. Gomis pushes death to its limits in *Tey*; and death becomes something other in *This Is Not a Death, It Is a Resurrection*. In his *Opera of the World* (2017), Manthia Diawara challenges us again with genre and questions of modern cultural authority by portraying the death of a child as though amiably agreeing with what he hears, while driving our feelings to the limit with questions that only cinema can pose to its viewers. "Do you see me, really, or is it I in the mirror looking back?" "Do you see the bodies now?"

Time cannot be measured in a vision caught in the abyss, in the mise en abyme, because as you catch on to the one image, its reflection carries the eye on to the next reflection, and seemingly on to infinity. This book is not intended as a denial of coeval temporality but as an attempt to catch a moment in the mise en abyme, to pin it down for a period, and to ask what we see and what we see as seeing, doing the seeing, for that time. We can call that time the period of global cinema, or "African cinema's" demise, or African cinema's resurrection in a time of globalization. At a time when "global cinema" threatens to englobe and diminish all national or independent cinemas, Africans working outside the law of the algorithm, working in their own non-coeval time, are producing films that continue to ignite that spark of the new Arendt saw as the sign of hopefulness in each generation. A "burial" and a "resurrection," as Lemohang put it in his brilliant film about a woman of many years, whose ending could be called only ambiguous.

This study attempts to track how we reached this point of signification by tacking on arbitrary points of beginning and ending—using *points de capiton*,[4] Lacanian upholstery buttons to temporarily halt the signifying chain; the better to open the question of any series of passages for cinema, and to question time's denial of clear punctuation to demarcate its cinematic eras. It is an attempt to portray African cinema as not reduced to a section of global cinema, but as continuing and shifting sets of works that are taking form beyond the market forces of the global.

Notes

1 Chris Rapu was the director. Nnuebe was the driving force behind the production and essentially deserves credit for the film coming out (see Haynes 2016).
2 Some of her major "African" films include, in addition to *Chocolat* (1988), *Beau Travail* (1999), *35Rhums* (2008), and *White Material* (2009).
3 Olivier Barlet's write up of the conference was relatively devasting. However, reports on subsequent iterations of FESPACO seem more favorable to me. Still, the cutting edge of African film festivals seems to have passed from Ouaga to Durban and Zanzibar.
4 https://nosubject.com/Point_de_capiton

PART ONE

The Long 1990s

1

WHAT THE 1980S BROUGHT

Kenneth W. Harrow

I.

The 1980s brought a new historical trajectory in African cinema (loosely defined here to include films "close to" Africa, like Denis's). In *Chocolat* (1988), Claire Denis didn't frame the narrative using anti-colonial or post-colonial binaries like metropole-colony or liberation/independence. For the first generation of African films *engagement* was the primary determinant of value. That started to blur with films that moved in a more heteroclite set of directions. Consider how all these disparate films came out in 1992: *The Blue Eyes of Yonta* (Flora Gomes); *Living in Bondage* (Kenneth Nnuebe); *Hyènes* (Djibril Diop Mambety); *Quartier Mozart* (Jean Pierre Bekolo); *Guelwaar* (Sembène Ousmane).

In this period of Structural Adjustment Programs that roiled the African continent, and with the global implementation of neoliberal capitalism, the film industry began to move in new directions. It wasn't so much the exhaustion of old themes, but new technologies that led to this historical cusp. Clearly there were anxieties over change in the world order/economic order in Africa, and in the manifestations of power. In 1993 violence would break out in Burundi and explode in 1994 in Rwanda. By 2000, much of Central Africa would never be the same. The "Suns of Independence" were no longer really relevant in this changing landscape. Mandela was released and then came to power in the same year that almost a million Rwandans were slaughtered, 1994. Authors like Boris Boubacar Diop would aver that their lives were forever changed. Filmmakers were bathing in the same waters of change. We could say there

DOI: 10.4324/9781003397595-3

was a "before-Nollywood" and an "after-Nollwood," or that the anticipation of "neo-" was not only for Nigerian cinema. A new generation arrived with auteurs like Haroun, Sissako, Nacro, Bekolo, whose world had come to know violence, disruption, and death. It was not possible to film as the grandfathers had done.

Ramon Lobato (2012) gives us a handle on how the film industry underwent monumental change. Demand for videos skyrocketed in the 1980s. As VCR machines became popular, "US production skyrocketed from around 350 pictures per year in 1983 to nearly 600 by 1988" (Lobato 22). He details the changes brought by neoliberal capitalism:

> [There was an] ongoing deregulation of broadcasting in Europe, Asia, and Latin America. As formerly state-run stations were commercialized and/or privatized, the demand for 'average or below-average American films' increased exponentially and a new market niche was born.
>
> *(Lobato 23)*

Half of the revenues for home videos went to independent companies.

The birth of this movement sounds close to what was occurring in Nigeria around that time, though there the distribution was initially handled by markets, which still continue to play an important role (Haynes 2016), though alternatives like streaming networks are gradually taking over much of the worldwide market. For the American independents, Lobato describes the birth of the video industry as chaotic: "These independents worked on a flexible model of dispersed, small-scale production and ad hoc distribution through the mini-majors, the larger independents, small fly-by-night operators, or through self-distribution" (Lobato 23). He says it was undercapitalized, but compared with Nollywood's early films would have seemed royally capitalized. Their predecessors in celluloid included porno and B-films industries. For Nollywood there was romance, occultism, and a range of genre films spelled out by Haynes in *Nollywood: The Creation of Nigerian Film Genres* (2016).

In tracing this shift, I want to suggest that it did not occur in a vacuum. The increasing costs of celluloid production and the increasing difficulty of studios to find the funding to create enough films to meet demand and to be profitable enough to support them led to a sea change in the industry. Video technology drove up demand enormously, so that the only way it seemed possible to satisfy market demand was to churn out inexpensive B films, with religious films increasing in popularity, as well as such genre types as porno, horror, martial arts, and drugs/sex/crime. This in turn might have encouraged urban grit marking lo-grade as well as hi-culture films, or both simultaneously like Scorsese's *Taxi Driver* (1976) or

Schlesinger's *Midnight Cowboy* (1969). *Taxi Driver*'s neo-noir approach to the mean streets and edgy-insanity of Travis Bickle indicated that studio budgeted A films could cross auteurist and commercial lines, but it also set a precedent for the B grade video films that followed in the 80s. Scorsese's heritage in B-films took the form of "sex, violence, swearing and other racy content" (Lobato 23). The market opened wide to B-film exuberance, ending up as Straight-To-Video (STV) inexpensive films, increasingly shown apart from Hollywood studio productions. The STV revolution spread, first to Canada, then the Philippines, Thailand, Romania, and Mexico (Lobato 24)—generating a global production side to be matched by the quest for markets abroad—wherever cheap videos could be sold.

Blaxploitation film (*Shaft*, 1971; *Superfly*, 1972) accompanied this shift, signaling a similar move away from "race" or "race-uplift" films to "entertainment" models. But on the cusp, again, was Melvin Van Peebles's *Sweet Sweetback's Baadasssss Song* that came out in 1971, the same year as *Shaft*. Both films spoke the language of revolution and popular entertainment, a combination very difficult to find in African films of that period, although we approach that model in Sembène's *Xala* in 1975.

There were some attempts at popular entertainment in African cinema, as with Moustapha Alassane's *FVVA: Femme, Villa, Voiture, Argent* (1972), Henri Duparc's 1989 *Bal Poussière*, and Mweze Ngangura's *La Vie est belle* (1987). These emphasized romance, comedy, and music, opening the way for films like Moussa Touré's *TGV* (1997). But the heavy influence of the "serious" filmmakers like Sembène, Cisse, Sissoko, Kabore, Ouédraogo, and Safi Faye, or more experimental directors like Mambéty, stunted the growth of this tendency.[1] SAPS were the African equivalents of the neoliberal capitalist policies that birthed video films in the west, and that led to the emphasis on world B-film genres. It seemed inevitable that Nollywood would be born, which happened fairly quickly following video film developments in Ghana that began in the late 1980s (Garritano 2013). Following Haynes, we can cite as an important moment in this endeavor Nnuebe's *Living in Bondage* in 1992, which opened the way for films with a serious claim to the market to emerge.

The 1980s globalization shift for cinema is marked by a twin imperative: cheap production, anywhere it could be replicated in established formulae; and correspondingly, video markets for genre films that required less a command of subtlety in language than easy comprehension of action, desire, and straightforward narratives. Again, the market driven features of early global video found close correspondences with African video films of the same decade. The turning point from the initial relatively amateurish endeavors to more costly and serious productions came with *Living in Bondage*, which was shot over months, not days, and cost much more than the subsequent commonly produced Nollywood films of the early 90s (Haynes 2016). It was producer and writer Kenneth Nnuebe's greatest aspiration to produce a quality film. He made the concept of the carefully marketed film possible; but the era of the cheap commodity, of local consumption and home viewing trumped his aspirations for a higher level of product (Haynes).

Lobato identifies this period as marked by the "transnationalization" of the video industry, and he alludes to "global tastes" (28) driving decisions about genre while regional forces, like Hong Kong films, sought pan-Asian markets for their films. Local tastes could influence the films produced with them in mind: the new binary of global and local was already there at the outset as cheap costs of production drove every decision about aesthetics—or simply content. What styles emerged might have been deliberately forged for their particular market—Asian comedy, say, from Hong Kong emphasizing its own particular tastes in coprophilia or cheap toilet jokes. But a corresponding low aesthetic level, mimicked in low-grade visual tones and grittiness, matched by the talk and look of the street, twisted loosely around the vulgar. The tropes of the trashy, from low grade to high culture, were easily fashioned, and the erotic entered on the world stage elegantly in Egoyan's *Exotica* (1994). It was *Living in Bondage* (1992) that set the stage for psychic violence, greed, luxury, and the psychotically esoteric, whose b-side as the occult would become the dominant genre type for Nollywood for the better part of the decade.

The tie between many of these early "global" efforts might be seen in Meaghan Morris's (2005) notion (borrowed by Lobato) of Kung Fu martial arts films, of roughly the same period (1985–1993), terming them a "minor" transnational media practice, as Adejunmobi was to do some years later, in her famous description of Nollywood ("Nigerian Video Film As Minor Transnational Practice" [2007]), a theme she picks up later ("Evolving Nollywood Templates for Minor Transnational Film" [2014]). The brief description Lobato gives of the Deleuzian take by Morris is of "a different, yet overlapping, way of 'handling the same material' as A-grade action" (Lobato 29). The description that follows matches Nollywood closely:

> The minor action mode involves such things as transnational film crews [not Nollywood here—but this will be true two decades later with New Nollywood], fast shooting schedules [Nollywood would perfect this with two-three days shooting, at its most inexpensive], a 'sleazy look' [like Nollywood with the bulk of the films shot with a single video camera, or later a single digital camera; filmed not in studio conditions but

on location, in a borrowed house, with street scenes, or downloaded footage of foreign locales], cheap shooting locations [what Lobato designates as situated 'often in the third world,' viz. Lagos or Accra and even earlier the Onitsha or other Igbo film sites] whose grittiness contrasts somewhat with the cityscapes in Nollywood, especially in its early years.

*(Morris [2004] all cited in Lobato 29, with
my bracketed comments)*

Originally Nollywood's mise-en-scènes were intended to convey luxury and occlude the mud in the streets that would soil the effect (Haynes). Over time the gritty began to emerge, and even dominate, as with Kenneth Nyang's hard-hitting melodramas.

Lastly, Morris's minor transnational videos had "informal modes of exhibition" (cited in Lobato 29). For Nollywood, distribution meant stalls in the market, street corner stalls or street vendors, and youths with handfuls of pirated videos and eventually VCDs, purveying often pirated wares to the public—sometimes with sellers standing at traffic lights, in the middle of the stalled traffic, or on the beach, wherever buyers might be found. Eventually market vendors became the largest distributors. In African terms, "informal" describes poorly these efforts at distribution when the market itself was central to the lives of most people, in cities as in villages. Stall after stall, rows of similar products are sold, be they vegetables, hardware, cloth, or videos. The sellers rent their stalls in the markets and establish their presence to their clients. These were the Video-To-Go and Blockbusters of Nigeria. Informal in global terms, these familiar venues in much of Africa approach more closely formal means of marketing.

Measured by Lobato's euro-centered notion of the transnational, in global terms, STV was marked by modes of production and distribution that crossed frontiers, and this was reflected in the films' content. But reading that content as framed for a multi-national Asian market might be seen as different from what we find in Nollywood's early attempts to reach Yoruba and Igbo audiences (and eventually Hausa as well) by competing with what had already been circulating and defining film in Africa for many years: Hollywood B gangster and action films, westerns, Bollywood musical romances, Kung Fu martial arts—genre as understood in Hollywood's notions of marketing—rather than A-films or auteur cinema riding the Art circuits. It was initially out of the question to imagine a Nollywood film being incorporated among the choices of "world cinema" on a transatlantic flight.[2]

Diawara's read of world cinema, in 2010 when he wrote on the topic, was that "World cinema, by which festivals understand everything that is neither American nor European, is a new invention of films from the non-Western world that comfort Europeans in their paternalistic supremacy vis-à-vis the Third World and in their struggle against Hollywood" (Diawara 87). Now Bollywood is commonly to be found on flights, in festivals, and on screens, and Nollywood is also available on the transatlantic screens—and more importantly, on Netflix and Amazon Prime.

The shifting informal or non-institutionalized practices of the early period in Nollywood, described as also fitting Asian popular films by Morris, or by the major commentators on Nollywood, beginning with Haynes, Okome, and a generation later Adejunmobi, Garritano, Adesokan, Onikoyi, and Tsika, amongst others, evoke something of James Ferguson's (2006) notion of globalization in Africa—a practice that hops over vast swatches of the continent, moving quietly below the great global flows of trade in minerals and arms organized and put into practice by violent men. For Comaroff and Comaroff ("Millenial Capitalism: First Thoughts on a Second Coming" 2001), gambling is the signal feature of this period of commodity capitalism. But in Africa, although every element of this global trade is marked by a gamble, its signal features are more to be found in extravagant markers of wealth, as in cars or jewels, and of necropolitics administered in lethal forms by militias, non-state and state actors.

The STV B-film world market, however different in its details from Nollywood and its African video counterparts, shared this one key trait with its African counterparts: the films were not blockbusters, marketed for theatrical distribution, costing many millions and aiming at ever higher profits in tens of millions, or eventually hundreds of millions. The difference in scale meant a difference in almost all features of production, distribution, and exhibition, features that can't be defined in terms of "professional" versus "amateurish,"[3] or first world/third world, or high/low aesthetics. Wherever greater sums of money came to be spent on celluloid films by 1990 (Lobato 2012; Prince 2007; Dirks n.d.), the relevant costs that began to define difference between studio celluloid cinema and video films involved advertising, the acquisition of and treatment of film stock, the equipment needed to shoot and to show the films, star salaries, and shooting locations, among other factors. In the 80s, the prices for these elements rose enormously, and only blockbuster films were deemed capable of generating sufficient profits for the studios to survive. STV films were able to skirt these expenses and the need to raise enormous sums of money for production.

A gulf was opened between the two worlds of cinema, the commercial STV and the gigantic studio films—a gulf corresponding messily and yet precisely to core values of the neoliberal age beginning with Reagan's revamping of the tax structure enabling the wealthy to become super-wealthy;

his deregulating of commerce, forcing the state to divest of its holdings when possible, opening state run enterprises to free market capitalism; his efforts at destroying unions—unleashing a model for what was to become, by the 90s, the reigning model of neoliberal IMF and World Bank practices, with their loans conditioned on the above features: the opening salvos for the "global age" (Geschiere 2009; Comaroff and Comaroff 2001; Lobato 2012; David Harvey 2005).

For the Comaroffs the era following 1989 in Africa, with the end of the Cold War and the promotion and prevalence of neoliberal thought, led to a now familiar conjunction involving occultism, concentrations of wealth among the few with greater immiseration of the masses, increased social uncertainty and street violence in cities, and the rise of violent campus cults, along with the ascension of Pentecostalism. The cultural representations that corresponded with and responded to these conditions frequently were marked by melodrama, blatant emotional colorings of narrative, and baroque plots and corresponding visual qualities. The sharp contrasts of light and dark that typified horror films like Sam Raimi's *Evil Dead* (1981) and *Evil Dead II* (1987) gave rise to Ndalianis's (2004) term neo-baroque.[4]

This was the scene in the 1980s, leading quickly to *Living in Bondage* (1992), the Ghanaian *Ghost Tears* (1992) and *Step Dad* (1994) by Socrate Safo, *A Mother's Revenge* (Ernest Abbeyquaye 1994), and dozens more. Perhaps most important was the inevitable and almost invisible termination of postcolonial political interpretations of the world, with its nationalist based binary of metropole and periphery. In place of late revolutionary ideals came a new sense of helplessness in understanding, much less, dealing with a world under the overarching discipline of neoliberalism. (Comaroff and Comaroff 2001: 24).

Goods flowing into the continent for the wealthy were glimpsed at a distance; the new Afropolitan cosmonauts were served by the cargo handlers of the world, while they continued to live behind their high walled enclaves, leaving the gleanings, the pickings, the trash for the common people.[5] Ideals of twentieth century revolution and freedom passed unperceived into oblivion. The Comaroffs write of the new dispensation and its wealth, bound up in the image of cargo goods and their cults of wealth:

At the turn of the twenty-first century, the cargo, glimpsed in large part through television, takes the form of huge concentrations of wealth that accrue, legitimately or otherwise, to the rich of the global economy—especially the enigmatic new wealth derived from financial investment and management, from intellectual property and other rights, from cyberspace, from transport and its cognate operations, and from the supply of various post-Fordist services. All of which points to the fact that the mysterious mechanisms of a changing market, not to mention abstruse technological and informational expertise, hold the key to hitherto unimaginable fortunes amassed by the ever more rapid flow of value, across time and space, into the fluid coordinates of the local and the global; to the much mass-mediated mantra that the gap between the affluent and the indigent is growing at an exponential rate.

(2001: 24–25)

The master-servant order results in the subaltern experiencing a "sense of impossibility, even despair, that comes from being left out of the promise of prosperity, from having to look in on the global economy of desire from its immiserated exteriors" (2001: 25). Where before it was freedom from colonial oppression, national independence, and the construction of the New African Man and Woman that we might have sought and celebrated, say at the time of Fanon to Fela, now the Comaroffs speak of the present conjuncture marked by "a loss of human integrity, experienced in the spreading commodification of persons, bodies, cultures, and histories, in the substitution of quantity for quality, abstraction for substance" (2001: 25).

The expansion of African film studies into the world of commerce and commodity, with international trade and transnational relations and contacts, interlaced with uneven crossings and encounters pressing against each other, lies in the corresponding death of the unfinished project of decolonization, the demise of the gods of postcolonial discourse. African films of the 1980s and 1990s—what we can call late FESPACO celluloid cinema to early Ghannywood and Nollywood video films— are framed by many of the concerns of the new globalized order, with sometimes mushy, sometimes satirical representations of the global. These include *Hyènes* (1992) and *Guelwaar* (1992), both tinged with a sense of loss. *Blue Eyes of Yonta* (1992), with its biting irony, also marks the new voice of youth culture along with *Quartier Mozart* (1992). Nollywood's *Living in Bondage* (1992) moves us off that stage completely, as it rises to the level of the grotesque with the question, what wouldn't you give to be rich?[6]

The millennium turns. The dominant voice in African cinema—old school—turns in a shocking new direction, and Sembène's heroine, Kine, the New African Woman, appears as the successful businesswoman (*Faat Kine,* 2000). Simultaneously, with the tenets of neoliberalism solidly in place, Comaroff and Comaroff publish the major opus of the period, *Millenial Capitalism* (2001), intending to dismantle the neoliberal apology for globalization.

These films I've been citing above bracket the period of the late 1980s to the early 1990s—with STV coming to Africa, transforming the world of African film, marking the inevitable demise of celluloid, signaling the obsolescence of a mode of filmmaking that had been given the misleading label "Francophone," and marginalizing their traditions and style. The changes can be measured by positing *Chocolat* (1988) and *Living in Bondage* (1992) as markers of different tracks of what World Cinema has tried to incorporate into its maw. "World Cinema" emerged in various iterations:

- World Cinema as non-English language films (French for *Chocolat*, Igbo for *Living in Bondage*);
- World Cinema as Global Art Films;
- World Cinema as cinemas of exotic Others;
- World Cinema circulating in festivals, on college campuses, at special showings of ethnic cinema, of New African or Asian or Latin or Gay Cinema, where they might have been tailored for the right festival circuits, airline film entertainment choices, or campus film series. Ultimately, they would provide the substance for course descriptions of often amorphous amalgamations of films into the generic rubric subsumed by the global or world requirement.

The focus of the films under study in this study include Claire Denis's *Chocolat* 1988, and Kenneth Nnuebe's *Living in Bondage* (Chris Rapu 1992). These will be explored in terms elaborated in Lobato's key claim that:

> . . . the films bear the legacies of their productions and distribution context *at a textual level*, and they are not directly comparable to the kind of Global Hollywood productions which seek to suppress these histories by making one place stand in for another, as was the case with other Philippines-lensed US productions such as *Platoon* (1986).
>
> *(32, my stress)*

In taking us to this claim, Lobato leans on hybridity and polyphony, as though a deconstructionist postcolonialism could translate directly the issues posed by the material conditions of production. Though the films might "ape" Hollywood, they are defined by these marks of difference: "the mixed-race of cast and crew, the polyphony of accents, [and] the curious cultural elisions that occur when 'local' talent is recruited onto international productions" (32). This fits into Hjort's notion of "strong transnationalism" ("On the Plurality of Cinematic Transnationalism," Durovicova and Newman: 13). For Nollywood, not being able to hire foreign crew members, nor to shoot in another yet cheaper country, the mixture has to be read in terms of the impacts of other influences, since all culture inevitably is marked by *différance* and hybridity. Yoruba Traveling Theater, Evangelical Christian movements, familiar occult practices grounded in village sorcerers or healers, along with the urban exposure to Hollywood B action or romance films, Kung Fu, Bollywood, and telenovelas—all leave their traces. Commodity capitalism's triumph can be measured visibly in Nollywood, even when constructed for symptomatic readings in the forms close to the auteur model, as with Tunde Kelani or Kunle Afolayan. It is manifest directly in the taste for the high life and what money can buy, figured in mise-en-scènes filled with extravagant accouterments adorning the homes of the rich, with their Benzes, guards, clothes, food, whiskey, servants, and luxurious beds (e.g., *Beyonce, the President's Daughter*, Arase, 2006).

Placing Denis's *Chocolat* (1988) in dialogue with *Living in Bondage* (1992) is intended to put pressure on the notion of World Cinema as it developed in the period following the 1980s when African cinema was generally not seen as an important component. However, World Cinema itself, challenged in the same way that the dominant ideological embrace of neoliberalism by the World Bank has been (Adesokan 2001), would have to negotiate with the positive face put on the globalization of cinema with the rise of the term transnational. The gradual retreat of hermeneutic analysis of film narrative, the rise of material studies, the focus on production and exhibition, all became central to the birth of Nollywood studies under the influence of Jonathan Haynes, with his groundbreaking *Nigerian Video Films* (1997) and later magisterial *Nollywood: The Creation of Nigerian Film Genres* (2016). He saw the break with postcolonialism, but had not yet anticipated how the emphasis on genre and production would also make room for transnational film studies that could displace the auteur cinema models he saw as having dominated African cinema in the past. His typologies of Nollywood had to begin with the telanovella and melodrama.

Claire Denis was functioning in another universe, one that had little awareness of the corresponding decline in its own forms of auteurism. The edge of New Wave was slipping into the past, perhaps as we might see in the career of Denis that began just as Wenders's and Jarmusch's were at their peak.[7] The films to which the 1980s and 1990s gave birth became foundational not only for the quick and dirty video industry models, or their counterparts in blockbusters, but also independent cinemas whose own roots lay in New Wave auteurism. For all cultural moments, marked with their various aesthetic and commercial ventures, there is a relationship of commonality and oppositionality. As Nollywood is being born, the transnational is marking the children of the New Wave, and in the clustering of films around Africa, many would fit into that schema. Godard travelled to Mozambique in 1978, at the government's invitation to try to start television station, and to assist in setting up a national cinema. Rouch also bridged the two worlds with his cinéma vérité African films, transposing France and Niger onto his screen—the bulk of his African films span the period from *Les maîtres fous* (1955) to *Cocorico M. Poulet* (1974). Chris Marker bridged the national divides with two remarkable films, *Sans Soleil* (1983) coming three decades after the controversial, anticolonialist *Les Statues meurent aussi* (Renais, Marker, Cloquet, 1953)[8]. Again, the decade of the change, the 1980s, where the borders of nations began to vacillate, proved the appropriate time for *Sans Soleil*, which stretched from Japan to Guinea-Bissau. The opening quote prefigures the awakening of the transnational: "L'éloignement des pays répare en quelque sorte la trop grande proximité des temps." (The distance between the countries compensates somewhat for the excessive closeness of the times. From Racine's *Bajazet* [1672]). The 80s brought the change, in this case the denial of coeval temporalities was always naturalized in "world cinema" when setting African vis-à-vis Western cinema.

The 1980s movements could not continue to hold in tension the coevalness. The rise of African cinema's video phase began as "New Wave" was in decline—Djibril Diop Mambéty's *Badou Boy* (1970) and *Touki Bouki* (1973) prefigured this encounter, and transformed his brush with the surreal into the transnational with *Hyènes* (1992). As Claire Denis's career was launched in 1988 after her apprenticeship with New Wave,[9] so too was Nollywood's prequel launching to come with the films leading up to *Living in Bondage* (1992) (Garritano 2013, Haynes 1997). Over time the video films underwent a series of transformations that shattered the singular definitions of the genres of each cinema, so that the early notions of what Nollywood was had to be recodified until Haynes was able to come up with his 2016 typography. Tracking Denis and Nollywood leads, in both cases, down a path that inevitably reconfigures the transnational. The filiations leading to New Wave or Nollywood were only ostensibly radically different. Over time, they began to operate on tracks that suggested convergences, or strange coincidences, that could be seen, in retrospect, as transnational. We can see something of this in the mechanics of formulating modes of transnational cinema that Mette Hjort attempts to accomplish.

For Hjort, it is less genres than a mélange of components involving nationalism, like the national identities of crew and production, that take priority in creating a typology of transnational cinema. The markers of intentionality along with perspective feature in Hjort's use of the terms "marked and unmarked transnationality" (2010: 13). When Hjort writes of the films' "authors," she means all those significantly involved in fashioning the film as "intentionally direct[ing] the attention of viewers toward various transnational properties that encourage thinking about transnationality" (14). Hjort goes on to assert that a film might have transnational themes, but could be made within a "national framework" for a national audience (14). She concludes that a film with "strong" forms of transnational filmmaking need not necessarily be characterized by "marked transnationalism" since the final product could be exhibited and received entirely by a national audience that takes its narrative as speaking directly to their own culture and society. *Hiroshima Mon Amour* (Renais 1959) was quintessential French New Wave, but its transnationalism was directly signaled from the title to the narrative, characters, and diegesis. None of those elements studied for their hermeneutic meaning was to be central to the reconfiguration of international art cinema's New Wave into Transnationalism or Global art cinema (Galt and Schooner 2010).

Struggling to give some coherence to the issue of transnationalism, Hjort settles on a typology framed by cinematic production that "links the concept of transnationalism to different models of cinematic production, each motivated by specific concerns and designed to achieve particular effects" (15). Hjort recognizes that her types would collapse when expanded onto the "global" level where "homogenization" would threaten any national specificity; and she wishes to validate a certain notion of cinema as striving for aesthetic, political, or intellectual qualities that are diminished when subordinated to purely commercial concerns. Her transnationalisms would have to be validated by hybridity which, as with Stam (2003), attests to the filmmaker's resistance to the reductive qualities of commercial or global filmmaking that eclipse the ultimate traces of the national when produced by an international crew and cast. The ideal transnational types would exhibit "genuine hybridity"[10] marked by distinctive national elements (15). Having established the claim that transnationality can be ascertained in production and intentionality, Hjort proceeds to a tentative typology with a range of "transnationalisms," some of which are driven by the content or implied purpose of the film, others by production conditions, and still others by economic factors, distribution, etc. There is little emphasis on genre, though the various types approach it.

The term transnational, now as indefinite as global or international, is used by Hjort, and throughout *World Cinema, Transnational Perspectives* (Durovicova and Newman 2010), as something that enables different national types, entities, or persons to meet in a space that bridges their national differences, without being immersed in the great seas of the global.

Global is assumed here to mean a flow that doesn't take note of national boundaries, whereas transnational passes or meets on boundaries and is aware of the meeting. Her usage can serve to bridge the films of the 1980s coming after the "art" films of the previous decades, but works only provisionally, given the Comaroffs's demolition of the economic structures that generated "world" or "global" cinemas.

Hjort wants to see her categories of transnationalism in terms that reflect a process, one that the creation and release of the film promotes. One might be the promotion of national consciousness that "overlaps with aspects of other national identities to produce something resembling deep transnational belonging" (16). Yet, her language of national identities, promoted, stimulated, or revealed by a film that operates within a frame of multiple venues of national consciousness, suggests a deeply help commonality. At the same time it functions amidst multiple identity positions that would seem to undo much of the work of using "trans-" instead of "inter-" as prefixes to national centered thinking. She softens this with "affinitive" transnationalism in which those who recognize difference do so gently, positively—seeing the self in the other, not so as to negate but to construct "shared core values, common practices, and comparable institutions" (17).[11] We can locate all of her transnationalisms, with their positive projects, as also examples of negative contact zoning, of global interactions that, when unveiled, entail national power relations that spill over internal and external borders; in the face of the ideal of the affinitive it would be deconstructed as an ideology that disguises/rationalizes material conditions. Hjort identifies those films as centering on "the tendency to communicate with those similar to us" (17), but with "us," "them," and "communicate" left for the diegesis to establish. The irony with which she laces this type of transnationalism's rhetoric can be seen in the description of its "concept of ethnic, linguistic and cultural affinity" that would "make cross-border collaboration particularly smooth and therefore cost-efficient, pleasurable, and effective" (17).

This is in line with the mode of cultural anthropology, with its recognition of the Other unproblematically bridging difference and power differentials. Johannes Fabian (1983) was particularly severe in reading the deficiencies of this approach. Communicating with "those similar to us" makes exhibition and reception easy, transparent, unproblematical. What vexed anthropology is very similar to what troubles the exhibition and reception of global south cinema in an age when globalization is always already weighted against the interests of the formerly colonized populations. It is precisely the impossibility of a transparent and equitable context for communication that troubles the waters—of cultural relativism in anthropology, of global cinematic interactions on all levels. The core of Fabian's argument is that at the heart of global inequalities is the notion that some people live in the present, i.e., in the modern world, and that others, who are also "other," have not yet arrived at the modern stage, and are thus deemed backward, primitive, and so on. This "non-coevalness" is manifest through Time, that is, the notion that there are modern "times" and backward ones. To ask whether anthropology (or cinema) has succeeded in breaking down this rather old-fashioned colonialist ideology, Fabian cites Maurice Bloch who argues against cultural relativism, claiming communication is universal:

> 1. Anthropology itself bears witness to the fact that it is possible, within certain limits, to communicate with all other human beings, however different their culture and 2. If other people really had different concepts of Time we could not do what we patently do, that is communicate with them.
>
> *(Bloch 1983, cited in Fabian 2002: 42)*

Communicating across cultures entails translation, which involves the mediation of the translator who must enter into the space of both languages. If language can be understood not as a universal system but as a relative construct, then what must be taken into account in every act of translation is the relativity of the translation both to the moment of translation, as words change over time, and the relativity of the concepts, as they are framed by the culture. Behind these concerns lies the more overarching question of the implied power relations between the implied-original and the implied-faithful-translation.

"Radcliffe-Brown, who stresses the structuralist-functionalist anthropological approach, claims 'the essentially social . . . nature of categories of thought'" (Fabian 1983: 43). This leads to two questions: how can one account for change, change of thought and thus values? How can one express oneself to an other in comprehensible terms if terms have meaning only relative to the culture/society in which they are formed? What cultural relativism fails to account for is that "social theory can account neither for new rules nor for new concepts; because 'if all concepts and categories are determined by the social system a fresh look is impossible since all cognition is already moulded to fit what is to be criticized'" (43). The second challenge, communicating in the language of the other, is made to appear almost hilarious: "if we believe in the social determinism of concepts . . . this leaves the actors with no language to talk *about* their society and so change it, since they can talk only within it'" (Bloch 1977: 281, cited in Fabian: 43). The leap here to the quandary of the anthropologist is captured by Fabian thus: "Paraphrasing that last statement, one might continue to reason that the anthropologist, inasmuch as he succeeds in entering another society/culture and comprehending it from *within* (which is the avowed ideal of cultural relativists), would be incapable of saying anything *about* it" (43). This Fabian describes as the *reductio ad absurdum* which requires faith in "universal translatability," something we are still awaiting from the gods of Google Translate.

Until that time, Hjort's unproblematic depictions of transnational cinema, along with the conventional acceptance of hybridity as a simple merging of culture, might be described as translation-without-*différance* and hybridity-sans-*différance*.[12] Such formulations are dysfunctional precisely because they avoid the key element of deconstruction, that is, the need to make visible power differences in cultures, in acts of translation, in that all such acts are inevitably ensconced in ideological freighting— the cargo ensconced in "cargo cults," as described by the Comaroffs, which underlie global exchanges.

The invisible factor of difference involved in translation marks cinematic apparatuses as well. The borders start to become visible when reflexivity is introduced into the role of the translator, of the anthropologist, the cineaste. That reflexivity can appear with the relationships inherent in the material framing of the acts of making and showing films when they are presented across borders. One thinks of the European Union's Schengen "open borders" as fitting this description. European cinema, traveling on the TGV, moves at high speeds: the train doesn't slow as one passes from Italy to France to Germany to the Netherlands. The train romance has a certified tradition in European and American cinema. The crossings in African films turn considerably darker with scenes of African migrants drowning in the attempt to cross the Mediterranean, as in *Frontières* (Djandjam 2002) or *An Opera of this World* (Diawara 2017); or with scenes of desperate people dying in the desert, as in *Bamako* (Sissako 2006).

The films invite the viewers to "board" the trains, but, as in relativity, one might imagine the TGV to travel at three times the speed of the local trains on the old tracks,[13] in which case the measured Time on each train would be different, as they would be relative to the stationary observer. Once on each train, it would be impossible to measure the Time on the one as if it were "coeval" with that on the other. There could be a compensatory factor added in, so that we could translate the Time from one locale to the other, but not without a translator needing to be situated somewhere, skewing the readings of the clocks since the time on each train relative to the observer would be different. In short, there couldn't be a moment that we could call simultaneous in each of the locations.

This might appear irrelevant for the reading of a film, let us say a film being read across one culture into the spaces of another. But the reading of a film, like the observations of the anthropologist, does not occur in a vacuum. Once we consider the entire apparatus, we can't help but notice the key role distance plays in the observation. One sits at a distance, say from the screen, or from the words being spoken, or the actions being portrayed, being lived out, and one writes about them, records them, interprets them, puts them down in black and white, and, in the end freezes them. The moving moment, the train in motion, the dance observed, the anthropologist breathing, in their imagination, in rhythm with the subjects, with the "informant" might manufacture a moment of self-awareness and record their breath, saying, I was there, but just like the present moment of "now," as that claim is being asserted it has changed. The distance, the time, however imagined or observed, is now lagging behind the consciousness of self of the observer.

This lies at the core of the problematic of the discourse in question: the anthropologist's, or alternatively simply the film scholar's, or the audience member's discourse functions as a text that seeks to place the scene in question into its Time, its World, or, its People-Nation-Race-Gender. For this impossible task, Fabian has described the conundrum as the condition of possibility for anthropology: "Could it be that the temporal distancing and denial of coevalness are not faults, but the conditions of possibility of anthropological discourse?" (Fabian: 50).

The question must remain, barred, as we pursue the vexed status of transnationalism, now translated into the barred basis for any African film. We mount the trains north on faith that there is reason to undertake the journey, that despite relativity and its uncertainties, a destination can be reached—*pace* Zeno and his paradox.

II. Affinitive transnationalism generates many types of narrative

For the global north voyage, affinitive transnationalism could entail narratives of affective barriers to be overcome for a young couple—the New Wave model for whom that mode of travel would be a metaphor for love overcoming difficulties. The couple might speak a common language only hesitantly as she could be Belgian and he Spanish. The language would have to be an accented English, learned during their Erasmus year in Denmark where university instruction is mostly in English—American English as they call it. But the boy's parents, living in Cordoba, report problems with their African farmworkers who are asking for better housing conditions, and what with the rise in food prices, can manage only barely, having to share housing etc.

A second film focuses more on the affinities of those collaborating on the journey from the south. In *Frontières* (Djadjam 2001), the obstacles prove deadly for many with the attempted reunion of a desperate couple resulting in the unhappy end to the trip, along with the exploitation, seediness, and corruption of coyotes (*passeurs*, in French). The "trash" that marks the South emerges in the depiction of racist Arabs in Mauretania, Algeria, and Morocco; the fat homosexual German in Morocco; the arrogant Spanish border police—all squeezing the immigrants dry as their illegal status made their lives precarious. The voyage was mostly an ending, not a beginning, much less an interlude.

These two movies mock each other. The needs and problems can be seen to arise from within a national context. For instance, in the Moroccan setting, like Tangier in *Frontières*, the local racism and hostility, the corrupt police, and frontier mentality constrain and permit the exploitation of the Ghanaian, Ivoirian, and Senegalese immigrants. The "border" here totally lacks the romanticism of much border theory with its focus on hybridity and mixing. Here it is the vast Sahara: between the initial crossing of the Senegal River into Mauretania to the arrival in southern Morocco the distance traveled is a good 2000 kilometers. The roles and mise-en-scène frame a series of encounters marked by violent contact and, ultimately, moments of affinity. In the narrative, the travelers are presented with a series of obstacles, with the road-movie's conventional emplotment, and with continual moments of "counter-affinity" that punctuate the action and mark the drama as dystopic. For Hjort, all of that becomes less significant than the approach of the filmmaker whose sensibilities might reflect a global cosmopolitanism, like that which she identifies with the urbanity of Evans Chan's films (2010: 20). His characters might be discoursing on a sophisticated level about worldly issues, even as they are unbuttoning each other in a stylish hotel setting in Copenhagen, meeting briefly as their flights cross from Hong Kong to London for the one, and New York and Brisbane for the other. This is a transnationality marked by long mileage and flights with multiple films; with laughter over the terrible wine on the flights, and with the sophisticated affect accompanying indulgence, flights of champagne, "just this once". . . This form of the transnational returns us to the conventional figures of world cinema, from Satyajit Ray to Truffaut to Scorsese, and the heirs of the New Wave who generated a worldwide phenomenon that eventually transformed Global North worldism into "cosmopolitan transnationalism."

Transnationalism, whose commercial side is now global, for Hjort becomes "globalizing transnationalism," featuring such factors as "global appeal" driven by cost, and "transnational appeal" entailing productions that drive "mechanism[s] for recuperating the high costs of supposedly unavoidable international co-productions" (21). For Hjort, Dogma disproves the assumption that high production values inevitably necessitate "astronomically expensive" costs requiring high audience numbers and ticket sales.

At this point the transnational becomes a weak feature in defining the core qualities of films that must reflect the production or directorial qualities. "Much as in the case of cosmopolitan transnationalism, the driving force in auteurist transnationalism is an individual director who is very much attuned to film's potential for personal rather than formulaic expression" (22–23). External factors, like collaboration across borders, become the add-on to auteurism, thus providing Hjort with the example of Antonioni's *Passenger* (1975), with which we might wish to set in contrast Kelani's *Abeni* (2006). "World" directors are described as finding collaboration across borders, along with the international financing options for the films. The audience becomes world travelers on a presumed higher intellectual and emotional level than that of viewers who consume travelogues. Talented individual directors signal this body of transnational auteurs, like Wong Kar Wai, Abbas Kiarostami, Steven Soderbergh, etc. This is "world" in its global, neo-liberal format, made possible by the technological revolution brought by digital formats, by global flows of finance, post-production, and exhibition. The anticipation of the next world to come is visible in the changes wrought by Criterion Channel, Showmax, and eventually Netflix and Amazon. "African cinema," having made it to this pinnacle, disappears into the global flow, lost in the trans-scapes.

Notes

1   For a full treatment of recent divisions of African films see Manthia Diawara's *African Film: New Forms of Aesthetics and Politics* (2010), where he brilliantly lays out the argument for three "waves" of African film: the Arte wave, La Guilde des cinéastes; the Independent Spirit; and The New Popular African Cinema.

2   Diawara situates African cinema within the wider context of "world cinema" by examining the politics of film festivals: "The European festivals' opposition to American cinematic imperialism is such that a newcomer to that scene would think the evolution of film language id solely defined by a dialectical contradiction between 'auteur' cinema and studio films; reflexive and meta-filmic narratives set against melodramatic and action-driven films; realist meditations about time and space against the artificial construction of narrative through continuity editing.

The question that springs to mind is, 'What does this have to do with African cinemas?' Plenty, if you consider the fact that *African Screens* are not only suffering from the same imperialist monopoly of Hollywood films, but also European cultural domination. French festivals and producers, in particular, practice a colonialist and technological paternalism when it comes to African cinema. They only have eyes for an African cinema that participates in the deconstruction of Hollywood film language and asserts the logic of a European humanitarian agency" (Diawara 2010: 86–87).

3 The terms Garritano identifies as part of the common discourse held on Ghannywood films in Ghana in the 1990s.

4 There is a wide range of neo-baroque texts in Angela Ndalianis's book, *Neo-Baroque Aesthetics and Contemporary Entertainment* (Cambridge: MIT Press, 2004).

5 See Forbes's description of "'Banana Island' in Lagos: The Most Expensive Neighborhood In Nigeria":

"A friend of mine met a really cute Nigerian girl at a nightclub in Lagos recently. He's got a certain *je ne sais quoi* with the ladies. So he approached her, chatted her up for about an hour or so, and was lucky enough to walk away with her phone number and her house address. She asked him to visit her sometime. He promised he would, but he never did.

The reason is this: The lady lives in Banana Island, Nigeria's most expensive residential area. There are only a few privileged men who can *afford* to date a girl who lives in Banana Island. My friend is not yet a part of the privileged few.

If you never heard about the Island, now you know. Banana Island is Nigeria's most extravagant and expensive neighborhood – on par with the Seventh Arrondissement in Paris, La Jolla in San Diego, California and Tokyo's Shibuya or Roppongi neighborhoods.

The exclusive playground of Nigeria's obscenely wealthy, Banana Island is an artificial island built on reclaimed land in Ikoyi-Lagos. From an aerial view, the island is actually shaped like a banana, hence its name. Sitting on 1.6 million square meters, the sumptuous island is divided into about 535 plots ranging in size from 1,000 square meters and 3,000 square meters.

Banana Island is a place of unrivalled opulence and grandeur. It's an entirely different world from other parts of the country. It's a gated community, and its inhabitants enjoy such luxuries as underground electrical systems and water supply networks, 24 hour-electricity supply (the only other place such privileged is the Nigerian President's residence), extremely tight security, good road layout, a central sewage system and treatment plant and the well-cherished company of fellow wealthy folks.

The island is the most expensive place in Nigeria and one of the most expensive in Africa to own a house. Property on Banana Island is dollar-denominated. The average cost of buying a three bedroom apartment is $2 million. However, if you're just looking to hang around the island for some time, and not to buy property, you can rent the same apartment for about $150,000 per annum. But there's a clause: you must pay for an initial minimum term of 2 years – in advance. And there are no refunds. Ever! Also, the tenant is also mandated to pay a 'service charge' of $17,000 per annum.

A typical plot of land on the island usually goes for between $4 million and $6 million, and the cheapest building on the island costs upward of $8 million. But because of the ridiculous prices of property on the island, about 60% of the completed buildings are currently unoccupied.

So, who are the people who occupy the land? The list includes multinational corporations, well-paid expatriate employees, corrupt government officials; their concubines (or mistresses), and wealthy businessmen such as Alhassan Dantata, Kola Abiola and Nigeria's newest billionaire, Mike Adenuga."

http://www.forbes.com/sites/mfonobongnsehe/2011/05/04/the-most-expensive-neighborhood-in-nigeria/ (Accessed April 16, 2015)

6 Set in motion by this new conjuncture, the films that follow carry the themes into the new millennium. Cf. Sissako's *Bamako* (2006), and Safo's *Amsterdam Diaries* (2005).

7 International New Wave art film vocabulary marks this remarkable directorial debut of Claire Denis: "Prior to this Denis had worked with Jim Jarmusch on *Down By Law* (1986) and Wim Wenders on *Paris, Texas* (1984) and *Wings of Desire* (1987). Denis credits their influence on the style of this film, as well as the Japanese films of Ozu and Mizoguchi." http://sensesofcinema.com/2001/cteq/chocolat-2/

8 Because of its criticism of colonialism, the second half of the film was censored in France until the 1960s.

9 She was assistant director under Wim Wenders when he made *Paris, Texas* (1984) and *Wings of Desire* (1987). He attributed the success in overcoming obstacles to the production of *Paris, Texas* to her work, and she clearly benefitted from the relation with him. In *1988* she made *Chocolat*.

10 "Genuine hybridity" was at one point self-evident; but with closer scrutiny collapses. The only hybridity that can sustained would be the ungenuine model of *différance* of better still the impurity of variations of trash. In the practice of translating the transnational into a typology its specificity largely dissolves, perhaps because national identity is also a concept that suffers when defining a type or identity, as was the case with the genre identities Derrida deconstructed in his "Law of Genre." Once formalized, say by legal citizenship, reified identities become useless for cultural analysis, especially as applied to films, except in the narrowest of senses.

11 She sees nothing of the dangers or alienation inherent in the encounter, as would be the model in working with Emmanuel Levinas (1991).

12 The virtue of Bhabha's formulation of hybridity is that it grounded precisely on *différance* (1994).

13 Although, as of this writing (February 2022), news of Senegal acquiring a TGV for the route from the airport to downtown Dakar has appeared in the press.

2

KENNETH NNUEBE, *LIVING IN BONDAGE* AND THE ONSET OF NOLLYWOOD

Kenneth W. Harrow

"What created Nollywood was the spectacular commercial success of *Living in Bondage*" (Haynes 2016: 55). The story of *Living in Bondage* (Chris Obi Rapu, Kenneth Nnuebe 1992) is apparently quite a simple one. Poor man bemoans his lot, will do anything to get rich. When he sacrifices his wife, he is able to join the millionaires club, but in doing so has lost his soul.

There are no real complications, subplots, nuances or complexities to this plotline. So the question is, why did *Living in Bondage* become so hugely influential, become, as Jonathan Haynes has said, the progenitor or ur-Nollywood film that finally succeeded not only in creating a successful model for the commercial cinema that Nollywoodian directors were aspiring to create, but a successful model for the plots of occult films for which Nollywood was soon to become famous? According to Haynes (2016), Nnuebe insisted on raising the quality of the production, taking longer, spending more on this film than was common at the time. The era of dirt-cheap 1980s video films was about to usher in more ambitious digital productions in the 1990s, as was to be the case throughout the world. But nowhere was there such an explosion of filmmaking as in Nigeria. Nollywood was born and *Living in Bondage* played a significant role in it.

There are a few obvious answers, besides production values, that might account for *Living in Bondage*'s success. Its theme touched on a crucial chord concerning the economic and political times (Comaroff and Comaroff 2000). The occultism was not coincidental but was a response to the vast changes experienced in the nation-states in Africa, again in response to conditions largely marked by Structural Adjustment, and with

DOI: 10.4324/9781003397595-4

it globalization (Geschiere 2013). 419 scams and Nollywood were of a piece; the figure of the conman, the feyman, the bushfalla, along with the cargo cults, were of a piece with the commodity fetishism of the 1980s (Comaroff and Comaroff 2000). And with these exotic practices and figures came a change in film culture induced initially by video filmmaking and then digital filmmaking, along with the use of video and digital viewing practices. African cities changed and grew; movie theatres changed and began to disappear; cultures and economies changed; nations lost control over much of their territory, and villages were buffeted about amidst these monumental developments.

A sea-change occurred in the 1980s, and the results have been well-documented by a host of anthropologists, political scientists, sociologists, and historians.[1] Nollywood's birth did not go unannounced! What this chapter will explore is how the key figures mentioned above were central to the appeal of *Living in Bondage*, and in particular how their roles resonated with the growing attention being paid to authenticity and inauthenticity as touchstones. Geschiere (2009, 2013) has been a guide to the issue framed in terms of autochthones versus allothones, the ones who stayed at home versus those who migrated, the "real" indigenous ones versus the foreigners.

All these elements will coalesce in *Living in Bondage*, but more than providing a sociological, or worse, a vulgar-anthropological explanation of the film, of the phenomenon of Nollywood, it is my intent to provide a way of setting *Living in Bondage* against *Chocolat*, so that we might see change across the larger sphere of the film universe at the times, to see simultaneously the radical difference between two films that appear as different from each other as possible, while actually being, in some other real sense, echoes of the same times, the same forces that bore upon society and film culture.

Every thread that leads from the changes in the economy and globalization tracks long lines that lead to insider-outsider questions. We can begin by following the construction of the autochthone in *Living in Bondage*, and in the process will be led to the other figures mentioned above, who sprang to life in the 1980s, who shipped out, shipped abroad, scamming us shamelessly as we learned to laugh or to cry at their machinations.

I.

According to Jonathan Haynes, Nnuebe's *Living in Bondage* (1992) set it all in motion.

"The 1992 Igbo-language *Living in Bondage* inaugurated the video boom. . . . [it] carries a deeply rooted and serious-minded popular discourse on values, intertwining what would remain fundamental Nollywood themes: economic morality and marriage" (Haynes 2016: 18). "*Living in Bondage* was like a seed pod: when it burst open it inseminated a whole industry" (30).

Haynes's description of this moment for Nollywood film, the incipient video boom, points to the first stage of the duping, that also associated with the Hollywood dream.

> The video boom occurred in the moment of neoliberal capitalist triumphalism after the collapse of communism, experienced in Africa as general distress and instability because of structural adjustment, accompanied (because of deregulation) by a flood of imported consumer goods available only to a privileged few and a flood of images of consumer goods, which washed over everyone.
>
> *(2016:44–45)*

Haynes cited Garritano who describes how "maddening these images were" (Garritano 2013, chapter 2, cited in Haynes: 45). The images of local wealth were irresistible, and the audiences were gulled into entering their hallucinatory lull:

> Part of Nollywood's appeal is that it provides images of specifically African forms of wealth and consumption: embroidered cloth, food served on covered plates, pampered African bodies, walled compounds with gatemen, expensive cars driven through familiar tropical landscapes or African-inflected English spoken into the latest cell phones.
>
> *(Haynes 2016: 45)*

He calls this the "Africanization of the pleasures of vicarious consumption" (ibid).

At the beginning Andy is trying to get his tape-player to work. He is at home, but dissatisfied. He checks the electric outlet. Since the 1980s the failure to have reliable electricity in Nigeria has become so notorious that simply shaking one's head and saying NEPA has come to signify jokingly technical failure or incompetence and corruption. ("Never Expect Power Always." Umez 2005: 36.). The setting for his living room, where virtually all the home scenes are shot, is bare. Two couches, a bare table, walls bare except for a calendar or picture of no interest: the space for us to interact with the principal characters, mostly Andy and his wife Merit, with little else. The door to the outdoors, opened often to let others in, or merely opened to knocks, as in the beginning when we hear the first tapping, is covered by a curtain, as is the case elsewhere. We don't see others entering; don't see the outside world. The room is shut in on itself, as is the action.

The home space might be said to be suffocating, and it is in that space that we soon see Andy drop with disappointment the letter that has arrived, hear him lament his fate of having had four corporate jobs come to nothing, of having nothing to show despite years of effort to have a career and make money. His words suffocate us, his sad face transparently conveys his unhappiness and vulnerability. He is not dispossessed: he has had four corporate jobs, and a banking job, and left the latter over unhappiness over his compensation. His wife Merit works, earns their keep, borrows money from her family so that he might invest and start over again. He is a failure, and asks God why.

The audience of his day, 1992, was living under the final days of the Babangida regime. In 1993 Abacha overthrew the government, instituting the most violently repressive government in Nigerian history (Bach, LeBeau, and Awumo 2001; Lewis 2007). Babangida had come to power in 1985 by overthrowing Buhari's government, which he accused of mismanaging power, and especially of not adequately addressing the economic crisis. When faced with IMF and World Bank demands for structural adjustment, Babangida held a referendum in 1985 and adopted a Structural Adjustment Program the following year. The program called for the deregulation of the agricultural sector by abolishing marketing boards and the elimination of price controls, the privatizing public enterprises, and the devaluation of the naira. Peter Lewis (1996) claimed that between 1986 and 1988, when these policies were executed as intended by the IMF, the Nigerian economy actually did grow as had been the hoped, but the real wages fell in the public sector and among urban classes, along with a drastic reduction in expenditure on public services. This set off waves of rioting and discontent in the cities. There was an attempted coup in 1990, with Babangida facing charges of corruption and authoritarianism. In 1991, Babangida moved the capital of Nigeria from Lagos, with all its chaos and violence, to Abuja, the new city of broad avenues and cleanliness. This followed the forced removal of some 300,000 residents of Maroko Town in Lagos to make way for the development of wealthy residential neighborhoods in Victoria Island Annex.[2]

In 1992 Babangida had organized elections that saw the victory of M.K.O. Abiola. Babangida annulled the election and threw Abiola in prison, where he died. Then Babangida clumsily imposed his own party's rule. By the time he left in 1993, the instability of the government, widespread civil disobedience, and massive disaffection paved the way for yet another coup, this time by General Sani Abacha, the most abusive and corrupt of rulers in Nigerian history (Lewis 1996).[3] "By the end of 1990 the adjustment package was in jeopardy. Economic management deteriorated during Babangida's final years, worsening sharply in the period surrounding the mid-1993 transition crisis" (Lewis: 79). The Abacha years read like a Nollywood nightmare: "Macro-economic uncertainty was accompanied by burgeoning corruption, widening social inequality, institutional and infrastructural deterioration, volatile market instability, domestic lawlessness, and international isolation" (Lewis 79).

These conditions of instability, violence, and autocracy, accompanying the years of neoliberal Structural Adjustment, were not unique to Nigeria. But when considering the local reaction in Lagos, at the time that *Living in Bondage* was being scripted, it is not surprising that story of the unemployed protagonist who was to catch Nigerians' imagination begins with his lament, "What have I done to deserve this miserable existence," and, "My god, did you bring me into this world to suffer? Am I bewitched or is this my destiny?" Yet when he explains, in the opening soliloquy, that he resigned from his bank job because "My body needs more money than the peanuts they were paying me," we are given to understand that his is not the case of the everyman who is suffering under Structural Adjustment Programs and authoritarian rule, but simply a greedy man who cannot bear with aplomb his modest conditions of life. His problem is quickly established: he is not as rich as others, and the other factors in his life cannot compensate for that fact.

The other feature to which we are quickly introduced is that his wife Merit is an ideal mate. All she asks of life is Andy's love, and she is willing to sacrifice much to get it. If they are short of funds, she borrows from her parents and brother. If he grumbles over his fate, she consoles and comforts him. She is tempted twice by wealthy men to become their mistresses, and in turning down the first, her boss Iche Millionaire, she has to resign her position. The second is Chief Omego (whose name means wealthy), who boasts of his generosity toward his mistresses. When she seeks advice from her friend Caro, and is told to accept her boss's offer, she responds, "Is this how you advise me? I thought you were my friend," and leaves Caro to her grasping ways. Caro later becomes a girlfriend of the millionaire who convinces Andy to join their club and to sacrifice Merit. The world surrounding Andy is filled with darkness, on the streets at night, in the worries he carries, the debts he incurs, and the insecurity that leads him to foolishly invest in a get-rich-scheme that leads to the loss of his in-laws' loan.

Relatively early in the film, Andy bumps into an old friend, Paul, who is driving past him in a larger sedan. Paul invites him out and convinces him that he can solve Andy's money problems. Shortly after, Andy attends a party at Paul's house, and is introduced to the club of millionaires, who are dancing and drinking with their women. Andy is attracted to one woman in particular, and Paul lets him know that it will not be a problem for him to pass her on to Andy, to Andy's delight. The stage is set at the outset: Merit will prove her fidelity to Andy, and in doing so establish her "merit." He has shown his lack of fidelity and failures in judgment. Although we are later presented with a flashback scene in which Andy remembers their initial falling in love, it is at the point where he is prepared to sacrifice her, literally, to become rich. There is nothing really complicated in this view of the two of them: good wife, bad husband, corrupt world, the need to resist evil, the failure of the morally weak, the price of sin. A Pentecostal formula guides the plot from the outset when Andy beats his chest in proclaiming his body's need for money. The only question becomes, what must he do to get it, what the price is to be. And even there, the sacrifice of Merit will come to the viewer as no surprise. We have been prepared for it and are surprised to see it carried out literally and not simply figuratively.

The moralism that guides these representations dictates the genre. Although the film is seen as setting the agenda for occultism, it is the occult in the service of religious morality, and the characters tend toward the allegorical to serve this purpose of the sermon. There are breaks, at times due to awkwardness, at times due to the irrepressibility of realism when representation is privileged. When Merit runs around a chair to flee her pursuing boss, the humor is inadvertent; when she pounds on him and throws tea in his face, it is skirting broad farce. When she looks Chief Omego up and down in the supermarket, chastising him and humiliating him publicly, as he attempts to shush her, it is a somewhat different Merit from the one who minsters to the depressed Andy and accepts his bad judgment. The strain lies in the audience of Nigerian women who would be continually urging her mentally to wake up.

When Andy recalls the time they fell in love, and paints an idyllic picture, their clothes matching, their romantic kissing, chasing each other around a garden, we are in still another genre of the dream world. But that is only to set off the horror of the sacrifice of Merit that follows. In all of this admixture of tones there is one steady drumbeat that governs, and that is the impending death of Merit that will satisfy the greed of her husband. And that drama is set within the wider one, which we might see as inevitably arising in the late 1980s and early 1990s where the spectacle of shooting thieves on the beach accords with the construction of mansions for the wealthy on Victoria Island (Haynes 2016: xviii). The times were out of joint, and it was especially the doings of men of power and wealth that were responsible.

The place of the men who constitute the millionaire's club is not made obvious at the outset. Paul presents himself initially as rich, owning several cars and able to make Andy wealthy as well. But the scene with Paul is soon followed by that of Robert. After eating out with Paul, Andy has returned home to Merit to tell her about his experience. "Sit down," he says,

"I have a story." The story is soon interrupted by the visit of Robert who tells the gullible Andy that if Andy only were to invest 10,000 he would get 70,000 in return, and that 20,000 would get him 140,000. After he leaves Merit begs him not to invest, but later learns that he failed to heed her advice and lost the entire 20,000 she had borrowed from her parents.

The spectator immediately recognizes that Robert is a conman. He appears shortly after Andy laments his own weakness and desperate desire to be as wealthy as Paul or those Paul describes as owning several cars, while he himself is reduced to taking taxis. His home is modest; Paul's swinging flat has a built-in bar, and room to entertain men of wealth and attractive women. There is no reason for them to have succeeded and him to have failed. They are not older "Big Men," but young like himself, starting out like himself from nothing—age mates. There must have been some force greater than ordinary human effort to account for their success and his failure. The ship that has come in for them contains cargo of value; the talents they display must have a backing that is not visible to all. Paul has guaranteed he can bring Andy into the fold of the wealthy. Robert comes knocking, as if the fable demanded that Andy be prepped one more time in order to become sufficiently vulnerable to agree to Paul's terms, to Paul's injunction that he be "strong."

If on the one hand there is the moral struggle of good versus evil, the Devil versus Jesus, the destruction of love, the sacrifice of the loving wife versus the Blood of Jesus (that saves the prostitute when Andy first tries to palm her off as his wife to the congregation of Lucifer worshippers), still the larger frame of the narrative depends upon an account of how the mysterious creation of wealth might be understood. Cargo cults, feymen, and bushfallas are a good place to begin (Nyamnjoh 2011; Fisiy and Geschiere 2002).

Robert is a "feyman", and the promise he holds out to Andy is that his investment in a cargo shipment will provide phenomenal returns. "There is a consignment that has just come in from overseas," he tells Andy, as he moves forward on the edge of seat, leaning toward Andy. Merit, to Andy's side, leans away from Robert, not taken in by appearances. Meanwhile, the camera, generally static, zooms in on Robert who is working his victim with the desire for gold. In fact, he appears immediately after Andy has told Merit about the meeting with Paul and the car they will have. Her response is, you will then get another girlfriend.

Robert tells Andy that when the Alhaji friend of his, who owns the container, opens it, it will contain every type of vehicle engine. "Pathfinder, Peugeot, name it." Merit, not hiding her feelings, looks down as if in disgust. "In the other corner," says Robert, "Video, TV, name it." He crosses his arms excitedly, to convey the image of excessive wealth. The scene of the wild carnival and array of refrigerators in Djibril Diop's *Hyenas* comes to mind, as an extravagant display of worldly wealth is conjured up in this scene. Robert tells Andy he must put money down to realize the profit from the container. 10,000 will get him 70,000 "cool naira." 20,000 will get him double.

The script for the conman is not new. But the lineaments for this "fey-man", the combination of the occult and the magical multiplication of wealth at a time of hardship, of neoliberal SAP, are traced with great precision by the Comaroffs (2000), as if they had taken the images directly from *Living in Bondage*! They begin the delineation of millennial capitalism in Africa with this account of "occult economies" which result in such practices as pyramid schemes like the one Robert was dangling before Andy. Occult economies, they claim:

> . . . have two dimensions: a material aspect founded on the effort to conjure wealth—or to account for its accumulation—by appeal to techniques that defy explanation in the conventional terms of practical reason; and in an ethical aspect grounded in the moral discourses and (re)actions sparked by the real or imagined production of value through such 'magical' means.
>
> *(19)*

For the Comaroffs, finance capital always had this "spectral" side, but in terms of the specific turn taken in Nigeria in this period—as Pentecostalism grew so rapidly (Birgit Meyer 1998)—the turn to video films at the same time meant that genre filmmaking could now be contemplated, and that amateur filmmakers, which the vast majority of early Nollywood and Ghanaian video filmmakers were, could step up. The beginning, the mystery of money, is summed by perfectly by Comaroff and Comaroff: "All of these things [schemes to acquire wealth] have a single common denominator: the allure of accruing wealth from nothing" (22). For the Comaroffs, that meant that they shared the same "animating spirit" as "casino capitalism" (23). The immorality of gambling immediately repelled Merit when Robert made his proposal. Further, his own immorality as a feyman also was distasteful to her: as he made his pitch, she turned her head away, as if not to be viewing the corruption.

About how much profit?

FIGURE 2.1   Merit turning her head away

The Comaroffs continue is this vein on the nature of gambling that characterizes this neoliberal turn:

> [I]ndeed, perhaps they *are* casino capitalism for those who lack the fiscal or cultural capital—or who, for one or another reason, are reluctant to gamble on more conventional markets. Like the cunning that made straw into gold, these alchemic techniques defy reason in promising unnaturally large profits—to yield wealth without production, value without effort. Here, again, is the specter, the distinctive spirit, of neoliberal capitalism in its triumphal hour.
>
> *(23)*

Just as the most successful expression of this turn in representation is Nollywood, so too is its religious counterpart in Pentecostalism, marked by the scamming sensibility of the feyman. Both offer what Robert held out to dazzle Andy with—the names of the big cars whose engines made up the cargo in the container he was selling: "Every type of vehicle engine." The Comaroffs describe the Universal Church's fashioning of "enterprise and urbanity," promising "swift payback to those who embrace Christ, denounce Satan, and "make their faith practical" by "sacrificing" all they can to the movement" (23).

Here Pentecostalism meets neoliberal enterprise. In its African churches, most of them (literally) storefronts, prayer meetings respond to frankly mercenary desires, offering everything from cures for depression through financial advice to remedies for unemployment; casual passersby, clients really, select the services they require. Bold color advertisements *for BMWs* and lottery winnings adorn altars; tabloids pasted to walls and windows carry testimonials by followers whose membership was rewarded by a rush of wealth and/or an astonishing recovery of health. The ability to deliver in the here and now, itself a potent form of space-time compression, is offered as the measure of a genuinely global God, just as it is taken to explain the power of Satanism.

(Comaroff and Comaroff: 23, my emphasis)

The technical language Robert deploys to hold out the vision of unlimited, inexplicable wealth, if only Andy had the courage to invest, appears anodyne. He mentions the container his El Hadj owns and wishes to dispose of. The details of the cargo are intended to evoke the signs of mysterious wealth, especially cars, which hold a particular attraction for Andy. Paul tells him about his expensive collection of cars, and the next one he will purchase. Andy pictures driving in his own with Merit. And twice in the film we see or learn of his not having his own car. He borrows one of Paul's to pick up the prostitute whom he hoped to sacrifice in place of Merit; and finally calls a cab to take Merit to her death in the Satanic cult ritual. Car engines, televisions, "Name it," says Robert, and Andy is hooked. In the end it is all cargo, that magical term that signifies the core of the capital upon which the entire mysterious system of import/export, profit, and glorious wealth rests, if only the investor had the courage to assume the risks. This is the global world into which the Comaroffs set their vision of millennial capitalism—the world to which Andy and Merit are so visibly outsiders. "To the degree that millennial capitalism fuses the modern and the postmodern, hope and hopelessness, utility and futility, the world created in its image presents itself as a mass of contradictions: as a world, simultaneously, of possibility and impossibility" (2001: 24). The magic of belief in the golden age at the end of the millennium, of time itself, comes with its cult magic centered in the cargo itself. Just as slaves turned their condition of filth and labor into gold, so too would cargo effect the miraculous. All that was needed for Melanesian cargo cults was the proper ritual act (Burridge 1969). The cults, beginning with colonial commercial networks that associated trade and wealth in some mysterious way, centered on the cargo that the ships brought, and the power and wealth of those who controlled the trade.

According to Burridge, cargo cults arose during times of crisis which saw the end of the old social order.[4] The Comaroffs complete the description that paints so well such a time as that of the world of *Living in Bondage*:

At the turn of the twenty-first century, the cargo, glimpsed in large part through television, takes the form of huge concentrations of wealth that accrue, legitimately or otherwise, to the rich of the global economy—especially the enigmatic new wealth derived from financial investment and management, from intellectual property and other rights, from cyberspace, from transport and its cognate operations, and from the supply of various post-Fordist services.

(Burridge 1969: 24)

The fortunes that were accumulated so quickly and mysteriously were also somehow joined to a logic that brought into play the mysteries of the market, of the new technologies that were responsible for "unimaginable fortunes amassed by the ever more rapid flow of value, across time and space, into the fluid coordinates of the local and the global" (Burridge 1969: 24).

Neoliberal wealth could only come with its negative counterpart: unaccountable poverty, the condition embodied by Andy as he felt "the sense of impossibility, even despair, that comes from being left out of the promise of prosperity, from having to look in on the global economy of desire from its immiserated exteriors" (Burridge 25).[5]

Andy moves between two orders. On the one hand, he is relatively poor and is an outsider to the club of the wealthy. But the more fundamental split lies between his original home in the patriarchal village and the riotous, unregulated world of Lagos. He was vulnerable to all that the cultists had to offer, and to the feyman's pitch. He was the naïve country cousin who fell for the city slicker's fast lines. This was his first fall, setting the stage for his ultimate downfall.

The "feyman," like the 419 scammers, came of age with the new capitalist world order. In the 1980s, the 419 scammers got their start following the decline in oil prices (Grinker et al. 2010). According to Grinker, Lubkemann, and Steiner, large numbers of the youth had acquired a good education, like Andy and his friends, and no longer had careers open to them. At the same time, the military rule had somehow enabled a smaller elite to acquire vast sums of money. Grinker et al. claim that just as the rulers had pilfered vast sums of money from the national economy, so too would 419 scammers dream of acquiring unlimited wealth. "Many of the scam writers' seemingly preposterous stories of huge sums of money somehow siphoned from Nigeria's coffers are in fact reminiscent of the actual methods corrupt Nigerian elites have used to steal the country's wealth for years" (617). Bayart's *L'État en Afrique: La Politique du Ventre* (1989) detailed the workings of these processes in the 1980s, and the language that accompanied its growth: "It's our time to chop" captures the dynamic of exchanging votes for "chop"; "cabritismo," a goat will eat where he is tethered (Bayart 1989, cited by Moorman). Mbembe (2000) completes the portrait of the autocratic ruler whose belly and anus mark his place in the world in his playing upon *Le Messager*'s cartoon representations of "Popaul," Paul Biya.

Fisiy and Geschiere's portrait, then, of the feyman could as easily be matched in any of the above texts that delineate the key figure of the times, from Babangida and Abacha to Biya, down to the anonymous 419 scammers whose inventive personae all come alive with Paul and Robert in *Living in Bondage*. According to Geschiere, the term feyman originated in Cameroonian pidgin to "faire quelqu'un," that is, to con someone. It gained currency in the global span of their operations" (Geschiere: 242). As with the cargo cults, if there is money in abundance, it must be due to grace or magic, and not just to the ability to win over the gullible. "[I]t is clear that the magical qualities attributed to their enigmatic accumulation of wealth" (Geschiere: 243). The rise of occult forces in the 1980s that came with economic neoliberalism was widespread. Unlike the 1960s and 1970s, when the rhetoric of development was subordinated to the logic of rational thought and progress, as understood at that time, with the economic downfall of the 1980s, the rise of SAPs, neoliberalism, and the declining state, came the surprising restoration of "witchcraft" once again as a credible factor in people's lives (Geschiere 2013). "Apparently the forms of enrichment that have come with economic liberalization have given witchcraft discourses yet another new lease on life" (Fisiy and Geschiere 2002: 243). For Fisiy and Geschiere, the reduced credibility of development rhetoric and the corresponding rise of belief in witchcraft are explained by the conjunction that marked the 1980s: "The subsequent proliferation of witchcraft and its many ambiguities seems to reflect seems to reflect the disappearance of a confident metanarrative about development's trajectory" (Fisiy and Geschiere 2002: 243). More significantly, this shift is not limited to Africa, but to the widespread consequences of neoliberal's impact on globalization more broadly. When we explore how autochthones and allothones interact in a film like *Chocolat*, it will appear striking how "entangled" the world-shaping forces of the period were.

For Cameroon in the 1980s as elsewhere, there was a "broad loss of faith in social engineering" just as there was a commensurate gain of faith in evangelical movements. Uncertainty had become:

> . . . a general phenomenon in our globalizing world with the defeat of the state—whether of the welfare or the authoritarian type—by the requirements of the 'market,' leaving society at the mercy of an economy that seems increasingly unpredictable and out of control.
>
> *(Fisiy and Geschiere: 243)*

The ascension of magic could then be explained in terms of economism, but also as a feature of modernism whose effects were "distributed" across various uneven global flows that were felt particularly in the technological changes of cinema. "[A]t the beginning of the twenty-first century magic seems to become a fixed corollary of modernism, not only in Africa, but also in the richer parts of the world" (Fisiy and Geschiere: 243).

The richer parts of Africa were of particular interest to Nnuebe in *Living in Bondage*. There would be no point in dwelling in Andy and Merit's tediously ordinary home. All the drama had to come from the chiefs. Ichie Millionaire was Merit's boss, and he was responsible for her having left her job, leaving her dependent on her family as well as him for an income. "Chief" Omego, like Ichie (whose name means chief), appears early in the film as a philanderer and polygamist whose reputation for wealth is widely attributed to his having sacrificed his mother (although precisely how is not stated). The two men who bear the titles "chief," along with the others whose club is based on the multiplication of money, exemplify the roles of success in the bloody competition for wealth in the city. They, like Andy, presumably have left home to combat powerful forces in order to become wealthy. Aside from the rituals and sacrifices, they are able to overcome others in the violence of the struggle. They enter into the bush and "fall" the game—bring it home and get the rewards. They are what Nyamnjoh has defined as bushfallas, and it is to become a bushfalla that Andy aspires and sacrifices his wife.

II Bushfalling

When we consider feymen and bushfallas, it seems obvious that they emerged in the convergence of two things—exactly like Nollywood itself. The first is the economic crisis that come in the 1980s, worsened by Structural Adjustment Programs in Africa, but still affecting countries throughout the world, including Hollywood where costs had skyrocketed. The second are the technological innovations of video and then digital filmmaking, whose new, inexpensive films generated the video revolution throughout the world (Lobato 2012), including especially Nigeria.

The digital age made it possible for 419 scamming to come about; the crisis made pentecostal appeals more potent. The Nollywood scenarios reflect both elements; the script for *Living in Bondage* appears as a model, with the ground prepared for Andy to enter the market ruled by "strong" men, as Paul designated them, as well as "Big Men," as Nigerians came to call the wealthy and powerful. Nyamnjoh opens his study of the figure of the "bushfaller," those who leave home to dare face the dangers away, with the "metaphors of choice among Cameroonians" being hunting and distance farming (Nyamnjoh: 701). His descriptions call to mind the Mande terms *fadenya*, father-childless, and *badenya*, mother-childless. I do not wish to refer to these terms as fixed anthropological categories, but rather broad ideological structures whose roots go back to lived experiences in the region (Bird and Kendell 1980). In the case of *fadenya*, it derives from the notion of brothers in conflict who seek "bushmeat," or wealth, outside the compound and village confines. Hunters abroad, like bushfallas seeking bushmeat, "eat" the prey they capture. Eating becomes the key metaphor for conquering, and bushfallas, like feymen, eat those whose wealth they have conned from their victims, eat those whom they have sacrificed in order to gain their wealth. In *Living in Bondage*, Merit has to be sacrificed for the aspiring bushfalla Andy to overcome his opponents. His prayers to God at the beginning would seem to be falling on deaf ears without the sacrifice.

The cult to which the sacrifice of Merit is to be made is called the cult of Lucifer, but in fact, the language of the high priest echoes that of the Christian preacher (Haynes 2016: 26). The act of drinking her blood echoes the sacrament of communion; the holiness of Merit, displayed in her giving nature, is made concrete in the materialization of the transsubstantiation of her blood. She embodies the virtues of *badenya*, one who gives for the community.

If *fadenya* involves the qualities of the brave individual who sets out to seek his fortune, he is in contrast to the more maternal figure of the one who stays at home and works in communion with others, those who sustain the community: those who are "mother-childed." *Fadenya* fosters change; *badenya* sustenance for the status quo (Jansen, Bird, Bagayogo). In Bird and Kendell's classical formation, *fadenya* is associated with "centrifugal forces of social disequilibrium: envy, jealousy, competition, self-promotion" (13–26). This is often seen as describing the world of men, the world in which only men can operate. It is the complementary opposite of *badenya*, with its "centripetal forces of society: submission to authority, stability, cooperation" (Bird and Kendell, 13–26).

Hunting for game is completed, like raids in warfare, when the game, the war booty, the loot, is brought back to the village. Nyamnjoh evokes this quality for the bushfalla:

> The mobile among them perceive the city and the "world out there" as they do hunting grounds or distant farms. The home village remains, however, the ultimate conferrer of social recognition and is the place of return at the end of the day. Fear of social invisibility among kith and kin compels individuals to disappear and subject themselves to the vicissitudes, whims, and caprices of worlds and forces untamed during hunting and farming expeditions into distant undomesticated lands.
>
> *(701)*

Nyamnjoh repeats his point that the hunter must bring home the "booty" so as to fulfill his social obligation, to win recognition.

This is the key point for my reading of *Living in Bondage*. The plot might well have entailed bushfallas and *fadenya*, containing all the action in the "wilds" of Lagos where Andy had to fight to prove his worthiness and win his battles. However, the key scene needed to establish the space/location of the wilderness lies in the trip to his home village. There one can reestablish the parameters of the insider/outsider, the autochthone and allothone, which make visible the work of the bushfalla.

For Nyamnjoh the logic of bushfalling lies in fulfilling obligations at home: in returning home with a large car and distributing wealth. Andy sets about to do all this, especially after he has finally gained admittance to the club of millionaires. However, he can't acquire the wealth without the loss of Merit, and that price proves too much for his decent family at home for whom *badenya*, seen in the need to take care of the bleating goats (the first scene that occurs when the action moves to the village), and caring for one's relations (Andy's mother pulls out a photo of Merit and grieves), take priority. Andy's father pulls up his porch chair and takes his accustomed position. The space is occupied as expected, with father, mother, and sister all assuming their familiar places. When that portrait of the family is completed, Andy can then show up, driven now by a chauffeur in a large expensive car. The "cargo" has come home. "Fulfilling obligations also demonstrates a certain level of success and guarantees survival and recognition" (Nyamnjoh: 701), which is what Andy expects from this visit.

Bushfalling, which Nyamnjoh calls a "metaphor for hunting" (Nyamnjoh: 702) is measured in terms that are commensurate with Pentecostal values, that is, "what in terms of money and material possessions they have gained" (702). "Bushfalling" gained currency in the 1980s with the "conjunction" that marked the economic crisis: it "coincided in Cameroon with struggles for multiparty democracy in the late 1980s and early 1990s, a persistent economic downturn, and mass unemployment (30–40 percent) compounded by a 50 percent devaluation of the CFA franc in 1994" (Nyamnjoh: 703–4). The earlier migrations of the 1960s and 1970s were characterized by the search for higher education and better career opportunities—the paths for gaining money. Communities of Africans living abroad became fixtures in the literature of the next generation that followed (e.g. NoViolet Bulawayo, Chimimanda Adichie, Dinaw Mengestu, Taiye Selassi, Teju Cole). Everyone who took that path initially, in that first generation, imagined that their stay abroad would be temporary, and that their homecoming would be marked by the ability to build impressive houses, to return with a family and all the signs of success. The downturn of the 1980s put much greater pressure on sending funds from abroad, and Western Union transfers grew enormously, at times reaching the point where the total sums surpassed any other source of local incomes. "Falling bush" became the greatest sign of success:

Responding to an article in the Post that was critical of bushfallers, a reader named Mukete, who has little positive to say about them, hints at just how popular and costly bushfalling has become: Friends have become enemies just because of the idea of falling bush. Families have separated, parents have abandoned children, children have turned against their parents, pastors and priests have abandoned their congregations, people have joined jojo and secret societies, civil servants have abandoned their duties with continuous salaries, people have stolen and have killed, just because they want to fall bush by all means. All the young want to fall bush!

(Nyamnjoh 704–5)

In *Living in Bondage*, "home" comes to Andy and Merit in the form of Auntie, whose role is to oversee the couple's travails, and bring Merit the moral support she needs to keep Andy in line. She begs Andy, with Merit, not to become like Chief Omego, but she fails, and is the only one present when Merit dies in the hospital. The return home is necessary, even if *Living in Bondage* confines that necessity to one scene. Still, Fondong's description of the typical return home sets the stage for our reading of Andy's return: "the bushfallers always endeavor to return home as often as they can, usually in December, to show off their latest catch: a futuristic SUV, a massive building project, an exotic business, etc" (Fondong 2008, cited in Nyamnjoh: 705).[6]

In the key scene of Andy returning home, he announces that he will be taking a new wife after the death of Merit. He brings money to the family and says he wants to take his sister back with him so that she can have an opportunity to make something of herself in the big city. All that could easily have been omitted without disturbing the basic plotline that drives Andy to sacrifice Merit in order to become wealthy. The return to the village gestures outward in two ways: it sets Andy off as an outsider to the autochthones of the city, reinforcing in a more meaningful way his status as outsider to the club of millionaires when the film began.

Andy's dissatisfaction with his lot drives the action, turns the villager to a city dweller, just as the call of the bushmeat turns the peasant farmer into the bushfalla, and the magic appeal of the cargo turns the colonized laborer into the assimilated African—the "civilisé" or "evolué." The story of the Africain *civilisé* was written by Cheikh Anta Diop at the outset of the period of independence, and he named that condition an "Ambiguous Adventure." The bushfaller's ambiguity might be seen as that of the close copy, imperfect yet essentially the same, creating the space for the "originaires," the autochthonous dwellers, the ones from home to argue that those who left for the bush, for Europe, for the city, return changed forever. They are now "ambiguous," marked by the double subjectivity of colonial hybridity indelibly engraved on their foreheads. This is how Nyamnjoh presents Igor Kopytoff's (1987: 3–17) reading of the newly created spaces:

> [Kopytoff] has argued that the largely "frontier" character of African societies has been ignored in the anthropological fixation on the elusive authentic insider firmly located in "the unambiguous heartland," to the detriment of the "uncertain peripheries" that represent histories of mobility, cultural encounters, negotiation, and flux. Straddling worlds the way bushfallers do in their capacity as "frontier persons" (Kopytoff 1987:17–23) is not always positively perceived by those who feel more embedded in either world, especially when bushfallers behave in ways that translate into opportunism, dishonesty, lack of loyalty, or impermanence in relationships with others.
>
> *(Nyamnjoh 706)*

Andy's initial encounter with new women making themselves available at Paul's party early in the film immediately places him in conflict with Merit, who demonstrates her fidelity to Andy in fighting off the advances of her boss Ichie Millionaire and in telling Andy about it.

We might wish to read with resistance the portrayal of Andy as untrustworthy. We can view his actions as necessarily marking his entry into the intermediary spaces lying between home and the millionaire's wealthy apartments, as signs of his status as an insider invited as a visitor; as one tied in the past to an original set of commitments, yet open to the future with its infinite possibilities. These factors can be interpreted as being responsible for the negative views of the old-school homebodies, like Auntie. This is precisely the tack Nyamnjoh takes in defending the bushfallas from those who could be called "fundamentalist" or "exclusionary":

> As many scholars have argued (Comaroff and Comaroff 2001; Geschiere 2009; Gupta and Ferguson 1992; Stolcke 1995; Wright 1998), some people are increasingly fundamentalist and exclusionary in their claims and articulation of belonging, in ways that pay scant regard to the reality of those who inhabit borderlands. Being neither an insider nor an outsider in categorical terms might have its blessings, but it does not inspire confidence or trust among those who see the world and configurations of belonging purely in black and white and in very rigid and frozen ahistorical terms.
>
> *(Nyamnjoh: 706–7)*

But in the analogy he subsequently constructs, the comparisons become strained when considering how far Andy proves he is willing to go in order to succeed.

Being a bushfaller is like being married but available, like cheating on or being unfaithful to one's culture, identity, and belonging. It is like subverting the boundaries within which one is confined. Bushfallers simultaneously belong and do not belong, are a present absence and an absentpresence.

(Nyamnjoh: 707)

A present absence and an absentpresence would seem to fit well with Bhabha's notion of hybridity where the doubled presence of the colonizer/ colonized generates an indistinguishable subjectivity, one always present after the fact, always waiting to be/return home. Comaroff and Comaroff evoke the models of semi-human subjective spaces as consequences of the alienation brought on by the new neoliberal age, where work and reward no longer seemed to have any meaningful relationship to each other, and more, where the generation of wealth seemed to arise as magically as the all-powerful state of the past seemed to be fading in its influence. What replaced those states were the fetish industries that drove the forces behind cargoes, cars with powerful engines, great houses behind walls, impenetrable containers for wealth that came with chieftaincies, with power. (At this early point in Nollywood, "Millionaires" digs might appear modest, in comparison with the mansions later leased for the films, like *Beyonce, The President's Daughter*, Arase 2006)

FIGURE 2.2 The "millionaires club" digs in *Living in Bondage*

With the consequences of the downturn in the 1980s, as the streets disintegrated and the population experienced impoverishment, ethnicities were increasingly set against ethnicities, region against region, and armed militia against militia. The turn to the occult multiplied: "There is a strong tendency for states to appeal to new or intensified magicalities and fetishes in order to heal fissures and breaches in the fabric of the polity" (Comaroff and Comaroff 2001: 36; see Geschiere 2013).

Nollywood film, dependent on Igbo producers and actors, on Yoruba audiences, or even Hausa, and those of neighboring states, typically would not stress the rise of identity politics (except for Kelani's *Thunderbolt* [2001], which is one of the few films to directly address the issue). But the projection of ethnicity onto class became notable, as the gulf in wealth became the signature of the changing face of nationhood in the neoliberal age. According to Comaroff and Comaroff, especially after 1989, there has been an explosion of identity politics. "Ethnic struggles, ranging from polite altercations over resources to genocidal combat, seem immanent almost everywhere as membership is claimed on the double front of innate substance and primordial sentiment, as culture becomes intellectual property" (2001: 37). In a powerful summary of the times, and its rising tide of xenophobia, Comaroff and Comaroff evoke the violence brought on by the changes due to neoliberal politics, economic crisis, and social unrest:

> The end of the Cold War, like the death of apartheid, fired utopian imaginations. But liberation under neoliberal conditions has been marred by a disconcerting upsurge of violence, crime, and disorder. The quest for democracy, the rule of law, prosperity, and civility threatens to dissolve into strife and recrimination, even political chaos . . . Everywhere there is evidence of an uneasy fusion of enfranchisement and exclusion; of xenophobia at the prospect of world citizenship without the old protectionisms of nationhood.
>
> *(2001: 8)*

The resulting turn to faith and the occult became tied to the desperate need and increasing desire for money bringing a great increase in "innovative occult practices and money magic, pyramid schemes and prosperity gospels; the enchantments, that is, of a decidedly *neo*liberal economy whose ever more inscrutable speculations seem to call up fresh specters in their wake" (2001: 2).

The bushfalla then is the reflected image of the speculative world created by SAPs and neoliberal economies. He is the imaginary figure of the warrior who can attract the youth for his daring and display of wealth, which matters more than the solidity of money in the bank (Newell 2012). The display must entail the car, clothing, and flash; it must involve the generosity of paying for the drinks.[7] The flip side of the bushfalla is the sad sap, the conman's victim, the patsy, who is Andy, twice over. Initially, we see him being taken in by Robert, despite the strong objections of Merit and Auntie, who speak for the audience in their warnings; and secondly, sacrificing Merit, acting with still greater foolhardiness in giving up the only real thing of value that he has. He tells Paul at their initial meal together in the restaurant that he has one thing of value, his wife, whereat Paul tells him he is to be congratulated, that it is not so easy to find and win over a good wife. That theme is accentuated when we see the conflict within the household of Chief Omego in the scene preceding this exchange in the restaurant between Paul and Andy; and it is accentuated when we see Andy's mother mourning the loss of the inestimable Merit. Andy himself is seen as being led to and manipulated by Paul throughout the initiation that leads to the sacrifice; and he is brought to the final decision by his recollection of the threatening words of the chief priest that he would die if he didn't bring Merit. In short, he lacks the courage or sense of the bushfalla. In submitting to their ministrations he embodies their flip side as an exemplar of the failures of neoliberalism.[8]

If Andy is a failure in the world of decent family life, he is a fabulous flirt who easily wins Ego and the women to whom Paul introduces him. Both men claim that women cannot resist them. "The bushfaller was a fly by night lover, saying all the right things a girl wants to hear and making her dream what was never to be. He dribbled her the way he did others in a football game" (Nyamnjoh: 707). Failures and scammers, the "club of the millionaires" are part of the transforming magic of the new frontiers where old restraints on conduct and limits are seemingly swept away.[9] They are seen as having no scruples, to the point of "being accused of having sacrificed kin" (Nyamnjoh 708). Like the entrepreneurs on the streets of Lagos they straddle two worlds: "seeking economic, social, and political capital in their quest for independence or favorable terms of dependence in the worlds they straddle" (Kopytoff 1987: 40–48, cited in Nyamnjoh: 709). Nyamnjoh calls them "borderlanders and border crossers," and instead of viewing them solely as exploiters, sees them also positively as "actively and creatively negotiating and navigating myriad identity margins and possibilities in their quest for flexible identities and belonging" (Nyamnjoh: 709). Andy the killer of women can thus be read two ways, like Lagos itself. *Living in Bondage*, after all, implies, in the title, that somehow, as Sethe discovers in *Beloved*, a sacrifice, a killing of one's kin, must be made if bondage is to be avoided.

III

There are two scenes that bring home all these values of the new world of the feyman and bushfalla. The first is marked by the banal existence of the village into which Andy tries to introduce the crude materialism and consumerism of the city, as we have seen. The second is the occasion for Andy's second marriage with Ego, whose name means money and whose family is joined not to Andy's family but to his new "family" of millionaires. The club in fact replaces the family just as he replaces "merit" with "money."

The two locales are linked by the coeval times of the present: modernity in its most corrupt face when involving the family, and in its most materially successful face when determined by business. The temporality of the family: with Andy at home with Merit; or back in the village; or with business, as when Merit is fleeing from her lecherous boss; or when Andy places Merit's body on the altar to be sacrificed and shares in the imbibing of her blood.

Similarly, the coeval temporalities of France's family in the past in *Chocolat*, when they are all together, as when arriving home at the commandant's *residence*, with Protée and the cook and other Africans all in their quarters. Then the temporality linked to France as a young woman arriving and departing from Cameroon in Douala. The arrival in the present moment, with Mungo Park picking up France when she is hitchhiking, in her jeans and with her knapsack. The earlier departure from the North when she was still a child, with the old Africa of horsemen and noble fons and elders meeting with her father Dalens on his *tournées*.

The temporality of the bushfalla is determined in both cases by the need to make the mark, to "faire" or dupe the target. *Chocolat*, the title winking at the French slang term *chocolat*, meaning duped, poses the question, who was duping whom, and when? France's father, the commandant Marc Dalens, is called a dupe by Luc since he turns a blind eye to his wife Aimée's desire for the African servant Protée. But Protée is duped by the confidence shown him by his *patron* Dalens, who remains the commandant du cercle, the good colonial figure who stands in contrast to the ugly colonial types. The Africans are duped by the French who tell them they are there to bring civilization, "la mission civilisatrice," while conquering them and exploiting their labor and lands. France, the young girl, is made *chocolat* by Protée who befriends her as her only comrade and servant, but who burns her hand at the end to force her to break her attachment to him, an African, where that friendship could not continue.

They live, all, as *chocolat*, or duped by their times, the times of modernity which the conquering country France, the metropole, repeatedly affirms as being "coevally" shared, along with their ancestry ("Nos ancêtres les Gauls"), while denying that shared time, place, and origin with the appurtenances of conquest. Chocolate is seen in the product of colonial cacao and Cameroonian labor; but also, simultaneously, in the lives of Africans living in Europe, dubbed chocolate, their images - on packets of hot chocolate and a dozen other products to be sold as authentically black.[10] "Chocolate" as in *Chocolat* from the minstrel shows and *bals coloniales*, and other forms of performances, including most notably that of the original "Chocolat" himself, the Cuban slave boy Rafael Padilla turned circus performer "Chocolat."

In 1895, Raoul Donval, director of the New Circus, formed a new duo, teaming Chocolat with a British clown, George Foottit. The two performed together for twenty years, popularizing clown comedy, especially with the burlesque sketch *William Tell*. This comedy relied heavily on "comedic slaps," making Chocolat a character consistent with the imagery and prejudices of that time; a character that gradually becomes the stereotype of the "Negro" scapegoat: silly, childish, and friendly. Chocolat, however, fought the stereotype by constantly diversifying his skills and careful observation of the skits shows a character not confined to the roles of the subject. The phrase "je suis Chocolat," meaning "I am deceived," was popularized by the dialogues in their sketches, introduced by the duo in 1901.[11]

FIGURE 2.3 Chocolat and the Clown.

The split between the "old Africa" Andy wishes to leave behind and the "new Africa" he aches to join can be seen as the signifier of modernity, visibly marking the career of Chocolat himself. Chocolat joined Foottit to perform in a circus act that brought together a Black and a white clown. They provided success for the New Circus for years, but when their contract was not renewed in 1905, some blamed the Dreyfus affair and politicization of racial issues. There were also questions at the time of black and Mestizo politicians representing the old colonies of the French empire. Their joint career reached its peak with the Folies Bergère until they were considered old fashioned with the arrival of a generation of American black artists bringing the cake walk to the stages of Europe.

In 1909, they returned to the New Circus with *Chocolat, aviateur d'Henry Moreau*. The first performance on 30 October was well received by the public. On 19 November, in an article by writer and journalist Pierre Mille, the Times erroneously announced the death of Chocolat. The next day, the Times retracted the error and published a letter from Rafael, curiously dated 17 November:

> Sir,
> The director read in your newspaper that Mr. Mille, the intelligent journalist wrote that I am dead like Augustus. I pray you, say that I am alive, and that I am playing every night in *Chocolat aviateur* at the New Circus.
> You can judge that I did not even turn white.
> Please accept my respect,
> Chocolat
> Please correct it, because it hurts me.
>
> *(Noiriel 2016)*

Chocolat had moved, like Andy, into the world of modern motion, of "Chocolat aviateur," just as Andy moved into the world of capital with containers and "cargo" capitalism, and its magic. That becomes the animating force of modernity, with its powers and wealth. Chocolat states, I am not "Augustus" but alive and moving in "Chocolat aviateur." He is ready for the moon shot of Méliès in his *Le Voyage dans la lune* (1902), and in fact Foottit and Cocolat become the subjects for skits filmed by the Lumière Brothers (Noiriel 2016).[12]

Nollywood is the aviateur cinema of Nigeria, "taking off" in the 1990s. Claire Denis's *Chocolat* is the tail end of the Nouvelle Vague of European cinema—post-New Wave— taking off from her work as assistant director with Jacques Rouffio, Costa-Gavros, Jim Jarmusch, and Wim Wenders. She and Nnuebe both give the death announcement to non-coevalness, stating in their films, each in their own way, "I pray you, say that I am alive, and that I am playing every night in Chocolat aviateur at the New Circus."

Though not a clown, nor "chocolat," in the pejorative senses above, still Andy is duped by the millionaires, since he sells his soul to get his wealth, and destroys his Merit. He is duped by the cars and apartments, liquor and clothes, the appurtenances of modernity and wealth in the city, and sets out to bring his sister into the same world of money. He is duped by his friends, foolishly. agreeing with Paul who says, "I don't blame you. Money is the emperor of the world. Whoever does not have it is as good as dead."

The dupes are there in all cases: the sincere dupes like Dalens and Protée, or the modernizing Cameroonian political types planning their actions on the eve of Independence, whose sunset—*Les Soleils des Indépendences*—is in the offing (the French had handpicked and installed Ahidjo before independence had even been declared). The millionaires in *Living in Bondage* include the corrupt Chief Omego, whose mother's blood paid for his wealth, and who thought his wealth was unencumbered. Above all, Andy is haunted by his wife's ghost when he wins the satanic bet and becomes a member of the club. Black and white, "chocolat."

The cynical face of *Living in Bondage* is seen in reverse in Claire Denis's *Chocolat*, which purports to portray her youth in the late colonial period as unmarked by the racism of her home country, yet whose reentry in the frame story at the beginning is marked by the ironic inversion of the colonial order: her character France plays a poor white hitchhiker, and her ride, Mungo Park, an older black man, clearly in charge of the relationship. Mungo Park is no less the dupe. His name is a cynical reference to the early European explorer, who paved the way for the Europeans to come. The character so-named is a black American who thought, in the post-colonial period, he could return home to Africa to find his roots, only to find that he was still a "blanc," a not-quite-white not-quite-African retournee—like Saidya Hartman (*Lose Your Mother* 2008).[13]

Finally, the dupe as the outsider, the allothone, who thought he could become an insider; an autochthone, a native [to "go native," to take on the local color as in the child in Francis Bebey's *Le Fils d'Agathe Moudio* (1967)].[14]

Could these figures of the faymen, the bushfallas, the dupes and their marks be elements of the morality tale to which the globalized film world has given rise? Haynes proclaims that Nollywood's central current is an underlying morality, like that of melodrama, which, in Brooks's (1995) famous phrase, exhibits the "moral occult."[15] Brooks attributes this to the desacralization of traditional values, and the loss of the religious undergirding of society. Haynes sums it up: "Nothing is more fundamental to Nollywood than understanding situations in moral terms" (Haynes 2016: 33).

The moral tale of the outsider who tries to cheat the simple villager often turns on the expulsion of the foreign corrupting agent so as to protect the original home and hearth. In both *Chocolat* and *Living in Bondage* the family home is either denuded of material substance, as in Andy and Merit's simple apartment where her desire for peace and love cannot fill Andy's needs; or in the colonial *residence* where Protée and Aimée's desire cannot reach fruition given Dalens's presence/absence. Under the watchful eyes of his small daughter, France, all he can offer for their need for a home and the security of love is the helplessness one experiences in the desire to reach the horizon, which continues to retreat as one seeks to approach it.

Chocolat presents a nostalgic look back at a home that could never be one for the French, for the whites, for the colonial family. *Living in Bondage* is a shocking "occult drama" that stages the bloody death of a loving wife caused by her own husband's greed. They both speak to the circumstances that gave rise to the permanent alienation of the autochthone turned allothone, the permanent condition of guilt forged in the presence of an unseen and unspoken moral order—a morality play lacking a central figure encompassing moral authority. Time in both coeval situations is the same, "out of joint," waiting for a return.

Both films play on the borders of Johannes Fabian's non-coeval time, meaning that the difference between the village and the city, the traditional and the modern, the autochthone and the allothone, is built on tropes that stereotype or conventionalize the superiority, the advanced status of the life and values of the "modern." More specifically, it is a refusal of the European, what Fabian calls the anthropologist, in his frame of reference, to acknowledge that his "subjects," the Africans he undertakes to study, are living in the same temporal frame of reference as the Europeans. "[T]he denial of coevalness [is] . . . a persistent and systematic tendency to place the referent(s) of anthropology in a Time other than the present of the producer of the anthropological discourse" (2002: 31). In neoliberal global terms, the compressions of space and time (Harvey 1989) in the city are played out in monetary terms, where time becomes measured in terms of monetary value. The denial of a shared experience of modernity forms the underlying basis for colonial world-making, what has morphed in the postcolonial times into globalization, "mondialisation." It is the denial of co-equal value.

When *Bondage* opens, Andy is sitting on the couch, bemoaning his fate, but basically doing nothing. It is not until he gets out, makes his contacts, and then takes action, that the plot is set in motion for him to become rich. The life in the village is static. In the city he is set in motion by Paul, who encounters him when driving his car. And later at the millionaires club party, when Andy is again sitting statically on the couch, Paul gets him up in motion, dancing. No time for sitting around, doing nothing.

The same division might be seen in *Chocolat,* where the old school Africa in the core story is centered on the *residence* where the commandant and his entourage are sitting around, as if waiting—waiting for the broken plane to be repaired, waiting for the missing part to arrive. When the commandant goes out on his *tournée,* he leaves the others back home with nothing to do. But when the contemporary frame story is occurring, beginning with France's arrival in Cameroon, we have cars, busses, planes, action, and modern talk about a life that is in motion—travelling, not sitting around, not static. Coevalness in time can't be achieved without coevalness in motion since time and motion are tied, as in relativity. At the core of the thought experiment of relativity, Einstein establishes that time dilates with acceleration; that time on the static train station moves faster than time on the moving train. By that standard, one should age faster in the village, where life moves more slowly—at least within the perspective of the one who "denies" coeval time.

These are the tropes of modernist cinema, and even if Sembène's cinema, the one he invented to capture the pace of an African world, moves more slowly, if the characters speak more slowly in Wolof than in French, still he could always be seen as resisting a certain non-coeval concept of modernity. Perhaps the most ironic example of this is in the two versions of *Mandabi* he was obliged to shoot.[16] The version in Wolof is longer than the one in French, despite the script being the same. Pacing and editing, speech, all the essential elements of mise-en-scene, establish a temporality that conveys coeval versus non-coeval time.[17] At the heart of Fabian's claims about the colonialist world view lies this central argument: non-coeval time is based on a colonialist temporality as opposed to that of "modern" mobility.

James Ferguson (2006) picks up the thread by affirming how from the young Zambians' perspective modernity, despite all the colonial or non-coeval baggage Europeans might wish to load it with, remains often enough the dream for the good life. When France wishes to move around in the south by car, going north by bus, and flying home by plane, she endows that motion automatically with the attributes of modern travel, unlike the ride to her school up north, when she was a child, sitting on a donkey being led by Protée. When Andy wishes to join his age-mates in their success, he bemoans his failure to buy a car for his wife, much less own the Benz and three other expensive cars that Paul already drives. He lacks the essential mobility assigned by global modernity to the desired life, as Lindsey Greene-Sims details so well:

> "Global modernity," as I use the term, is therefore a paradoxical, sometimes aspirational, and often uneven experience that has much more

to do with "relations of membership" (Ferguson 2006, 187) than with teleological projects of modernization or with a deterritorialized, new (capitalist) world order. And it is my contention in this book that automobility is a paradigmatic experience of a global modernity, that it affords particular insights into West African economics of desire and modes of belonging. . . . I see automobility, like global modernity itself, as an experience infused with both "violence and pleasure" (Bayart 2007, 251), precariousness and prestige, and exclusion and inclusion. . . . [A]utomobility, as a claim of autonomous, unfettered mobility, remains a powerful discourse to the construction of the modern self, just as the automobile continues to give meaning to the ways that African citizens inhabit their global world.

(2017: 21–22)

As a proper bushfalla returning home to the village, Andy demonstrates his success by coming not in bush taxi but in his chauffeured limousine. He paid dearly for it. But in the modern economy, the global world order, he knows it is not possible to arrive without having made the proper sacrifices, without being strong, as Paul told him. The rest is to be discarded by the wayside—trash, as it were, of little worth.

These are the moments of globalization's incipient marks upon African cinema. It reveals a world in the process of transformation, like that seen in Cervantes's *Don Quixote* when the figure of picaro was created to navigate the uncertainties of a world undergoing magical disruptions caused by the new pressures of an economic order that would replace the orderliness of feudalism with capitalism (Bjornson 1977). The end of the old colonial order in Cameroon is figured unforgettably in the scene of the airplane flight from the North when France and her family depart from Mindouf and the residence, leaving behind the galloping horses and the dust of the savannah. Nollywood is no less marked by a vision of society in the throes of violent change, a world with its demons, zombies, magical reproduction of blood money, of its ghosts that Ferguson calls "global shadows" (2006). The global side is all too visible. It is, as always, in the shadows that the loss of home and the journey to the new occur, not with complacency but rather as marked by terrors, loss, and ultimately, with the birth of a new cinema.

Notes

1 Lobato's *Shadow Economies of Cinema* (2012) does a good job in documenting the path toward digital cinema, and the effect of piracy on the industry. The Comaroffs's *Millenial Capitalism and the Culture of Neoliberalism* (2001) contains a host of key essays on this critical moment. Haynes (2016) documents the change in Nigeria. Geschiere's many works (see 2013) document how the

social shifts under the duress of structural adjustment plans created havoc in Cameroon and elsewhere. James Ferguson's *Global Shadows* (2006) is a key guide to the shifting movement toward "modernity" in Africa, and the tensions it entailed. See also David Harvey (1989; 1996); Appadurai, A., 1996, *Modernity At Large: Cultural Dimensions Of Globalization*, and Michael Hardt and Antonio Negri's *Empire* (2001).

2 This was the setting for Chris Abani's *Graceland*, 2004.

3 Economic management deteriorated during Babangida's final years, worsening sharply in the period surrounding the mid-1993 transition crisis. After ousting civilian caretakers in November of that year, General Sani Abacha turned economic policy over to populist elements in his cabinet, who quickly dismantled the vestiges of the adjustment programme, promoting further decay. Macro-economic uncertainty was accompanied by burgeoning corruption, widening social inequality, institutional and infrastructural deterioration, volatile market instability, domestic lawlessness, and international isolation (Lewis 1996: 79).

4 This is the theme of many Tunde Kelani films, from *Thunderbolt: Magun* (2001) and *Arugba* (2009) to *Dazzling Mirage* (2014).

5 Comaroff and Comaroff (2001): "More and more ordinary people see arcane forces intervening in the production of value, diverting its flow toward a new elect: those masters of the market who comprehend and control the production of wealth under contemporary conditions. They also attribute to these arcane forces their feelings of erasure and loss: an erasure in many places of community and family, exacerbated by the destabilization of labor, the translocalization of management, and the death of retail trade; a loss of human integrity, experienced in the spreading commodification of persons, bodies, cultures, and histories, in the substitution of quantity for quality, abstraction for substance" (25).

"To be sure, occult economies frequently have this bipolar character: At one level, they consist in the constant quest for new, magical means for otherwise unattainable ends; at another, they vocalize a desire to sanction, even eradicate, people held to have accumulated assets by those very means.

Occult economies, then, are a response to a world gone awry, yet again: a world in which the only way to create real wealth seems to lie in forms of power/knowledge that transgress the conventional, the rational, the moral—thus to multiply available techniques of producing value, fair or foul" (26).

"As all this suggests, appeals to the occult in pursuit of the secrets of capital generally rely on local cultural technologies: on vernacular modes of divination or oracular consultation, spirit possession or ancestral invocation, sorcery busting or forensic legal procedures, witch beliefs or prayer" (26–27).

"As the connections between means and ends become more opaque, more distended, more mysterious, the occult becomes an ever more appropriate, semantically saturated metaphor for our times" (27).

6 A classic, hilarious example is in *Abena*, which I analyze in *Trash: African Cinema from Below*. The sons—439 scanners—return "ruined" from America.

7 In *The Modernity Bluff: Crime, Consumption, and Citizenship in Côte d'Ivoire* (2012), Sasha Newell describes how the young men of Abidjan dress to the nines and buy rounds of drinks for their friends, even when they are broke. Style, modernity, keeping up with the best, at all costs—echoed here with the "Millionaires Club."

8 Nyamnjoh: "Back home on brief visits, male bushfallers, in particular, are both an attraction and a disappointment, hardly to be trusted even as they

are trusting. They are seen as ready to lie and exaggerate their profession, status, and achievements to obtain what they want, prominent among which is sweeping a girl off her feet, perhaps to the detriment of an established relationship" (54).

9   "Many young students and unemployed graduates seek bushfalling opportunities through age-mates, friends, or relations abroad and also through Internet scamming—popularly known as 'feymania' in Cameroon and '419' in Nigeria" (Nyamnjoh: 707).

10   This is an old, common story, perhaps best exemplified in the chocolate pastry "tête de nègre," which it took the French decades to rename in the relatively recent past. "Of course" *nègre* did not mean what the pejorative usage connoted; yet the stain of the term could not be ignored indefinitely. A comment on the French website "quora" dated before 2009 sums up the attitude. It is a response to the question, if you were a pastry, which one would you choose? "Un Forêt Noire ou un Opéra, c'est délicieux et c'est tout noir, bien d'actualité pour le moment, puisqu'il ne faut même plus dire Tête de Nègre, Oncle Benz ou Banania. Même les 10 Petits Nègres d'Agatha Christy Changent de nom . . . Du délire." https://fr.quora.com/Si-vous-%C3%A9tiez-une-p%C3%A2tisserie-laquelle-seriez-vous-Et-pourquoi-Faites-moi-rire

11   Noiriel, Gérard (2016). *Chocolat, la véritable histoire de l'homme sans nom.* Paris: Bayard Culture. *ISBN 9782747068826.* https://en.wikipedia.org/wiki/Chocolat_(clown)

12   https://en.wikipedia.org/wiki/Chocolat_(clown);   http://www.circopedia.org/Foottit_%26_Chocolat

13   Hartman discovers on her "return" to Africa, to Ghana, that in the eyes of the Ghanaians she is still the "obroni"—the white, the European, the outsider.

14   Bebey's "fils d'Agatha Moudio" was black by his mother and white by his father. The lines go, it's more than a month since the baby is born, and up till now it hasn't decided to take the "couleur locale." https://greatsong.net/PAROLES-FRANCIS-BEBEY,AGATHA,102678357.html

15   Jane Tompkins sums up Brooks's basic argument thus: "The authors of melodrama sought to illuminate daily existence in a post-Christian world with references to a clash of moral absolutes that lay behind the domestic and social façade. Melodrama's mode of excess, with its inflated rhetoric, its sententiousness, its constant reaching toward sublimity, justifies itself as a literary form by reinvesting ordinary life with a sense of transcendent moral significance" (Tompkins 1977: 262).

16   The famous story tells of Sembène turning on the funding provided him by his producers, Comptoir Français du Film Production (CFFP), who were surprised when they discovered the dialogue was in Wolof. He was required then to reshoot the film in French, under the title *Le Mandat*, and at a pace that shortened the length of the film. The World Cat website shows a length of 1 hour 25 minutes; IMDB shows 1 hour 32 minutes.

17   An ideal scene that captures this occurs in *Faat Kine* (2001) where the dishonest Frenchman and his African partner attempt to pressure Kine into releasing their car while paying their gas bill with a counterfeit bill. The "modern" couple belabor Kine as backward—out of their time.

3

CLAIRE DENIS'S *CHOCOLAT* (1988)

Auteurism and African Cinema

Kenneth W. Harrow

"Agha se edo, Edo re"—having arrived in Edo, Edo is distant.

I. Wim Wenders,[1] Claire Denis

The "world" in cinema d'auteur, as in Nollywood, exists in a tension that carries over its beginnings and anxieties into the present. The post-New Wave auteurism, like the post-Fespaco Nollywood, was not born whole cloth. Even if Nollywood seemed to have sprung directly from Eshu's head, even if Claire Denis simply burst on the scene after *Wings of Desire* (Wenders 1987), the "New Wave" in which she was formed had always already been there, going back to the films of Renoir and Vigo, with the influence of Bazin and Langlois. Already there in the *Maîtres fous* (1955) of Jean Rouch, scenes of which are serendipitously echoed in *Living in Bondage* (Nnuebe/Rapu 1992) (eating the sacrificed dog in the one, with one celebrant licking his lips in delectation; drinking Andy's wife's blood in the other, with a crazed look of pleasure in the drinkers' eyes). Already there in the eye of the director whose "cinéma vérité" set the stage for some other kind of witnessing for Africa, *both distant and close*, that defined the particular combination of home movie and testimony that we see as marking the tone of *Chocolat* (1988). Like all genres, of all periods, it was all there already, waiting to be picked up and put together again, creating similarity and difference.

Not only was the same true of Nollywood, of "video films," and STV films, but in some strange way they seemed to respond similarly, "coevally entangled" to the same pressures of the 80s, of the times that sought to

DOI: 10.4324/9781003397595-5

impose divisions ever more completely between the fortress up north and the declining nation-state in the south—two worlds that had known too intimate a congress in their former pre-1960 encounters, and now were coming to meet again, at least in cinema, despite the growing distance in their structures of power and wealth. Ironically, Wenders's sequel to *Wings of Desire* is titled *In Weite Ferne, so nah* (1993) (*So Far, So Near*)—a title that would seem to fit much of Denis's own work.

With the struggle to find ways to mark transnationalism in film types, with the taste of bitterness that comes with contrasting such pleasurable, comforting types as affinity transnationalism that marks "world cinemas" in the global north with their more stressful or difficult counterparts from the global south, it would be instructive to ask how the Claire Denis's classic, *Chocolat* (1988), is marked by affinities between Africans and Europeans. She sets the stage for Europeans' entry into Africa, both with the return to the past marked by divisions between colonized and colonizer, and in the contemporary frame story set in the present, exhibiting a racial distribution of roles between black African/African-American and white European. The absolute space between "African" and "European" is crisscrossed with those on both sides of this divide who share traits with the other to a greater or lesser extent.[2] In both cases, the "affinities" of the transnationalism could best be described as relative: relatively open, relatively blocked.

We want desperately to believe in Denis's cosmopolitanism, but she increasingly frustrates that desire with her increasingly dark encounters, contact zone frictions, macabre loves, brutal slaughter, corruption, and fin de siècle pessimism that marks the relationship between Europe and Africa, between white and black. What is adumbrated in *Chocolat* (1988) develops more fully in her work from *Beau Travail* (1999) to the completely dystopic *White Material* (2009). The protagonist of *Chocolat*, named France, appears in the opening of the frame story as a young white woman in her twenties, returning to Cameroon, where she had lived as a child. She reaches out, trusting the driver who picks her up when she hitchhikes on the road to Limbe, just as she had trusted her parents' houseboy Protée in her childhood. She trusts that the bus from Douala can take her back to her past, up North. We want to see her trust rewarded, her freedom restored.

Chocolat (1988) deliberately eschews the 1980s world of commodity capitalism and its vulgar embrace of the life of wealth and ease. Its absence is conspicuous, made visible in the beat-up jeans worn by the grown-up France who presumably can easily afford to hitchhike outside Limbe, formerly Victoria. We "enter" her world, the world of "France," focalized through her character—a world left in the wash of the former colonial masters, of which her father, the colonial *commandant du sous-division* (district officer of the sub-district), was one. The "return" of France carries, always already, a debilitating irony. At one point in *Chocolat*, Protée, the Dalens's houseboy, offers an ant sandwich to France, the little girl who is his charge. At the peak of the film's idealism, that scene offers the gestures of giving and receiving in their tenderest mode. As we approach the last few scenes of the film's core story, as we close in on the exit from the past, Protée feels the need to have France break that tie they had created, and he tricks her into burning her hand, ending the affinity—the "transscending" of the barriers between French and Cameroonian, European and African. What was shared is brutally separated. Colonial incestuousness returns as post-colonial schism.[3]

Denis frames the return to the past with France's memory of the colonial times when her father was "king"—the kind of gentle, enlightened king who could not bring himself to wield power. She carries in her name her past, and in her demeanor the values of her generation's liberal modernism. As Mette Hjort would have it, she figures the cosmopolitanism that would mark the ideal work of coming-together that characterizes transnationalism. Denis's production team reflects a 1980s vision of diversity. Though Denis drew upon a largely French crew, there was a mixed assortment of African, French, Italian, and Scottish actors.[4] The film crew and cast fit perfectly with Hjort's definition of "strong transnationalism." Made in 1988 before the term "global" became fashionable, before "transnationality" was critically deployed, *Chocolat* was "postcolonial" only in the sense that "international" would have been imagined at the time. This came before the final demise of the term "Third World," although the latter, positioned alongside late New Wave would probably best describe the new director and her entry onto the stage of postcolonial cinema.

African cinema in 1988 was very distant from the worlds of Ozu or Wim Wenders, who had recently returned from Japan where he had shot *Tokyo-Ga* (1985)[5] with Denis as his assistant. She remained with him as assistant director for *Wings of Desire* (1987)—the year before Sembène's *Camp de Thiaroye* (1988) premiered in the Venice Film Festival. In 1988 *Zan Boko* came out, and the following year it was *Yaaba*. It was not clear at the time that these films were bringing a certain "African" cinematic generation to a close, although a few years later Bekolo's *Quartier Mozart* (1992) and Teno's *Afrique, je te plumerai* (1992) made the punctuation visible.

Chocolat also seems to have been marked by Oyono's *Une vie de boy* (1956) so closely it is impossible to imagine Claire Denis's Protée without Oyono's Toundi, who was, after all, also a houseboy in love with his commandant's wife. More importantly, Oyono's novel is intended to demystify colonial rhetoric, appearing when the anticolonial movement was in full swing. Denis's film looks back at the era, not so much with nostalgia, nor really with the kind of historical perspective that Jameson would have said was no longer available to the postmodern late capitalist, but with the bitter-sweetness of displacement. With the dispossessing of the masters at the moment of the inevitable rise of the servants, it captures the turning moment in the dialectic colonizer-colonized. To introduce the perspective that would mark the gaze back in time with loss, the film begins with France's return to Cameroon, and the voyage back up north, to the past—a journey of return not to her home but to the scene of her youth where the possibility of her family establishing a home had been eclipsed.

At the time of her youth, the struggle for independence was underway, with the backlash against white privilege accompanying the rise of an indigenous African political consciousness. By the time *Chocolat* had come out in 1988, Cameroon's President Ahidjo had long since set out an official policy of Cameroonization, with Africans replacing Europeans in businesses connected to the government whenever possible.[6] In the film's diegetic present, when France's plane lands in Douala, Paul Biya had already been in power for six years, having replaced Ahidjo following the latter's resignation from the presidency. Cameroon would know considerable strife in 1991 with the *villes mortes* campaign, but in 1988 the country was relatively calm under the strict rule of Biya, and we are presented with the image of the African state having undergone the transition to postcolonialism with African men now behind the wheel, and Europeans no longer visibly in charge.

One such driver is the man who picks France up when she is hitchhiking, William "Mungo" Park, who is clearly more financially solvent, older than she. She has a knapsack and wears jeans—he already has a child. It turns out he is an African American, which completes the racial role reversal. These opening framing scenes suggest more than a reversal of racial positions or fortunes compared to the earlier colonial period, as they emphasize that France, the child of a couple whose relationship was in trouble when she was a young girl, has now become a woman in search of her own center. She is vaguely caught in the dispossession suggested ironically by her position as the retournée, the returning ex-colonial child. The title *Chocolat* means something like duped. Her trip awakens the memories of the past that inevitably carry with them the shadow, so near, so far, of the *revenante* with its ghostly powers coming from her former life.

We would be at home with this situation, this narrative and cast of characters being remembered in times long gone by, in a New Wave setting like that of *Wings of Desire* (1987) with its magical angels and the conflation of times past and present when seen from the angels' point of view. But we become more confused as to the location of New Wave angst and anxiety given the colonial history within which it is played out. The flashback, cutting across time, bridging past and present in architectural landscapes that mark time's passage in both change and absence, becomes the central device for bridging the frame and core stories in *Chocolat*.[7] The film itself functions somewhat as a bridge into the memory of Denis herself.

Claire Denis grew up in West Africa, and her father was a colonial civil servant. She lived as a child in Cameroon, as well as in Senegal, Somalia, and Upper Volta (now Burkina Faso). Author and auteur meet character in the imaginary realm of the transnational, a space that accommodates the entire range of extradiegetic factors in the effort to create some solid material basis for claims to transnationality. The composition of the production unit, the target audiences, the experiences of the director, the film's financing,[8] and the sites of exhibition have increasingly displaced the complex analyses of content when we raise the question of what constitutes transnational or world cinema. The attempt to bridge a "modern" and "colonial" Cameroon—in a sense the core of Denis's African films in general—is "blurred"[9] if not blocked, as though the meeting of the young white woman and older black man could not shed itself of the past.[10] When France asks Mungo to take a drink with her, he looks at the palms of her hands, and sees that they lack lines. For him, perhaps, that is a sign of there being no future. By the end, we learn that the lines were effaced when Protée had the little France take hold of a burning hot pipe. His hand, too, was burned. The traces of erasure for both, presumably, were all that remained. Her "return" was complicated by her relationship with her father—the two were enmeshed in the sorrow engendered by her mother's alienation from her father, and in his attachment to their shared time in Cameroon.

On one level, one would want to see Denis's idealized commandant father as the locus for affinitive affect. He loves his Cameroon, "his" natives, "his" Africans. Like the anthropological cultural relativist he wants to visit them in their "native habitat," to invite their presence into his home, to join in the debates of the intellectual class, even as it plots the removal of Europeans from the colony, even as he is the "commandant." Simultaneously, he rejects the crude colonialists who bitterly face their imminent departure, who look back nostalgically on the good old days as they don their formal dress dinner, take drinks on the veranda, and reiterate the ironic banter of those whose identities derive from feeling themselves as world-weary sophisticates.

The passing beauty, France's mother Aimée, embodies desire and transgression. Despite the idealized traits of Marc Dalens, the papa-commandant, despite the affecting scenes at the beginning portraying their family as beautiful and adventuresome, by the end all we see is the wreckage of the colonialists' marriages, the failures of the colonial adventure, the wrecked scene of the past perceived by Benjamin's angel of history as it retreats from our gaze. The colonialists constitute a closed world, and are set in contrast to Luc, an anomalous white outsider, who speaks truth to a power that has no intention to challenge him.[11] He fails to break into the circles of the colonial community, or that of the African servants. Both sets live in their own bubbles, which he highlights by his presence. They fade, with time, into a past that can survive only in France's memory. It is as if Luc belonged to the world of France when she hitchhikes as an adult wearing jeans. He is out of place, the classical definition of trash by Mary Douglas—like the cultural relativist anthropologist who has studied the native language, but fails to get past the door.

II.

How far we are from Comaroff and Comaroff's "global triumph of capitalism at the millennium, its Second Coming" (1). The Comaroffs want us to see "history at the end of the century." Instead we are seeing it back in some other century, twice over. The frame story places it in a present moment commensurate with the postcolonial gaze, i.e., when the film is made in 1988 and when the independence of "modern Cameroon" is best signaled by the country's ambitious project of creating a national airline, Cameroon Airlines, whose Anglophone name was the result of a compromise initiated by Bernard Fonlon.[12]

The frame of *Chocolat* smoothly fades, at the beginning and end, into and back out of the past—a relatively romanticized and painful, poignant and yet wounded period where the best of the Europeans who lived through the late colonial period inhabited a "dying" world, which was punctuated by the ugliness of colonialist policies and relationships, mostly rendered in pathetically mocked figures. At its best, it is ironically embodied in the term *chocolat*. In a key scene Aimée, who had just sought to seduce the houseboy Protée and was "corrected" by him, tells Marc, "tu te fait toujours avoir," you are always letting yourself be taken in, though it is unclear who she means as the one doing the taking in.

Of course, we could treat the triumph of capitalism at the end of the millennium as a logical continuation of the "plagues of the 'new world order,'" (Derrida 1994: 91), that the Comaroffs evoked in citing *Spectres of Marx*. The long view sees colonialism as the purest form of capitalist domination—capitalist colonialism with its industrial heart at a distance from its material resources, its cotton and palm oil, tea and coffee plantations, its gold, ivory, rubber; its foremen and police and officialdom, brutal in enforcing its rule. It dated to the long 18th century and 19th century when it began to commandeer recruits for the colonial police forces and army, the *tirailleurs sénégalais*, the conquest, World Wars I and II, and then the colonial wars in Indochina, Madagascar, Algeria. It encompassed the soldiers who would eventually turn against the officers,[13] who wouldn't settle for the same old ways, the educated teachers and politicians who would mobilize and meet and discuss and speak up, and eventually create a new logic: independence. The problematic vision, looking backward from the airplane departing the past at the end of the film, provides us with the reflexive distancing of Denis in her embodied roles as France in the film.

Chocolat could not have anticipated a change that saw the French beating their retreat in the 21st century.[14] Its focus was still on the familiar world constructed in the logic of postcolonialism and the traces of Fanon's *Black Skin, White Masks*. In the core story within the frame, the colonial world of northern Cameroon at Mindif, 30 kilometers south of Maroua, the film's historical reconstruction is simple. In the frame story's diegetic present the cinematography presents conventional images of the south (the obligatory shots of Mount Cameroon), but in the scenes set in the past the camera lovingly dwells on the north with its Muslim culture, its idealized figure of the local Waziri types, capturing the majesty of the riders on their galloping horses. This is a "certain Africa" rendered with enormous affection: an Africa where elders still exist, where the landscape, dry, hot, open to the horizon, is physically challenging but ultimately an ideal.

Into that world comes the posting of the liberal humanist Marc Dalens who rules over his sub-district in the fading days of colonial rule. Dalens, himself swept up by that Africa-scape, records its features in his diaries with sketches and descriptions of the land and people. Set on its margins of history we witness the drama of his family. The two women in Marc's world have to face the break: Aimée is brought up short by Protée when she places her hand on his leg, and he abruptly ends her advance. France, too, having accepted him, is brought up short when Protée allows her to place her hand on a burning hot pipe, betraying her trust, so that she learns that she can no longer be his affectionate charge, no longer assume the safe place allotted her in the old world order. The new break into modernity is built on the pain brought to the two, the mother and daughter, as the hapless father learns something about unhappiness.

The painful entry into modernity, seemingly experienced by the past generation, is reiterated in the present, in the frame story, where the incomplete process of ending colonialism is developed. For "Mungo" Park, the return "home" to Africa brings regret and the discovery of the gap between Afrocentric ideology and African realities.[15] The incomplete project of decolonization might be seen as less obvious with France, now an adult who returns, she says, in order to see a house, and not for her people, who exist only in memory. The figures from that time constitute a mixed conglomerate of retrograde colonialists and a handful of progressive individuals; yet in every case, they do not represent unmitigated good and bad. The repulsive colonialist Delpich, at most times caricatural, demonstrates both his dependence upon and affection for his African housekeeper-mistress. He approaches most closely the image of a slave-owner, with his coffee plantation; yet at the same time, in private, exhibits a dependence and caring tenderness toward her. Dalens appears the old-school anthropologist-administrator and broad-minded colonial officer, the model for the cultural anthropologist. His freethinking attitude extends to his wife's independence, which he won't try to control any more than the freedom of the people under his country's rule. He appears to be a liberal in an age of colonial rule, somewhat like Gide, open to the experience of Africa; or like Rouch, witnessing a world whose passing he seeks to record in great sympathy. Or more like Paul Marty, administrator turned scholar of African Islam.[16]

In the frame story France is returning to a country that was the place where she passed her youth, but is now no longer under her own country's rule—under "France's" rule. She is a person whose identity might be called that of the outsider who doesn't belong to two countries: France, hollowly echoed back to her in her given name, and Cameroon which doesn't deny her, but which exists for her only in a past that is revealed in being demystified, and ultimately lost, to France. She is thus like, and different from William Park, "Mungo" Park, whose ironic given name turns not on an Africanization of his naming, but in the ironizing of the link to the past. As a black man he can lay claim to belonging because of his race, which she can't do. As an American he is all the more alienated, more than she is, despite having married a Cameroonian woman and having a child. His accent, his manner, his freedom betrays his outsiderness. They are both dispossessed—the descendant of the master and of the slave; their roles reversed, as he is the one in charge, older, more commanding; she more supplicating, inviting him to a drink, which he declines. For him, she is "la petite;" she is attracted, but not really disappointed, ready to leave and take the bus up north. Thus they are both independent, both kind of admirable in their ways: he open enough to Cameroon, despite being an American, but disappointed in the closed door he finds; she free enough to take the bus up north on her own, the backpack on her shoulder, the traveler not burdened by the ugliness of privilege, yet clearly bearing the scars of her past which he reads in the smoothness of her palm.

Her parting from Mungo marks the transition, back up north to the past. The scenes within the core story are turned into memories that are revived, and enter into a second level of meta-diegetic memory, looking back to that level of film of the late 80s, when New Wave had passed, when the highpoint of global art film culture was riding in the wake of Ozu and Mizoguchi, Resnais and Marker, with Denis's generation now led by her mentors Rivette, Jarmusch, and Wenders. Denis was to add her own name to this list, not so much with *Chocolat*, but with the films that followed,[17] establishing her on the roll of those whose queered desire and oblique violence drew on a postcolonial anguish frequently appearing in various configurations of racial mixing. In fact, not just *métissage*, but adumbrations of broader and more violent acts of queering, terminating in scenes of abjection that probe the limits of what can be shown (cannibalism rape murder mayhem butchering, the vortex of spinning desires and punishments—*Trouble Every Day* [2001], *White Material* [2009], *Les Salauds* [2013]). More significantly, she approaches her limits of the cinematic act with a sense of certainty: she is following the central trope of *Chocolat*, which is that of the horizon. Marc, le bon père, tells France what "horizon" means.

III.

The horizon functions as a trope, so it turns and twists according to the axis. For acts of sex, it is overlaid with the line that is defined by race in colonial terms. For Oyono's "boy" Toundi, it is the invisible barrier between himself and the commandant's wife who is attracted to the forbidden black servant, as is he to the beautiful white woman who is strictly off-limits. He enacts Fanon's drama of desire, even to the point where others perceive his anguish and have to advise him not to be indiscrete. In the case of Protée, Luc calls out publicly for all to hear that Aimée is attracted to him, that Protée is attracted to her, and that both are too cowardly and conventional to be open about it. We see Protée hammer the walls in his shower in frustration when Aimée's bath water comes pouring down the pipes, and we see their exchange of glances when he dresses her for the formal dinner with Jonathan (see Fig 3.1). We see black servant, white madam, and remember the scene played out over and again, in *Rue Cases nègres*, and in the secondary relations in *Une vie de boy* as well as in the conversations in *Chocolat*, the colonial gossip.

But the desire comes mixed with their differential statuses, is unevenly experienced and crossed by the social horizon. When Fanon critiques Mayotte Capécia, it is for her unabashed acceptance of the color line: "For after all we have a right to be perturbed when we read, in *Je suis Martiniquaise*: 'I should have liked to be married, but to a white man'" (1967: 42). He rehearses his disdain for her sense of inferiority (à la Adler), placed within the economic frame of the islands, and constructs a psychology for her of

FIGURE 3.1   Protée and Aimée

resentment and false consciousness: "It is in fact customary in Martinique to dream of a form of salvation that consists of magically turning white" (1967: 44), and of finding acceptance that will pass over the color line by rendering its barriers, the money undergirding it, invisible: "Her resentment feeds on her own artificiality" (1967: 44). "It would seem indeed that for her white and black represent the two poles of a world, two poles in perpetual conflict: a purely Manichean concept of the world; the word has been spoken, it must be remembered—white or black, that is the question" (1967: 44–45).

If that world is defined by race, if the niceties of the insular society are heightened to the point that desire cannot be expressed except within the anxieties surrounding the crossing of racial barriers, if mulatto mistresses, skin color, passing, guilt, and shame turn the black woman into the servant of the free white man, that particular scenario might be seen as both reflected in but also contrasted with the sexual relations in the African colony. Oyono's Toundi will be called by Sophie to sleep with her, while her white *patron* maintains the fiction of their separation by sleeping in a different *case* while *en mission*, and Toundi's fidelity to the dream of the Commandant's wife will set him apart from the other mixed race couples of master-servants. His dreams are also all too visible to the others, to the washermen and other servants who warn Toundi that desire for the white woman mistress can't carry beyond her own decisions of where to regulate the line between them; that he has no propriety rights; that he cannot pound the wall in frustration and anger when she turns her gaze on another white man while her husband is away *en tournée*. What is seen in African eyes must be kept unseen in European eyes, even when it is obvious to all. The African story becomes one of compensation: we may be servants, but we know the secrets of the whites, which they themselves try to keep from each other. But it reads too much like a Nietzschean notion of Christianity: the weak compensate for their subjugation by denying it, and construct an ideology of Negritude that occludes the underlying distribution of power. Negritude as a reverse worlding, that becomes a worlding in its own right when seen on the level of the frame story. France may belong to both worlds, but the commandant's wife cannot, in both accounts.

While *she* can use or abuse her position by enjoying her desires and satisfying his desires, the two don't even dream of going beyond those moments in secret, the pleasure even depending upon the secrecy. But *he* plays out a different drama since he is either the *commandant* or the *commandant's boy*, and the enjoyment of desire can't be completed without the boy acceding to the position of the father. For that to come about, he must accept his subjugation with patience, knowing that his fate will be to supplant the father eventually. One day. But when the commandant is white, the *boy* is black, and in this case the language of servant, the *boy*, can be a man or woman of any age—inevitably still called "*mon boy*"—then the horizon of expectation disappears, and another narrative is framed. This is how Fanon begins the framing in Martinique, in his original colonial world: "Out of the blackest part of my soul, across the zebra stripping of my mind, surges this desire to be suddenly *white*" (1967: 63).

For Fanon *white* means the ticket to the barred place imposed on his desire to rule, to be able to rule, to be able to recognize his desire, and in his desire, his own self. A self that can't be acknowledged. "I wish to be acknowledged not as *black* but as *white*," and, he asserts, "who but a white woman can do this for me. By loving me she proves that I am worthy of white love. I am loved like a white man" (1967: 63). The transformation, like that of the black woman in her dreams, but to the superior position: "I am a white man" (1967: 63). We read this like intruders. Embarrassed. In resistance. No, you shouldn't be saying this, writing this; I shouldn't be reading this. We are back with Richard Wright's *boy*, now Bigger Thomas, whose name evokes the shaking, quavering line of the color markers that were intended to prevent such a language from being heard, acknowledged, avowed.

Protée is not Bigger; Toundi is not Protée. But each of them rises and falls because the white woman and the path to accession to the role of the father are in deadly conflict with their desires, with *his* desire, and with the guilt and prohibition that ride them under the colonial whip: "When my restless hands caress those white breasts, they grasp white civilization and dignity and make them mine" (Fanon: 63). *Propre, propriété*, and what's proper[18] cross the color line, mixing genres in their improper behavior. The framing of the key moment, when the father will tell his daughter about the secret of power and desire, must come when Aimée puts out her hand, reaches for Protée's leg, and crosses the unspoken barrier of which Luc, that is, the incarnation of Segalen, had earlier spoken aloud for all to hear. Embarrassing all, Luc's role is to sleep and eat inappropriately with the Africans, to work with the Africans, not to be in his proper place. He is the anachronism that puts *Chocolat* into a time frame that is neither here nor there, but in both—occupying both in France's memory of that moment which she herself and her father did not see but knew about, saw but could not openly acknowledge, as if they were the blacks repressing their desire for the whites.

Protée has just chased Luc off the porch, has thrown him away from the house, silently, angrily, and closes the veranda doors. Crouched in the corner, next to the curtain, her head bowed, and her thoughts somehow swirling, Aimée waits till Protée approaches her side of the doors, and as he reaches for the curtain she stretches out her hand and grasps his leg. He is standing over her; she slowly looks up, and then down, in disappointment or apprehension, at what she has dared to do. He walks the curtain over, drawing it; we do not quite know whether it was to shield what he would be doing from view, or to ignore her indiscretion, or to hide from himself his own desire. After all, it was to him that Marc had entrusted what he held most dear, his child, his wife; and now that Marc was back, that trust was no longer needed, in a sense. In the other sense, it was all that Marc had.

The next moment strikes me as one of the more memorable of cinematic events—one that creates the unruly new. Protée returns to Aimée's side, crouches down, and grabs her shoulders. He jerks her to her feet, restoring her to some stature that would enable them to carry on. She ceases to be the colonial mistress, but in being so abruptly, so physically handled, manhandled, she is shaken into a new relationship with him.

She can no longer keep either the desire, or the pretense of not desiring, or the position of authority, as a cover. Neither can she remove Protée from her presence, since now that Marc is back, they are once again within the circle of the *Commandant* of the Sub-district, or more accurately, the District Officer, whose authority, always borrowed, on borrowed time, has now been removed by his wife's willful crossing over the barrier, the horizon. Their time is foreshortened, the airplane comes for them, the visitors all leave, their lives up north at an end. They come to an end; the old passes away as the plane rises into the air, and the magical transition back to the present is made.

This scene of transition is one of my favorites. Early in the film, when France heads up north, after being dropped off by Mungo, it is conventionally shot. But the departure by plane from the past has been prepared by the key scene between Marc and France, immediately following Aimée's attempt to have Protée come to her. It is the moment when Marc tells France that all she desires can never be reached; that they must leave their world, their secure lives and the safety of who they are, for an unknown, unknowable self. He conveys this to her with the metaphor of the horizon. [19]

They are both lying in her bed, and he is putting her to sleep. "Do you still want to know what a horizon line is?" he asks. "Do you remember, are you sleeping?" She is still wounded by the memory, not yet fully comprehending, of her mother's actions, which, we can say, she would have sensed fully by then, maybe right at the moment when Protée draws the curtain so abruptly and pulls her mother to her feet. When you look beyond the hills, the houses, Marc tells her, now standing by the window, and looking in her direction, almost directly into the camera—as if confessing, rather than informing—where the sky meets the earth, it is the horizon. The horizon can be the asymptote, visible, approachable, but at a limit point, like the one Zeno evoked in the failure of the hare ever to arrive at its destination. Or in time studies, it is the present, which we always approach without ever arriving at. This is the moment "now," elusive like a limit or horizon, dependent on the location of the observer whose attempts to reach it, increasingly desperate at every moment, reveal the frantic failure of power to affirm its dominion—a colonial moment for which the conquest is never completed; or a liberation from the colonial, equally out of reach, incomplete. This is Denis's point of the perspective on a colonial past in which she had been ensconced in her youth, as elusive as the quest of France to recapture it by her return. A horizon of distance, but more of time that can never quite become "here."

That's why France's attempt to reach back into her memory of the past carries a trace of failure: its ultimate lesson was given by her father, when he was in pain over the loss of his wife, or of his place in the country that was never his. France is always on the outside, observing, never acting. Her recollection of the past is the same: that of an outsider hitchhiking back to a place that has long since disappeared. The relationship between that memory she evokes, and her place in the frame, duplicates what Derrida says about genres—in fact about most deconstruction claims—that what gives the genre its presence depends on that which is seeing it, defining it, from the outside, as it attempts to inhabit it; the location of that which sees and defines it, we could say the perspective that imposes an uncertainty on all its claims about location or motion.

When Derrida (1980) says there is no law of the genre, he means that when we stand outside that genre, looking at how it is being constructed by the law of the genre itself—by its rules, its own structuring frame—we can't see the contents of the genre itself without having the framing device implicated, simultaneously engaged in the picture. And that picture is marked by a frame that is subject to the invagination of the genre, of the contents of the picture.

Marc stands by the window; it is night; his life, his wife, his love for that moment in his life—the moment at the point where that specially beautiful family and life are all disappearing. The colonial dream has ended for him, for Protée, for "his" African subjects, and above all for the ideals that he had constructed in his presence there as father, commandant, lover of Africa, father of France. Colonialism and its black and white desires have invaded his life, and he has to find a way to tell the story to France so that she can understand and perhaps return one day, to remember its contours and tell it in this film. The frame is the horizon, and this is what he tells her: "Tomorrow, when it is day, I will show you something. The closer you get to that line, the further off it goes." He looks desperate, or quietly unhappy—not like a father telling his daughter a bedtime story, but as someone who must finally confess to his failures. The camera holds him, now in the space of the hymen—behind

FIGURE 3.2 The horizon

him on one side the ridiculous blue and white polka dotted curtain; on the other, the window, the shutter half closed.

"If you walk towards it, it moves away." The light from the moon falls on the edge of his face, the rest is in shadow. She must be listening, like us; saying nothing. *Il te fuit*—it flees from you. We see her feigning sleep. He has just said, this too I have to tell you. We expect to learn, from the father, how to take what Aimée has just done, about the line and her desires and indiscretion. But he says, "You see it [*tu la vois*]. And it doesn't exist."[20] This is the feminine law, for Derrida, that renders us mad, and that in its embrace makes it impossible for the genre to obey the law, to keep its separation clear. Our attention to Marc has shifted, with the focalization of the camera, to France, who lies there in bed, barely stirring. The daylight comes; the mountainous hill outside the window appears, the sounds of the insects is heard. The law of the genre has been enacted.

IV.

The scene of departure, viewed from inside the airplane, is evocative of Benjamin's "Last Angel of History." But more than the colonial past was at play. The long ride of European high art, following African *engagé* cinema, the final heirs of Third Cinema, and especially the post-New Wave films that had learned to incorporate its African faces (Isaach de Bankole, Alex Descas, Sotigui Kouyaté), was about to come into contact with another kind of film: Nollywood in the one case, and in the other a transformed world art or "global" cinema, whose elements of desire, locality, and anomy marked a shift in auteurism. Now it is Tunde Kelani as precursor to Genevieve Nnaji, Kunle Afolayan, Wanjuri Kahiu, Oumar Sy, and the Esiri brothers, whose names are appearing on the marquee.

The horizon line, retreating as you approach it, plays the same role as a mirage on the horizon of world cinema. It separates two things, but is an illusion. Like the hymen in deconstruction, it is part of the two things, but is outside of them since it separates them. The frame in Derridian analysis participates in what lies within and is outside its contents. Derrida uses the term "invagination," as it can denote the line that circumscribes or merge genres. The "law against mixing genres" (Derrida 1980) itself mixes and contaminates what it purports to stand at a distance from as it defines its object.

And suppose for a moment that it were impossible not to mix genres. What if there were, lodged within the heart of the law itself, a law of impurity or a principle of contamination? And suppose the condition for the possibility of the law were the *a priori* of a counter-law, an axiom of impossibility that would confound its sense, order, and reason?

(57 "Law of Genre")

The law that defined the line of the border was contaminated, "always already," with the colonial mandate, but equally so in the post-colonial memory with which France marked her return. The past was not only inaccessible, like the immediate moment of the present, but equally enfolded within her present return, not simply mixing it or rendering a temporal hybridity, but contaminating it, as in the list Derrida provided for his notion of invagination—contaminated by "an internal division of the trait." The horizon not only proved inaccessible, but as being both here and there, impure: "impurity, corruption, contamination, decomposition, perversion, deformation even cancerization, generous proliferation, or degenerescence" (57). All these terms would have been used to define the métissage that followed the colonial enterprise, and marked the affair between Protée and Aimée.

This strict law was marked by the moment of its enactment: the colonizer Delpich and his African mistress crouching in the dark, away from the sight of the notable guests when the commandant returned from his *tournée en brousse*. The guests who took their places, as if issued formal invitations, but were in fact transient travelers who never belonged, under the law as Derrida defined his law of genre: "I shall call the law the law of genre. It is precisely a principle of contamination, a law of impurity, a parasitical economy" (59). Shockingly, his treatment of the genre of the narrative, the "récit," might have been transposed onto the colonial account directly. Using the language of set theory, he continues: "I would speak of a sort of participation without belonging—a taking part in without being part of, without having membership in a set" (59)—or without belonging to the company, we might say; nor in the soiree, nor in the world whose order was established for the soiree.

> With the inevitable dividing of the trait that marks membership, the boundary of the set comes to form, by invagination, an internal pocket larger than the whole; and the outcome of this division and of this abounding remains as singular as it is limitless.
>
> *(59)*

More than the inaccessible horizon, now, we are in the space of the Moebius strip that turns over on itself without ever reaching the other side—or we might say, with always being the other side.

Racial lines function similarly. Fanon's depiction of Mayotte Capécia's claim was to occupy physical spaces that are black and white, folded within black skin; or Fanon's desire expressed as "I am loved as a white man," the drama of "Black Skin and White Masks" for which the outside and inside are similarly invaginated. Genres function like the colonial law: belonging and not belonging at the same time. Dalens and Protée: commandant, *boy*, exceeding those roles at every turn. Thus, the invaginated pocket when Dalens visits the old men in the village, or when Protée looks in the mirror at his "madame" with undisguised desire and unhappiness. Even the out and out racist, colonialist plantation owner Delpich, crosses the public line of "patron" when in private with his woman servant. Aimée and Protée, Marc. Luc. Being duped, taken for *chocolat*, each thinking they are part but as they get closer realizing the line has moved off. The colonized and colonizers as *chocolat*: cheated, and being dark.[21] But also, like chocolate, a sweet that is eaten.

The *fold*, for Derrida, comes with the *récit* that denies its identity as a *récit*, and more importantly, where its frame sets the stage for, and in so doing establishes the nature of the content. Without the frame, for instance, France's journey wouldn't be back to her memory. But when the present day story of France gets "folded over," so that only the images of the past are visible, are reenacted, we are within what the fold encompasses. If the fold is big enough, if it comes over the past heavily enough, if it covers it by entering into its space, it invaginates the core story of the past. Reenactment becomes enactment, until we pass out of the core back to the frame.

At the point of the family's departure from the north, leaving the fold, the shape of the fold matters less than the horse and riders behind the airplane. We return to our point of departure. Initially we moved around by car with Mungu driving, appropriately, since Mungo Park (1771–1806) was, after all, a traveler, a voyager who came to Africa from Scotland to seek the headwaters of the Niger River, and died in the effort. Our "Mungo," the African American "retourné" driver, moves us around the edges of the fold, until France straddles it. He drives her to the bus station in Douala where she will catch a bus up north. But in the car, Mungo's son Sawa has turned around in his seat, watching France look at the pictures of the north in her father's diary, moving us textually back to a place still unknown to us, but not to her. The fold covers from our eyes what she will open to us, but not before the memory of her own efforts to learn the language Protée teaches her are reiterated in Mungo's own efforts to learn the language of parts of his body from Sawa. When Mungo, with his American accent, asks France what her name is, he responds to her "France" with "Vive le France." She looks out the window, disinterested in this man who pretends to be what he isn't, whose weak French comes out so awkwardly. A native speaker. A native guide. Their roles already reversing, like the time frame across the fold. The fold returns: she looks out the window, the wind blowing her hair, and the non-diegetic music comes up, carrying us across the time to another ride, this time with France the child in the back of the pickup with Protée, as her father drives with her mother sitting across from him, back in *l'Afrique*. The sight of the villages with the thatched peaked roofs, like her flashback, is conventionally done with the musical accompaniment. The point of view from the back of the truck gives us the sight of the dust coming up from the truck, to be matched by the dust kicked up by the motors of the plane when we return from the folded contents of the core story, back out to the frame, in the final segment.

But in reflection, we can gather up all the images of motion—the plot driven by a plane whose motor had given way, whose motor part had to be brought up eventually; the cars brought the visitors, including Jonathan. Her father on tournée traveling on horseback; the "noble" northerners on horseback, herding their cattle; their trucks, as well; and the donkey that little France rides to school. The motions that cross the landscape up north are significant because they establish the incapacity of the colonial order to control the changes occurring already with the local Cameroonians organizing for independence; the inability of the colons to control the herds; for Delpich to get a ride with a Cameroonian who refuses to take him; the failure to connect another racist colon, whose wife is ill, with the African doctor whom Marc has brought to the residence.

Folded within these motions are the memory of what happened back in the residence when Marc left on one of his official trips. The journeys were recorded in the diary, of a past unfolding while his wife gradually turned her affections away from him, from the place where her German predecessors had died. Motion, change, or dying. The only alternatives, to cross the fold or to be trapped within the covers of the diary, a memory that can be evoked, but that ends as the plane takes off. The motion marks temporal displacement, just as the dust blurs differences and lines. The haze of memory that sharpens into precision with the family members before the camera blurs again in the form of a displacement where the objects of the desire are now played out by actors who perform as the parents, as the guardian-substitute Protée, and as the minor players caught in impossible yearnings, desire, and despair. With the image in the mirror, the image at the edge of the horizon of memory, there comes into focus and returns as the gaze of recognition, exposing the desire and the bar, the "méconaissance" of the two transformed into, or rather stepping into, the canvas painted by Ingres, where the figured object returns the spectator's gaze.

FIGURE 3.3   Jean-Auguste Dominique Ingres, *Odalisque*, circa 1830, Los Angeles County Museum of Art, gift of the 2014 Collectors Committee (M.2014.64) photo © Museum Associates/ LACMA.

Aimée models the same gaze back.

FIGURE 3.4   Aimée's gaze in the mirror

V.

At the end of the film we get one more glimpse of Protée. Now free and open, laughing or joking with his fellow workers at the airport in Douala, as France is on the verge of flying up north, he is seen at a distance. The camera centers on his figure, with the two mates on either side—with only the indistinctness of a long shot. The adieu to the past is completed with the glimpse of this "modern" worker at the airport, in contrast to the young man who had been the colonialist's houseboy. But by that point, with our reentry back into the present, we are carrying the full weight of the past; like the heavy sculpture Protée and his mates load onto the loading ramp, to be shifted home to France for some tourists. The rain starts to fall, the three African airport workers, on break, smoking and peeing, are gesticulating and chatting while the highlife music carries us away. The moment between Aimée and Protée remains to haunt the present, with its beauty and violation marking a colonial encounter where, just for an instant, all the curtains of division fall away leaving the two caught in the mirror's image.

This moment of their gaze stops time. It thus echoes the scene that brings an end to their ties to Cameroon where France burns her hand. Reading it as trauma forces us to revisit France's return to Africa, at the beginning, as the return of the colonial spectre. In her chapter "Palimpsests of Trauma: Excavating Memories in Qurratulain Hyder," Ritu Mitra cites Laura Marks's *The Skin of the Film* (1999) where Marks creates a table of "recollection-objects" where the return of the past might haunt the present. These might include: "(Benjaminian) fetishes, (Deleuzian) fossils, to transnational objects . . ." (Mitra 2015: 77). She uses Deleuzian terminology to explain how when an image surfaces from another place, another culture "it disrupts the coherence of the plane of the present culture . . . and brings its volatile contents to the present" (77), a process she describes as radioactive. Marks argues, further, that the meaning of objects is not encoded metaphorically but through physical contact (1999: 80). According to Marks's reformulation of Walter Benjamin, "aura is the sense an object gives that it can speak to us of the past, without ever letting us completely decipher it. *It is a brush with involuntary memory that can only be arrived at through a shock*" (81). It is characterized especially by its seeming ability "*to look back at us*" (80, my stress).

The memory can look back at us only through its distancing action of separation from the present, thus resembling that same distinction the observer makes when defining the object observed, say the location of an experiment, or a figure posing for a photo, a painting. That distinction that enables the viewer to come into being is the cut, the marker that enables one to perceive distance. It marks the space so that it can come into view: defines the horizon that delimits the shot. This is how Henrik Gustaffson calls upon Nancy to delineate the role of the landscape in *Chocolat*.

> The single most definable feature of the landscape is the horizon, which is emblematic of the withdrawal and suspension of presence through which Nancy defines landscape: 'The division itself is nothing: it is the separation, the interval, the insubstantial line of the horizon that joins and disjoins earth and sky.' It is 'at once a closure of space,' the outer limit of earth, depth and presence and 'a flight into infinity . . . which never stops drawing back.'
>
> *(Gustaffson: 207, cited in Vecchio 2014)*

He continues describing the metaphor as Marc did for France, echoing the painful relationships of his family with those he attempted to govern. Drawing near, so far: "Thus the horizon performs a double operation of joining and disjoining, of bringing together and pulling apart, of closing and opening" (207). The figure provides a metaphor for the image which, according to Nancy, "is not a bond but a cut separated from the invisible ground that surrounds it." As with Marks's "radioactive" process, this:

> . . . releases a hidden force that makes the image stand out, clear-cut against this background, discontinuous with the world and remaining always at a distance. The line that sets it apart is also referred to by Nancy as a mark, or a scar.
>
> *(207)*

The blurred lines of France's hands are the scars of this sort, the cut that brings into focus the scars of the past.

Focalizing narratives through Aimée results in three levels of "herstory" centered in the protagonist. The first is with France, the young woman, who appears at the outset, on the road to Douala, the retournée. She is both at home as one who grew up in Cameroon, and alienated, like former colons, or former pieds noirs would have been in their lives in France after the end of Algerian colonialism; or like the French foreign legionnaires, depicted in *Beau Travail* (1999) in Djibouti and Marseilles, not at home in either place. Inside and outside—posing the question of the line between them. She carries her father's diary with her, the maps and drawings "looking back" at her, France, records of the power that once ruled over the *cercles* with their district officers. The text now lies open to her with the painful moments of her past holding her in their gaze. For Freud, the trauma sustained within is like a bodily wound being mourned without healing.

When she returns up north, a second level is created. In Cameroon the line between south and north is traversed gradually, but it is quite definite: the forest in the south, from the coast, with its mountain, on up to the interior, until you reach the borders of the Sahel, with the train stop at Ngaoundere, the savannah, and then up further to Maroua and Garoua, and the country of Mindif, where the Hausa riders and fons had ruled. The borders of the Sahel. The distance between whites there was greater; the life imagined and remembered creating a greater distance between African subjects and French administrator, and his family. A past that remembers its child in the present.

More significantly, the line between two worlds forms a hazy frontier between the time remembered and time in the present. France, the young woman, takes us back to the past, through the flashback constructed by her alter ego, with another alter ego, the young woman looking back at her through the camera's lens having her re-enact the experience of Denis/France as a child growing up in Cameroon. The spaces here grow more distant as Denis approaches more her doubleganger self figured in France.

There is nothing inherent in this film that asks us to make these connections. But in this third moment someone had to stand outside the scene and direct the camera recording the return, telling the young woman and then the young girl to recite their lines and reenact her life. Instead of asking how these two characters are reenacting Denis's past life we can ask how Denis re-enacts the lives of these two characters, embodied by actors who must look back at her as Olympe looking directly at her viewers, the spectators. Nowhere is the effect of the Uncertainty Principle more spectral than in this unlawful effect. Unlawful because it is in violation of the genre, that is, the rule of realist cinema that demands complete separation between biography, physical embodiment, and fictional story—narrative, *récit*. The spectator is only human: she sees the look of France in response to Protée's, the seductiveness of Velasquez's nude, and responds with questions about who they are and why they are looking back, across the barrier established by the law, undoing the anonymity and safety of the gaze.

That reflexivity turns on an awareness of the present-ness of the gaze and the past-ness of the action. In both cases the Arrow of Time continues its motion forward, until the end to the sojourn up north ending in dust.

What if *Chocolat* had no frame story, and simply began with France the child on the dusty road in the pickup truck driven by her father, with her in the back with Protée? We would be no longer focalized with France as adult remembering, but with France as child reenacting. The cut between the two levels, frame-core gone, the effect of the frame gone, it would no longer be "invaginating" the core. It makes us aware of its presence in the core when we imagine the scene without the frame; with how it invades the core at every moment, opening up a space that is extraneous to the present moment in which the remembering is occurring. And that space, secondary to the "now" of the frame, i.e., the past, becomes the new "now" when the frame is gone, becomes the past only as an effect of the frame.

Derrida calls that relationship a fold ("The Law of Genre": 70), about which he writes:

> Suddenly, this upper or initial boundary which is commonly called the first line of the book, is forming a pocket inside the corpus. It is taking the form of an *invagination* through which the trait of the first line, the borderline, splits while remaining the same, and traverses yet also bounds the corpus.
>
> *(70)*

The pocket belongs to the narrative of the past, yet is there only as a memory in the present; and thus belongs and is split, is seen from a perspective outside it. Invaginated in the past, there is no arrival in "Edo," which remains distant.

Notes

1 Denis's affiliation as assistant director with major directors before her first feature film venture included Wenders (*Paris, Texas* [1984], *Wings of Desire* [1987]), and Jim Jarmusch, *Down by Law* (1986).

2 The works of Simon Gikandi have best elaborated this theme. See *Maps of Englishness* (1996), and *Slavery and the Culture of Taste* (2011).

3 In his interview with Denis, Jean-Luc Nancy stresses this theme of separation as the fundamental quality of her films. "Interview with Claire Denis." Jean-Luc Nancy, in Vecchio 2014.

4 Getting his start on a stellar career, the houseboy in *Chocolat* (1988), all so reminiscent of Oyono's houseboy in *Une vie de boy* (1956), was played by Isaach de Bankole (Cameroonian). François Cluzet (French) played the commandant Marc Dalens, and his wife was played by Giulia Boschi (Italian). The rest of the cast was constituted by a good number of Cameroonian and French actors, with the role of Boothby played by a Scot, Kenneth Cranham. (The music was by the famous South African Abdullah Ibrahim; cinematography by Robert Alakrazi, who worked primarily in France; editing by Monica Coleman, who worked in the U.S. as well as France; a second unit, in Africa, was headed by the Cameroonian director Bassek ba Kobhio; the film was shot largely in the north of Cameroon).

5 The juxtaposition of an internationalist modern landscape, set against the traditional Japanese past, seen in *Tokyo-Ga*, is replicated in *Chocolat* which sets the diegetic modern times in Douala against the colonial past in northern Cameroon to which France returns.

6 On a personal note, my wife Liz Harrow worked for the sole remaining French architect in Yaounde during our two-year stay in 1977–79. I taught in the English department of the Université de Yaounde, where many French instructors remained.

7 In a sense the issue of coeval Time is presented as having a double valence: in the present, in the relationship between "Mungo" Park and France, the "othering" of the past is no longer visible; in the past, the exceptional character, Luc, is different from the other whites because he no longer accepts the role of colonial white vis-à-vis Africans.

8 Production companies include: Caroline Productions, Cerito Films, Cinémanuel, La Sept Cinéma, Le F.O.D.I.C. Cameroun, MK2 Productions, TF1 Films Production, and Wim Wenders Productions. https://www.imdb.com/title/tt0094868/companycredits?ref_=tt_dt_co Accessed February 4, 2022.

9 This term, "blurring," functions as a trope for time for Vlad Dima in his *Meaning-Less-Ness in Postcolonial Cinema* (2022). It is drawn from Carlo Rovelli's use of the term in quantum gravity studies (*The Order of Time*, 2018).

10 A reversal of the non-coeval as this particular "Mungo" Park is a very modern African American whose insertion in the African world is completed with his having a son, and being divorced; whereas the white Claire relives the past, whose primitiveness resides largely in the colonial society she recalls.

11 He eschews colonial privilege, dresses in African garb as one would expect a Peace Corps volunteer of today to do, and converses in pidgin with the Africans. When he visits the residence he chooses to sleep and eat with the African servants. But they, too, do not accept him in the final analysis.

12 Fonlon was an important West Cameroonian figure in Ahidjo's government who gave up his post to become chair of the new department of African languages and literature, a major accomplishment for African universities most of which, as in Kenya (Ngugi) did their best to incorporate African literature into English or French departments where it could be duly controlled by Eurocentric thought.

13 *Camp de Thiaroye* (1988).

14 Two key markers of this retreat can be seen in the ascendancy of the Chinese, and the failre of "Operation Barkhane," the attempt to defeat the Islamists in the Sahara.

15 Like Aidoo's *Dilemma of a Ghost* (1965).

16 "Toute la vie de Paul Marty, mue par un idéal supérieur, a été vouée à l'action. Il a compris l'Islam et l'a aimé, ainsi sut-il obtenir la confiance de tous ceux qui l'approchaient." [All throughout his life Paul Marty was animated by a superior ideal, he was devoted to action. He understood Islam and loved it, and thus knew how to obtain the confidence of those who approached him.]

"Lyautey disait de lui: 'esprit cultivé. profond observateur de l'Islam. capable des missions les plus délicates.'" [a cultivated mind. a profound observer of Islam. capable of the most sensitive missions.] A fine brief view of this administrator and author of numerous texts on Islam in African can be found at the blog http://rol-benzaken.centerblog.net/185.html, "Qui Etait Paul Marty," by Arthur Pellegrin, May 27, 2014.

17 I am thinking in particular of *S'en fout la mort* (1990) with Alex Descas and again Isaach De Bankole; *Beau Travail* (1999) with Denis Lavant; *35 Shots of Rum* (2008) with Descas again, and Mati Diop; *White Material* (2009), with a co-script writer shared with Marie N'Diaye, and de Bankole again appearing along with Isabelle Hupert and Christophe Lambert. Descas will also appear

in other roles in her films. The ones I mentioned in particular are located in Africa, or in the diaspora, and signal some continuity with themes adumbrated in *Chocolat* (especially in *35 Shots of Rum*).

18 "1. TN. Throughout this book I will translate *le propre* as 'the proper.' Derrida most offen intends all the senses of the word at once: that which is correct, as in *le sens propre* (proper, literal meaning), and that which is one's own, that which may be owned, that which is legally, correctly owned—all the links between proper, property, and propriety" (Bass, in Derrida 1982).

19 "Points of Flight, Lines of Fracture: Claire Denis's Uncanny Landscapes." Henrik Gustafsson. In *The Films of Claire Denis: Intimacy on the Border*, edited by Marjorie Vecchio. (2014, 207+esp 209.])

20 As Marc shifts his eyes toward the camera, us, he says, where the earth touches the sky, "c'est l'horizon." Looking serious, unhappy. The closer you get to that line, "plus il s'eloigne." If you walk toward it, it moves away. "Il te fuit. Tu vois cette ligne, tu la vois, mais il n'existe pas." Her eyes are open but her head is turned away from him, as if embarrassed to see him . . .

21 For the term "chocolat" as being cheated, duped, see http://sensesofcinema.com/2001/cteq/chocolat-2/

PART TWO

The Problematics of Modernity in African Cinema at the Millennium

4

MODERNITY IN THE WORK OF TUNDE KELANI

Ti Oluwa Ni Ile (1993) and *Thunderbolt: Magun* (2001)[1]

Kenneth W. Harrow

Tunde Kelani has long constructed his films around issues of modernity. Nigeria has undergone rapid economic and social changes since oil transformed the landscape and presented the government and military with the means to create a powerful and corrupt oligarchy. The Biafran war ended with the crushing of the independence movement by 1970, and three years later oil prices began to soar. A military coup by Murtala Mohammed followed in 1975, and then quickly enough with another coup by Obasanjo in 1976. Elections, coups, instability, oil, and the deep stains of violence by military leaders culminated with Babangida torpedoing elections in 1992 and Abacha taking power from 1993–1998.

In this period of chaotic reign and the flush of oil money, Tunde Kelani had to negotiate the equally dramatic shifts in film production and distribution, shifts from the relatively limited opportunities of serious celluloid filmmaking to popular video and then digital films. Kelani had been schooled in the belief that films were to rise above the level of mere entertainment and aspire to addressing social ills as well as reflect the dramatic realities of society. He believed Yoruba culture was necessary for this challenge, and that to bring Nigeria into full independence and modern values the past had to be honored.

Modernity is a vexed term in African studies. Its usage is blemished by association with colonial discourse, as the Europeans claimed the sole rights to deploy the term "modern" to describe their societies. In general, the colonial rationale for conquest was based on the "mission" to "civilize" Africans. With the work of V.Y. Mudimbe (1988) and then Simon

DOI: 10.4324/9781003397595-7

Gikandi (1996), we can begin to understand what was obvious from the start: not only are these terms loaded so as to valorize European thinking, but the construction of these very notions was also done in collaboration with Africans themselves who joined in the "mission civilisatrice," even as they attempted to modify its most blatantly exploitative features. Kenyatta's collaboration with the anthropologist Malinowski and his monograph *On Mount Kenya* (1938) evoke similar notions of western modernity and African traditionalism (Gikandi 2001). Mudimbe is correct in claiming, in *The Invention of Africa* (1988), that what the West invented was a notion of modern disciplinary education whose values became absorbed into African social thought and practices, so that attempts to resist Western dominant values were contained within the very Western frame whose horizons of expectations remained intact. Decolonialism, under these circumstances, remains impossible.

Kenyatta and Kelani bring to the fore the question of modernity, and when collapsed into the binary of modern versus traditional, the differences created across history tend to be obfuscated. The worlds wrought by capitalism between the early twentieth and early twenty-first centuries highlight this difference. Gikandi frames the question of Kenyatta's positioning across tradition and modernity in terms of alienation. Gikandi begins his analysis in his "anatomy of colonialism" (2001) by affirming the Comaroffs' claim that the colonized subject was not silenced or ensconced within a closed universe of tradition, but rather that the Tswanas (the Comaroffs' prime examples) spoke with agency in utilizing the colonialists' tools: "They were still able to speak through the European text; . . . their telling of stories of self through the text of the other did not necessarily negate the agency of the colonized" (Gikandi 2001: 356). The location for Kenyatta, for the colonial subject more generally, and specifically for the native elites, was to be found in an in-between location (see Bhabha 1994) generated by colonial spaces ("colonial governmentality (the semantic and material conditions of colonial politics)" [Gikandi 2001: 357]) and what Gikandi calls African traditionalism, where the African subject identified him or herself as belonging—the place where he or she could come to recognize themselves: the "realm of subjective desires (the colonial subject's cultivation of their self-hood through the mastery of the trappings of colonial modernity)" (Gikandi 2001: 357). In his typical refusal of the powers of this binary to capture "The West" and "The Rest of Us," Gikandi positions the African native elite, and in this case Kenyatta, in that alienating non-space that lies both between and in alternation with those spaces dubbed native/European, or traditional/modern: "one that had been produced at that liminal scene where the self becomes the other and the lines between the two were blurred or folded into one another" (Gikandi 2001: 357).

As Gikandi put it, if Kenyatta had become the great national leader on whom Kenyan, and Kikuyan, identity was to be based, it was not by a simple rejection of any dialectical pole, but rather by a negotiation between the two. In Kenyatta's day, the poles were set up by the colonial discourse as inevitable and natural so that the entire corpus of colonial and post-independence literature would assume that perspective: "colonial subjects were structured by paradigms in opposition to either modernity or traditionalism" (358), but the patterns of expropriation practiced by the colonized subjects continually generated liminal spaces that produced tensions with the simple notions of modernity assumed by the paradigms. Gikandi continually evokes these patterns of agency that not only generated the colonial subject—as Bhabha also posited—but attributes to this liminality the rise of alienated subjectivities, the products of incomplete modernization, indeed the defining quality of the modernization project: "what made such [colonial] institutions potent agents of the modernization of the colonized was their incompleteness" (358).

One way of accounting for the consciousness of the colonial subject is not simply to show how they were plotted by colonial narratives, or how they adopted mythologies of tradition to counter their displacement, but to foreground their alienation from both the institutions of the "tribe" and those of colonialism, to call attention to these subjects' self- consciousness cultivation of this alienation, and their ability to locate themselves in the unstable zone between the two competing entities represented by the signposts of modernity and tradition.

(Gikandi: 366)

Gikandi sees this scenario as generalized, though his focus lies with the Kenyan nationalist leader: "This rehearsal and cultivation of alienation as a mode of identity was not restricted to Kenyatta" (Gikandi: 366).

I want to read Kenyatta's position as echoed in that of Kelani, whose oeuvre returns to the liminal spaces of alienation as the condition for the formation of subjectivity. Unlike Gikandi, I want to explore a reading in which the conjuncture of "modern" and "traditional" is to be set against the material base, the capitalist formations of the times. Kelani's position, like Kenyatta's, lies in the conjuncture constructed by the radical changes in production of capital at the moment of their generations' coming to consciousness. In Kenyatta's time the colonial economy was based on various types of extraction and cash crop development. The ties that linked Kenyan crops to the world market lay in the routes taken through Kikuyu highlands that were expropriated by whites whose crops were transported down to the coast on the newly built rail lines. The economic order corresponded to the form of state capitalism analysed by Žižek, to be described later in this work.

Kelani's career came along as Nigeria's economy shifted from one of agricultural and small industrial production in the years following independence to the entry into global markets with oil production (Falola and Heaton 2008). The violent conflict that marked this crucial time with the entry into a global economy brought the traumas of ethnic conflict usually given as the principal cause of the Biafran war. But the significance of the oil, for this analysis, does not lie in how it might have generated conflict, but rather in how it changed the social landscape in repositioning the population into an economy dominated by oil extraction. The modern economy ceased to be located in cacao and other cash crops, but in the relations with Shell Oil and its competitors.

The liminality to which Gikandi alludes lies between what he dubs the cosmic orders of the traditional and the modern—the uncertain, incompletely framed space of modernity (Gikandi 2001: 368). The positioning of Kelani in terms of the contemporary reconfiguration of Nigeria's economic order from state capitalist to global, from agribusiness to petroleum, is intended not simply to reflect the effects of the growing oil economy and its accompanying order of wealth and power, its disruptions of the rural productive order, the shift to urbanization, but the liminality that the conjuncture brought in the cinematic industry. The earlier means of producing celluloid films, their distribution in both urban theatres and travelling companies that brought projectors to villages, functioned as the "Old Africa" of the movies (Haynes 2016, chapter one). What was to come in the 1990s represented a sea change.

Nollywood, the "New African" wave in the production of video films, with their distribution in Idumota and Ataba markets of Lagos, their popularity as home videos, as well as their new genres, all combined to produce notions of "movies" as sharing both old and new elements. The conjuncture generated considerable alienation and anxieties with old school African filmmakers and critics who attempted to ignore or denigrate the commercial forms taken by the new films—especially in Ghana and Nigeria (Garritano 2013). Kelani experienced both worlds in the course of his career, initially resisting inclusion under the label of "Nollywood" and then succumbing, while simultaneously identifying himself as unique (Haynes 2016). With *Thunderbolt: Magun* (2001), *Dazzling Mirage* (2014), and others, he continued the old tradition of making films with pedagogical intent, yet couched in the clothes of popular melodramas or family films (Haynes, chapters 4 and 5). Simultaneously he produced *Abeni* (2006), *Maami* (2011), *The Campus Queen* (2004), and others that emphasized cultural transitions, romance, and especially family values. Corrupt politicians and military figures (*Arugba* [2008], *Saworoide* [1999]) were represented in his critiques of contemporary governmentality, but invariably within a universe peopled with old and new style Kabiyesis and bearded babalawos chanting Ifa verses and throwing the cowries for their clients.

What is of interest then is why Kelani, imbued in Yoruba values and thought since his childhood ("We have a rich cultural heritage which is of great interest to me, our ways of life are threatened but it is my responsibility to document as much as I can before they fade away" [Interview in *Nigeria.com*: "My Challenges, Successes, Life as a Filmmaker—Tunde Kelani"]), was driven to give expression to modernist tropes in his films. In fact, it was almost inevitable that he did so, not because any African creator must come to terms with modernity when situating his or her dramas in the contemporary scene, but because the highly dramatic issues he evokes, from the conflicts on campuses to government corruption, to death and medicine, made the most sense to his audiences when framed in terms of modernist epistemologies.

I. *Thunderbolt: Magun* (2001)

A compelling example is disease. In *Thunderbolt* (2001) the protagonist suffers from magun (the "African AIDS"),[2] a disease that has brought significant trauma to much of Africa. AIDS has dramatic qualities: it is associated with homosexuality, immoral lifestyles, profligacy—in short, with the stuff of melodrama. Its sexual transmission guarantees revelations of private matters. It was also regarded as incurable in 2000 when *Thunderbolt* was made. The two competing major themes in *Thunderbolt* concern the inter-ethnic struggle embodied in the marriage between Yinka, a Yoruba man, and Ngozi, an Igbo woman, and the struggle between modern medicine and African herbalism.[3]

Although the cross between Yoruba and Igbo had a particular resonance in 2000, that is, 30 years after the Biafran war, the real political backdrop that framed this film had to have been the gradual disintegration of the political processes of rule and governance that followed in the years after the war. In particular, 16 years of military rule, culminating in the disastrous reign of Sani Abacha (1993–98), introduced state violence and insecurity that marred the lives of ordinary citizens. Kelani frames the issues of politics in terms of power.

At one point Kelani has one of the chiefs aver in *Saworoide* (1999) that power exists in three areas: with the demos—the body of the citizens—in democracy; in the state, that is, the governing bodies and their instruments of power; and finally, in the realm of world ruled by spiritual forces.[4] The latter was the dominant factor in *Thunderbolt* (2001). As Nollywood films emerged in the 1990s, that spiritual realm was represented overwhelmingly by occult forces marked by evil, forces that prey on human weakness such as greed and desire and that require countervailing forces of divine goodness to trump them. When the power of the people or of the government fails, then justice must go searching among the spirits to find its defender.

For the sake of the drama in *Thunderbolt* (2001), the evil figures must prevail through most of the film, so that the forces of goodness might triumph at the end. What people come to see on the screen is the temporary triumph of the forces of evil, their horrific features, and then their defeat. Should the defeat come early, there would be no plot and no thrill. Similarly, as Haynes has shown (2016), with the ascension of family films as a genre, as seen in telenovelas, and with melodrama shaping the narrative, what drives audience interest has to be an apprehension that a situation that is in need of correction is untenable and must lead to corrective measures that will right the imbalances and injustices. In family films, that means whatever is keeping the family from coming together harmoniously under the proper authority and power within the family, must be overcome.

The marriage of Yinka and Ngozi is torpedoed when an unscrupulous friend undermines Yinka's faith in his wife, in her fidelity, especially as she is becoming financially independent. It is further undermined by Yinka's mother's desire to see him marry a Yoruba woman, not an Igbo. Despite their love, despite Ngozi's patience with Yinka's abusive behaviour, the dissolution of the marriage in the end occurs because of his weaknesses and greed. Magun serves as the device that led to their rupture. Magun also supplants the theme of ethnic division. It grows in the course of the film from an underlying reason for her dreams and fears, with her hallucinatory experience of encountering a ghost who warns her of the danger, to embody the increasingly chaotic disaster that Nigeria seemed to be courting with Babanginda, Shonekan, and finally Abacha, who introduced more and more corruption and violence in society. It was as if the fundamentals needed for ordinary life were being undermined as corruption, armed robbery, and a dysfunctional social order. This insecurity marked the need to have films create a sense of what is lacking in ordinary lives: a decent social order. Haynes detailed this in his overview of the prevalence of cinematic moralism: "[T]he demand for moral closure comes from the audience's aching need for order and justice. The reality of contemporary Nigeria does not provide either order or justice" (2016: 54–55). This is ingrained in the filmic imaginary as well: "The moralizing is kept real because it is lived all the time. The temptations and instabilities that make the theme prominent are built into the structure of the industry itself" (55).

Magun overwhelms Ngozi, to the point where much more than her marriage is at stake: she has to confront a mysterious, evil force whose destructiveness extends to the very sources of fertile reproduction, to life and the libido itself. Ngozi must have sex to be cured; men who dare attempt to copulate with this dangerous Mami Watta figure risk annihilation and destruction.[5] Her survival can be assured only at the price of her sexual partner's death. Here is the heart of the film, the annihilation of life: the figuring of the destructive force that infects ordinary existence, that threatens even the best intentions at reconciliation between opposing peoples, that overcomes all efforts to bring together those marked by difference ("There are only two tribes, good and bad people," are Ngozi's last words of the film. She might have added, never the twain shall meet).

Magun is a destructive force that can be read as symptomatic, but the most compelling reading should preserve its qualities as both a trope and a material object, one that takes on gigantic, monumental proportions, as we can see in the final scenes of the film where Ngozi's cure is matched by the violence of the disease and the magical forces. When Dijemi, a Yoruba doctor enamoured with her, finally consents to undertake the challenge of copulating with her, it is not represented as a sexual act in the erotic sense: the partners are awkward, diffident to the point of dissociation. Although the act is carried out in a medical facility, with Dijemi's doctor friends and the traditional herbalists present, there is none of the usual cinematic sex imagery that conveys the arousal with groans, pleasure, and flesh. Rather, we have the staging of the ultimate confrontation between the truths of scientific medicine: Dijemi's friends are dressed in white medical gowns and hold charts; the herbalists are dressed in traditional robes, equipped with their magical lotions that they will be called on to apply in the event that magun strikes Dijemi. At this moment—the film's climax, so to speak, rather than that of the couple—there is a material encounter involving physical bodies whose relationship determines the outcome of the threat to life. Magun, as in Slavoj Žižek's schema of Hitchcock's films (1991), functions as a McGuffin that brings the protagonists into relationship, one involving life and death. What is normally performed in privacy as providing the ultimate pleasure, bringing the culmination of desire, and assuring the reproductive, generative side of humanity, becomes perversely turned to death. Perverse salvation bought at the price of generosity and sacrifice. Furthermore, the significance of the act for the question of how and how far to go in representing sexuality in a Nigerian film can't be separated from considerations of the passage of the film before the censor board, and before the public whose expectations of a Kelani film would seem to prevent this representation of sexuality from being sexy!

We need to read this scene in two ways: as a medical cure, presenting the limit of the powers of modernity in preserving life from its threats, and simultaneously as demonstrating the workings of pre-modern "herbalism" preserved by the traditional elders. More is at stake than the power of modern science or traditional practices. The healer charges 60,000 naira, a fortune that the headmaster qualifies as more than his annual salary. Ngozi, educated and employed as a teacher, reacts to the threat of ma-gun by scoffing at the superstitious practices mobilized by her landlady to counter it. She is the heir to a small fortune when her grandmother dies, and would seem to embody the goals of the modern state to bring together the conflicting ethnic populations of Nigeria and to ensure that their meet-ing will result in a new future, represented by her son Hero (like Junior in Afolayan's *Figurine*). The reproduction of the state, of the principals, of the epic orders of the past, present, and future, cannot be evoked outside of the capitalist economic and social order—the world into which Yinka and Ngozi have entered with their careers and marriage. The framing can no longer be reduced to a hypothetical modern west versus a hypotheti-cal tradition-bound Africa. That doesn't account for the economic forces that frame the drama in *Thunderbolt* (2001), or *The Figurine* (2009) for that matter. The issue of modernity in Africa needs to be rethought. And Kelani's films allow us to do so.

Conventionally we have always associated notions of modernity with colonial discourse, which means we've accepted using the colonial frame to shape the argument. However, it would serve us better to demystify the colonial discourse not simply as racist, or not only as racist, but as a capitalist mystification. After all, the racism was not what drove the colonial mission or even the power structures of the colonial era: it was the economics. With time, racial arguments followed as rationalizations for colonial conquest.[6] Minerals and cash crops became central factors in offsetting the costs of supplying the colonial state with materiel and troops, administrative personnel and infrastructural development. These costs preoccupied the colonialists in the 1850s and delayed by decades any government decisions to intervene (Young 1994). By the time Sir George Goldie and his competitors convinced the British and French gov-ernments that there were serious economic incentives to intervene—after ending the slave trade in the 1830s and 1840s—others began to see the possible profits in the ivory, rubber, cocoa, coffee, and tea trade (Falola and Heaton 2008; Hochschild 1998). More importantly, as the decisions of the 1880s following Berlin were implemented, the home office's de-sire to limit costs of running the colonies led to the use of forced labor, reinstituting forms of plantation slavery, as on Zanzibar (Cooper 1977, 1980), in the Sahel under French-Touareg agreements (Klein 1998), and their equivalents in the use of child labor with mining practices in the Congo (Amnesty International reports[7]). Road gangs using forced labor built roads and railroad lines, at times with brutal practices. Race was not driving the decisions to arm native subalterns and impose colonial sovereignty; it was the possibility of utilizing steam power, coal, steel, and electricity to create train lines, communication systems, radio networks, etc (Larkin 2008), all of which entailed collaborations with elements of the local population. Northern Nigeria was not the exception, it was emblematic. Modernity and development meant capitalism—and in the instance, state capitalism and private ownership with state subventions. The 1870s saw intense competition among British and French companies for trade up the Niger River. Ultimately, the Royal Niger Company was granted a charter and, operating under Goldie, functioned as the effective ruling party from 1885 till the British government decided to turn the territory into the colonies of the Southern Nigerian Protectorate and the Northern Nigerian Protectorate in 1899.

The introduction of capitalism threatened every component of African social life, upending the economic order involving local production and commerce (Rodney 1989; Wallerstein 1979, 2004). Roads and trains transporting military troops, cash crops, minerals, rubber, ivory, lumber, and other products down to the coast, to be shipped to the metropoles, reordered the fundamental structures of life, the basic patterns of land ownership, and thus the relations between rulers and ruled. The peanut trade in Senegal, for instance, came along with the intervention of the powerful Mourid and Tijani brotherhoods, with state control over costs and prices, and with foreign investors, like the Lebanese, entering into the field (Curry-Machado 2013). All these factors point to one conclusion, that the representation of modernity could not be configured properly without taking the material conditions for production, distribution, and consumption into account.

Magun is the material trope that embodies the anxieties over modernization, and by modernization here I mean to challenge the conventional notion of anxiety—what Cheikh Hamidou Kane depicted as the "aventure ambiguë"—following the colonial imposition of western values and social structures, including women's roles, public education, and official language use, European thought, etc. Here my concern is not with the superstructure, which has dominated theorizations of modernity in Africa, but the materiality itself associated with an economic order, and embodied in biopolitics. Magun is not only a "thing," but a violent, enormous, unstoppable "Ding" (Žižek 1991), its force experienced as devastating.

At one point, we might have imagined these great forces as figuring globalization, the enormous pressures of a capitalist neoliberal global order, with gigantic container ships taking over the entire universe with their wealth and power (Comaroff and Comaroff 2001). But the shipping, the wealth, and the power were already there in an earlier exchange system that brought in goods and guns, and that shipped out slaves under the impress of state capitalism. The goods changed in the course of the late 18th and 19th centuries; and they continued to change in the late 20th century when items like coltan and "blood" minerals emerged, when tin and lumber replaced copper, when labor and agricultural goods were replaced by other "modern" extractive metals and oil that made the communications and commerce of a global economy work. But the revolutionary effect of capitalism that Marx signalled in the Manifesto—upending everything in society[8]—proved completely true for the 20th century (Rodney 1989; AbouMaliq Simone 2001, 2004; Comaroff and Comaroff 2001).

II. *Ti Oluwa Ni Ile* (1993) [God's Own Earth]

Modernity in Africa means changes on fundamental levels that capitalist production and ownership brought—as well as those that are "profoundly ideological and profoundly historical" (Comaroff and Comaroff 1993). Changes in human relations, as seen when market women in Ghana began to pay for their "small boy" pleasures. The powerful figure who saves Chief Otun in *Ti Oluwa Ni Ile* (1993) is in fact a very large, wealthy woman—an impressive figure, like the even heavier passenger who causes the motorcycle to fall over when she gets on back.[9] The women dance bent over, their behinds in the air—signalling not sexuality but, with their size and motion, their dominance of the space, their central place in the circle of the dance, their weight in society. Next to them, the impotent Western-educated Kabeyesi appears truly a frail small boy, a thin twig of a figure whose worries pale to inconsequentiality as with his place in the final celebratory dance where he is merely another participant.[10] His "grammar" fades to insignificance before the generous shapes of the wealthy capitalist women when they are dressed in their Dutch wax prints and elaborate head wraps.

Ti Oluwa Ni Ile (1993) begins with the images of modernity—not, as in Sembène's *Moolaadé* (2004), or Kelani's *Abeni* (2006), with the worries to be anticipated when the next young man or woman returns from France, or Europe, or the USA, having imbibed the magical brews of modern society. In the conventional thinking of the West, they should be carrying back its technology, knowledge, and assurances of what the New African Man or New African Woman should represent—especially with the means to become wealthy. But here, with our more grounded, material notion of modernity in *Ti Oluwa Ni Ile* (1993), the focus turns to a mere gas station, one that involves a convenience store, requiring electricity and good paved roads. It will bring in money by selling the one commodity that in 1990 would make work for the whole country: petrol. Oil nearly destroyed all other forms of production, exactly as Marx had predicted capitalism would do, and replaced them with the deathly effects of extraction: dependency on a world market that no one could seem to control, the magical rise and fall of the market prices, and enslavement to its powerful institutions (Comaroff 2001, Geschiere 2013). It also brought, as Mbembe (2000) has noted, necropolitics, along with devastating practices and extractions, pollution, controls by the state, corruption, and by 1991, death to those who dared challenge the pattern, the ownership, the wealth—the cocktail of elements that conspired to bring the death of Ken Saro-Wiwa and the Ogoni Nine. In *Ti Oluwa Ni Ile* ownership is finally decided and the filling station gets built. The only question that really matters within the capitalist order will be who will profit, whose bank abroad will receive the cash profits and payoffs. When the confrontations with death, disease, and corruption are all acted out, even in *Dazzling Mirage* (2014), at the conclusion of all the dramatic confrontations, we are left with an office, workers, telephones, professional dress, management, everything that has put in place an order that conveys a "modern" business practice. Capitalism, its conquests and malcontents, these are the issues that define the realities of modernity in Africa, then and now, and all that has changed is how it is represented. This is the location of biopolitics in modern Africa.

Modernity is central to Kelani's thought. As Haynes puts it:

> The blending and coexistence of past and present, tradition and modernity, is a nearly constant theme in Kelani's work . . . The call in *Thunderbolt* for a synthesis between traditional and modern/Western medicine is perhaps the most programmatic example . . . The traditional and the modern are expected to go on being poles, fountains of meaning that do not run dry or lose their difference from one another. Kelani is distressed by the general failure of modernity in Nigeria to produce the expected enlightenment, but he remains dedicated to that project.
> *(Haynes 2016: 134)*

We can read the early, the middle, and the late films through this vector of modernity and its representations, and to do so we will turn back to cinema and to Slavoj Žižek's model in his analysis of Hitchcock's films (Žižek 1991, 1992).

The cinematic features that correspond to modernism's socio-economic order and its subjects can be discerned using Žižek's analysis of the relationship between the films' McGuffins, the protagonists' subjectivity, and the capitalism order. Žižek traces the evolution of the three stages of Hitchcock's films within the conceptual limits imposed by the changing capitalist order that produces representations that work on three levels: the subjective; the relational functioning among protagonists; and the economic.[11] This model associates the intersubjective relations between people with the dominant ideological and economic orders, giving us a meaningful basis for understanding the kinds of subjectivities that are embodied in the protagonists.

Žižek links the first stage of Hitchcock's films to liberal capitalism, the second to imperialist state-capitalism, and the third to "post-industrial" state-capitalism. The first is grounded in the "classic ideology of the 'autonomous' subject strengthened through ordeal" (Žižek 1992: 5). The autonomous subject progressively declines in each subsequent phase. "The resigned paternal figure of the second stage evokes the decline of this 'autonomous' subject to whom is opposed the victorious, insipid 'heteronomous' hero" (Žižek 1992: 5). Finally, Žižek tells us, "it is not difficult to recognize, in the typical Hitchcockian hero of the 1950s and early 1960s, the features of the 'pathological narcissist,' the form of subjectivity that characterizes the so-called 'society of consumption'" (Žižek 1992: 5). Although what Žižek has in mind is centered on Hollywood or European cinema, and European or American stages of capitalist development, its relevance to Africa appears significant to me.

The forms of capitalism Žižek focuses on are grounded in industrialized Western states. For us the IMF and World Bank's push to liberalize African economies, and their ill-fated Structural Adjustment Programs, correspond to the temporal stages that we are linking roughly to changes in African cinemas. Nothing is more vexed than dividing cultural production into "stages." Here my question will be very limited: when the impact of SAPs was felt in Africa, when loans and their repayment squeezed African economies, what effects were felt in the society and in cultural production? By the time Sissako had made *Bamako* (2006), African economies had reacted dramatically, jobs had become harder to find, and large numbers of youth were emigrating north. The "ages" of African cinema that preceded Nollywood were coming to an end. FESPACO tried to sustain the old Sembènean ideals of an *engagé* cinema and Third Cinema, but the costs of production and especially the obstacles to distribution could not be overcome. In parallel fashion, SAPs promises were also failing. We can regard the development of video films in the late 1980s and especially 1990s alongside the shift toward informal economies throughout much of Sub-Saharan

Africa (and elsewhere, see Lobato 2012). From the relatively crude images and themes implemented in the earliest years of Nollywood, down to the formulaic, algorhythmically driven projects now being generated by Netflix and Amazon, and the other major platforms, we can correlate large shifts in culture with the rise of new genres and styles. From *Living in Bondage* (1992) to *Thunderbolt: Magun* (2001) to the latest works of Mahamat-Saleh Haroun (*Lingui* [2013]) or Abderrahmane Sissako (*Timbuktu* [2014]; *Le Vol du Boli* {theatrical piece}, [2022]) enormous changes have occurred. The three generations of Hitchcock's films that Žižek detailed are discernible in the films of Kelani, in the dominant tropes and relationships between characters, in the genres, in the new approach to serious films with a popular appeal.

Žižek associates the three phases of capitalism with characteristic *objects* whose crucial role in each film is determinant of its mode (1992: 5–6). The first of the objects is described as the "McGuffin," the familiar invisible Hitchcockian device that is actually a pretext whose "sole role is to set the story in motion" (1992: 6) (e.g. El Hadj's "xala," or magun in *Thunderbolt*). In this phase the possibilities of taking action within an economy of the autonomous subject correspond with liberal capitalism (1992: 5). Not surprising, this was the form of capitalism that so confidently implanted its development programs in the thinking of IMF and World Bankers, resulting in neoliberal structuralist programs.

The second kind of object Žižek describes has a material form, and its function is to bring the characters into relationship with each other. A key example might be the plots of land in *Ti Awola Ni Ile* (1993) that function precisely to bring the developers and the members of the royal court into a relationship. The relationships make sense and motivate the action in the film, thus setting up a symbolic order. The struggle over who owns the land sets the stage for the protagonists to appear less as autonomous subjects functioning in a liberal capitalist economy than what Žižek terms the "heteronomous" subject. The latter, especially Chief Otun (played by Adepoju) in this case, is no longer quite in control of his situation, his actions or his relationships which would normally provide the basis for his subjectivity. Haynes describes the role often played by Alhadji Kareem Adepoju ("Baba Wande") as that of a "wily rogue": "a deeply cynical, greedy human being, a congenital liar steeped in corruption, a traitor . . . [who practices] *wuruwuru* and *gomago* [tricky business]" (Haynes: 122). In Žižek's schema, the protagonist here functions within the system of imperialistic state capitalism, and especially in its immoderate quest for money. By the 1990s the empire had long since been removed from its direct rule in the 1950s; neocolonialism had morphed into neoliberalism, and the international banking and financial institutions and larger EU structures took their place. Imperialist state capitalism, with weakened African nations genuflecting before loan-granting international agencies, had become the norm.

If we focus on the diminished powers of the paternal figure, or Law of the Father, on whose authority is constructed the symbolic order, we could observe how in films like Jean-Marie Teno's *Chef* (1999), or Bekolo's *Aristotle's Plot* (1996), such figures had been reduced, like the burlesque "Popauls" of Mbembe's postcolony (2001). The Kabiyesi in *Saworoide* (1999) follows this model. When he enters onto the scene, early in the film, he interviews the men who are logging the forests, and states, "I'm a modern king. What's your gross income?" Impossible to parody this version of the modern capitalist. We see the neocolonialism of the early period of independence exacerbated with this far more debilitating klepto-capitalism of the postcolonial failed state, with its far greater dependencies and incapacities (see Bayart [1989], 1993). In Kelani's *Saworoide* (1999) we have General Lagata who overthrows and succeeds the Kabiyesi, carrying the grotesqueries of power to even greater degrees. The original Kabiyesi's chiefs have corrupted power and taken their share of the logging money to buy cars; the General who succeeds him has the soldiers and guns, and could well have been played as Soyinka's Kongi—although the reference is clearly to Abacha, whose portrait appears in the king's reception room, behind the Kabiyesi. From the Law of the Father to the lawless, heteronomous father.

The third and last of these phases considered by Žižek involves the figure of "pathological narcissism" associated with late capitalism. We are now on the terrain of the late postcolonial period where globalization has taken hold in Africa, with SAPs's debilitating effects having wrought their damage. African nations systematically battled for and often lost control over their territory with the rise of local militias, banditry, and predatory international merchants or even mercenaries now prevalent. Naturally in cinema this is accompanied by the inevitable disappearance of the paternal superego altogether and its replacement with the completely dominating figure of the maternal superego.[12] In *Looking Awry* (1991), Žižek describes the disorder in the family generated under these circumstances:

> The father is absent, the paternal function (the function of the pacifying law, the Name-of-the-Father) is suspended and that vacuum is filled by the 'irrational' maternal superego, arbitrary, wicked, blocking 'normal' sexual relationship (only possible under the sign of the paternal metaphor).
>
> *(1999: 99).*

For Žižek, the mother in *Psycho* (1960) presents such a figure, attesting to the "unresolved tension in intersubjective relations" (99). In *Dazzling Mirage* (2014) it is "Mummy," Sanya's overbearing mother. In Moussa Touré's *La Pirogue* (2012), the pater familias Baye heads out to cross the seas to Europe, leaving his wife behind and in charge of the family. His return as a failure comes as a fulfilment of normalized expectations. This description fits closely the return of Mory in Moussa Absa Sene's *Ainsi Meurent les anges* (2001), where the close to the "ambiguous adventure" is seen in the father who abandons his mixed-race family in Paris, and returns home to Dakar penniless.[13]

The autonomy of the dominant male subject and the sense that his choices can determine his fate are gone. Correspondingly, the kinds of objects that come to inhabit Hitchcock's landscape now assume gigantic and monstrous proportions: the birds in *The Birds* (1963), or the airplane, and then Mt. Rushmore in *North by Northwest* (1959). In *Thunderbolt* (2001) it is magun; in *Dazzling Mirage* (2014) the dreaded sickle cell. In Afolayan's *Figurine* (2009), it is the statue itself. And in *Living in Bondage* (1992) and thereafter, the figures responsible for monstrous crimes become commonplace. In *Jezebel* (Agu 1994), she rises out of the water like Mami Watta, having seduced the female protagonist, overturning the paternal order, ready to wreck the household and its old order:

FIGURE 4.1   Jezebel

For the figure of monstrous subjectivity in African cinema, we would not turn to the standard failed despots, the Popauls of the second phase, but to those multitudinous shocking figures of disruption and fearfulness that embody the spiritual realm of evil forces, the favoured haunt of contemporary video filmmakers in Nigeria and Ghana. This is echoed in many films of the post-millennium period, where fighting in Sierra Leone, Liberia, Rwanda, and the Democratic Republic of the Congo, and other regions like Darfur, the Central African Republic, and others, has led to brutal violence and genocide.

FIGURE 4.2 *La Nuit de la verité*

The colonel grilled:

FIGURE 4.3 Bill in *Formidable Force*

Demonic figures, insurmountable forces motivated by acts of excessive greed and lustfulness—all the markings of the absence of the paternal superego—were translated into an African imaginary. In the universe of Nollywood often we find portrayals of the infinite machinations of Satan, with phantasmagorical blood rituals, and the ghostly magic of evil forces. Francophone cinema led to the same pattern, with zombies and predatory capitalism thematized in Mati Diop's *Atlantiques* (2019), though not as gory as Nollywood.

Kelani's modernity can be traced through the appearance of these features highlighted by Žižek, though there is considerable overlap; more than one stage might be present at the same time. Given the underlying material base for this approach, the question of modernity is posed in the ways it is embodied. This is magnified in the diseases and treatments that sustain the bodily form in the face of threats of disintegration, both physical and phenomenological. The circle must turn. When we arrive at the end of the journey taking us from Otun's death in *Ti Oluwa Ni Ile* (1993) to Dijemi's bare survival in *Thunderbolt* (2001) to Funmi's unexpected recovery in *Dazzling Mirage* (2014), the spectre of death appears as to have haunted all the phases of the modern. It is a spectre, like that of capitalism that haunted Marx, when considered under the aegis of an economic order that could not advance without destroying what was there before.

A number of the key elements of Žižek's first and second stages are strikingly present in *Ti Owula Ni Ile* (1993). The action takes place at a distance from Lagos and the engines of power and wealth, in a city governed by the Kabiyesi. His modernity is made clear by his infusion of English words and phrases into his speech, his liberalism and enlightened values,[14] and his seeming devotion to an equally attractive, thin wife. He speaks the language of liberal capitalism throughout the film by advocating the development of the community in economic terms, inviting investment, even at his own expense when he donates or is willing to accept the loss of his ownership of a parcel of land on which the outsider, Mr. Johnson, another visibly modern businessman from the big city, wishes to build his filling station.[15] The locals seek to cheat Mr. Johnson, as well as the Kabiyesi, the legal owner of the land, work to defraud the king, and eventually to overthrow him. The decision about who is the rightful owner of the land, and of the throne, is made by a judge who dresses in the English manner with black robes and a wig. We are clearly launched into the world of liberal capitalism with the king as the autonomous subject who must overcome obstacles that test his agency so as to validate his status as the figure of modernity, the modern African—the New African. Old Africa is represented by his enemies, the false chiefs, with their continual recourse to babalawos to enable them to survive and succeed in their nefarious schemes.

The film is not really about the Kabiyesi, but Chief Otun, the villainous schemer who is closer to a trickster, more like Žižek's second stage capitalist than a clearly delineated individual entrepreneur. His name changes; his motives, and especially relations with others, change. He is more heteronomous than autonomous, incapable of deferring death indefinitely, yet working his schemes and resisting his due punishment throughout the film. He lies and perjures himself; yet he also begs and wins forgiveness and absolution from the punishment he merits. He isn't all bad; he is far from good. He wins some, loses some, and most of all sustains the plot as we wait to see when and how he will get his comeuppance.

Where is the McGuffin, the object that drives the plot? It is the ownership of the land, and in its materiality, the land itself, which is anything but invisible at the beginning. To the contrary, we see the parcel the realtor tries to sell Mr. Johnson at the opening. When the first plot offered is turned down, we see the alternate plot he offers to sell, the land belonging to the Kabiyesi, and ultimately to the community whose lands and life, we are told, are in the hands of their benevolent ruler. We see the terrain measured; we see the building; and in the end, we see the abuse of the lands, as Chief Otun attempts to build on a portion that would impede the flow of the river and damage the environment. The land lies passive, but its value, and the fight to obtain and use it, drive the plot from the outset. It is a figure that appears to be incapable of defending itself, like tradition in the face of modernity, or Africa in the face of outside forces that control its resources, wealth, development, and enlightenment as conceived in Western terms. The attempts of the enlightened elements of society to drive the Kabiyesi's decisions are thwarted continually by the unscrupulous figures who lie and abuse the power of the courts. The plot flips frequently, with the enlightened king supported by the people early in the film, but nearly overcome by the machinations of the evil pretender to the throne, who mobilizes mobs to attack the monarch, and conspirators deploying legal trickery to win the right to the land. In the end the judge who had appeared to accept their bribes comes through with justice, exercises his autonomous judgment, and saves the day. With ownership restored to the king, liberal capitalism and democracy prevail.

What makes this happen is a deus ex machina, the intervention of spirit forces conjured by the babalawos. Chief Otun's fate is sealed by the spirits; he is pursued in his dreams by two ghostly figures identified as ghosts. Ultimately he is taken by them, again in his dreams, through a mystical doorway that lies between life and death, and crosses over to the other side where we had known all along, following the babalawos, that he was fated to wind up. He dies, but in death his fate doesn't end: his body is taken to a mortuary where science and legality will determine its disposition.

We are granted a glimpse into the disposition of his immaterial spirit, just as earlier we had been provided much fuller access to the sight of his body, pressed hip to hip against his fulsome benefactor, Madame Akere, the widow. He is welcomed into the weighty world of her home, with two female house servants, a gatekeeper, the luxuries of lush quarters and copious quantities of food, lodged in a guest room with an en suite bath. The materiality is commensurate with the physical consequences of the spirits' attacks on the four evil conspirators—the two businessmen, Otun the corrupted chief, and their lawyer, all of whom are shown to fall ill, with foaming mouths and horrible deaths. The autonomous king's modernity fades far into the background as we are entertained at great length with the depiction of conniving chiefs, wealthy schemers, illegal crooks, and a corrupted mortician.

If the modern gas station is presented to our gaze at the end, as the king celebrates with his followers, it is not because his use of English, his education, or his modernity were able to prevail over his enemies. Rather, it was due to the conspirators' inability to resist their fate, their demise ordered by the spirits or the ancestors whose patience with their machinations finally came to an end. The supernatural beings, Orunmila and Ifa, work invisibly behind the presence of the babalawo priests, along with the Gelede ancestors whose presence is hidden beneath the costuming of the dancing masqueraders. The world of the spirits, their presence seen in the continual occurrences of ghostly interventions in this world of modern cars and hospitals, creates a heteronymous notion of subjectivity that matches the heteronymous mix in the McGuffin itself, the land and its relationship to its owners, and its final disposition.

The land was initially stolen from and then restored to the king, his rightful ownership invisible but still a presence, like the McGuffin of the first stage. In all that, the physical land came between the major antagonists in the film, and thus functioned as Žižek described it in the second phase, where it acts as "the object of exchange between characters whose relationship takes on a meaningful dimension as a result of that exchange" (1992: 6). In that phase, pure liberal capitalism is gradually supplanted by "imperialistic state capitalism," the order that efficiently describes what Babangida and Abacha were determined to establish, with their own rule secured by the military forces. Even when the immediate threat of Chief Otun and the conspirators is overcome, the world order displays its own tenuousness in resisting threats to legitimacy. The community dances at the end, but future threats are as inevitable as the need for a sequel to any telenovela series, as if to say that a nation founded on oil wealth can only be unstable. Though Chief Otun is finally defeated, the instability he and his co-conspirators initiated has taken hold. Abacha hanged Saro-Wiwa, but the violent campaign in the Delta was launched, to remain for years to come, down to the present.[16]

III. *Dazzling Mirage* (2014) and the Modern African Woman

Thunderbolt (2001) and *Dazzling Mirage* (2014) bring us firmly into the world of modernity, of the modern educated woman, and of the successful, urbane, businesswoman.

Ngozi, from *Thunderbolt*, is the predecessor for Funmi in *Dazzling Mirage* (2014). Ngozi's education and national service as teacher foreshadow Funmi's role of important advertising executive, like Sembène's Faat Kine, the business woman of the New Africa (both *Thunderbolt* [2001] and *Faat Kine* [2001] came out around the turn of the new millennium!). Both of Kelani's female protagonists are infected with a modern disease that is sexually or genetically transmitted, and the educated Ngozi rejects the attempts of herbalists to treat her by calling their cure "ridiculous, preposterous." The presumed audience shares her view of their potions and prescriptions as superstitious. In contrast, her semi-illiterate landlady, a surrogate mother who is "old-school," tells her, "Stop this grammar and think of your life," before taking her to the herbalist.

In *Dazzling Mirage* (2014), Funmi's introductory scene concludes when she has a sickle cell attack, and rushes to the pharmacy for medications. There are no more consultations with babalawos, no more herbal cures, ghosts, or satanic forces. In *Thunderbolt* (2001) the doctors in hospital gowns are defeated by magun, the "African AIDS," but the thunderbolt itself, now transmogrified into sickle cell anaemia, must conjure modern methods for its cure and is defeated by modernity.

Perhaps one of the best ways to understand feminism and modernity in these Nigerian robes is in the anxiety caused by the notion of the liberated woman. Ngozi, the carrier of a disease that kills men who dare to have sex with her, cannot survive unless she transmits that death to some male partner. This is the myth conveying the dangers of women's liberation, which we can track back to poems like Frank Aig-Imoukhuede's "One Wife for One Man" that represented the dangers represented by the figure of the westernized African woman, with patriarchal complaints voiced for many years. In the poem he states his father has wife "borku," but doesn't get any "equality palaver." He lived well as boss ("oga") in his own house. The famous line that follows is that those days are gone when there was "One Wife for One Man."[17]

The fearful figure of the "one wife for one husband" comes close to what Žižek called the maternal superego[18]—the woman whose power, without the Name of the Father, leads to the familiar figure of the "mère dévorante" of African folktales. As women entered fully into the educational system and workplace, men experienced the challenge to their roles, in the workplace, in the home.[19] In Žižek's model, the ascent of global capitalism led to the inevitable disappearance of the paternal superego and its replacement with the dominant figure of the maternal superego. Already prefigured, in some sense, in the figure of Mami Watta, she has evolved in *Dazzling Mirage* (2014) where we will see her split into the positive figure of Funmi, the liberated New African Woman, and the negative embodied by the virago "Mummy," the mother of Funmi's first fiancé Sanya, who has reduced her son to the pathetic figure of a "mommy's boy." When Funmi has an attack from her disease, she calls Sanya, who comes over to help. He puts on an apron, starts chopping tomatoes, and tells Funmi he is there to do everything for her. Then his mother calls, and he makes lame excuses before leaving Funmi to cope with her pain alone. When his mother tells him he must wear the tie she has picked out, instead of the darker one of his own choice, he succumbs to her orders while she smiles in contentment, in triumph. And so it goes. Eventually his mother succeeds in having Sanya's relationship with Funmi broken off by promoting his affair with his docile research assistant. Just as the dangerous figure of the modern woman is split into two halves with Mummy and Funmi, so are the men split between the emasculated figure of the fiancé Sanya, and Funmi's eventual husband, her boss Dotun (played by the incomparable Kunle Afolayan).

Ultimately Funmi marries Dotun, and they have a child. Before this occurs, Funmi has chastised her parents for having conceived her knowing they would likely pass on the imperfect gene. She becomes an activist for a sickle cell support group and leads a campaign of awareness. When she has a child in the face of the physical dangers this presents to her, the audience is left in suspense, fearing that she will die in childbirth. This theme, the dangers of modernity now marked by "modern" diseases like AIDS and sickle cell anemia with their modern treatments in modern hospitals, is brought to its climax when the dangers of transmitting deadly genes or viruses to the children are evoked.

Dazzling Mirage (2014) might have had a stronger ending if Funmi died in childbirth so that the audience could empathize with the surviving father and child, and identify with the father's commitment to dedicate himself to the struggle against the disease. However, as the film embraced the goals of the infomercial more than the melodrama, we are granted the complacent ending of a family film—the triumph of which Haynes so beautifully traces in his study of the genre in Nollywood films (Haynes 2016: chapter four).

IV.

The new global city has modern medical facilities, above all. The new global age is best conveyed in the scene in the hospital where Funmi is being treated after her first attack. Her worried parents are gathered, along with the doctor, and her assistant who brings her the files she needs to work on. As they discuss her treatment she demonstrates her impatience with the hospital stay, and decides to discharge herself. Her parents worriedly encourage her to return home with them since she has no man to take care of her. During this scene we see a television screen behind her where an old-school Nollywood film is being shown. The drama there needs no words, as a woman sobs and shrieks while men grab her, and she is seen being dragged along, begging. The scene has nothing and everything to do with the modern medical world that now frames the mise-en-scene. No one in that room is watching as this "Icarus" falls, as yesterday's cinema is now replaced by something new, and if for Kelani it isn't easy to adopt the mantle of "Neo-Nollywood" for his work, it is because his goals far exceed, have always far exceeded, those of a film like *The Figurine* (2009) where Afolayan merely aspired to make a successful film. For Kelani success meant more than commercial returns. His intent in this, as generally in all his films, was social amelioration. His means of accomplishing this have been forged through the tools of modernity, which include not only representation of a modern world, but in the very form and message of the film itself, an idea never embraced by the commercial world of Nollywood. Perhaps the difficulty in accomplishing this can be seen in his venture into television with the online TV channel *tundikelani.tv*, where entertainment and sturdy Yoruba values might be promoted.[20]

We return to Gikandi's assessment of Kenyatta where the grand old man sat between two worlds, ruling over his new nation:

> Kenyatta's post-coloniality was not predicated on hybridity or a play of differences, but a calculated deployment of a set of values from both colonial and African institutions. He was a product of the structural ambiguity inherent in the modernity of the African.
>
> *(Gikandi 374)*

It is in that sense that Kelani, too, is a product of an African modernity which he both perceives and defines, at times with resistance, at times embracing it.

Notes

1 Originally published in Tunde Onikonyi's *The Cinema of Tunde Kelani*. Newcastle Upon Tyne: Cambridge Scholars Publishing, 2021.

2 Although Magun is used in the film, and is its subtitle, the reference to the "African Aids," and especially to its symptoms, made clear Kelani's intent to associate the references to magun with AIDS, which was becoming endemic in parts of Africa at the time Kelani made the film.

3 Its American distributor was California Newsreel, which described the film in these terms in their blurb:

> Yinka and Ngozi met in the National Youth Service Corps. The seeds of jealousy are planted when a friend of Yinka suggests that Ngozi is having a secret affair because 'Ibo are untrustworthy.' Adding to Yinka's suspicions, Ngozi has recently inherited some money and so is a financially independent woman. In the second half of the film a distinctly West African emphasis on the supernatural comes to the fore; curses and ritual cleansing take the place of psychological explanations. An old man warns Ngozi that her death is imminent. We later learn that Yinka has placed the curse of magun upon her, a curse reserved for those suspected of infidelity. Magun is described as 'African AIDS'; any man who has sex with a woman infected with it will die . . . On the other hand if the woman does not have sex within nine weeks she will die. Despite her scepticism Ngozi undergoes a long and painful treatment by a herbalist. This introduces a subsidiary theme in the film - the efficacy of traditional African medicine. A scene is interposed where a doctor scandalizes his colleagues by suggesting that the West has been arrogant in rejecting the wisdom of traditional healers. As the time for Ngozi's death approaches, neither her husband nor an old lover can be induced to have sex with her. She finally convinces Dimeji. He is immediately stricken and only saved by the herbalist. Ngozi and Dimeji are reconciled and will apparently become a couple and live happily ever after. . . . Dimeji says he hopes Ngozi will not think all Yoruba men are cads; she replies with the moral of the story: 'there are only two tribes, good and bad people.'" (http://newsreel. org/video/THUNDERBOLT)

4 Chief to military ruler who overthrows Kabiyesi in *Saworoide*: "Of the three sources of power, you have just one. You have the gun being a soldier; but you need money to buy people. And metaphysical power against your enemies" (*Saworoide*).

5 If not precisely "Mammi Watta," she shares enough of the traits of the femme fatale—or the woman married to a deity, and who brings both wealth and risk of disease and death for those daring to establish romantic relations with her.

6 The rationalizations for colonial conquest morphed into the commonplace slogans justifying and disguising the nature of conquest. In French, the common expression was *la mission civilisatrice*, with "mission" implying something of an obligation or appointment to a task, i.e., a beneficent enterprise. In English, "the white man's burden," in German, *kulturarbeit*, and so on. The irony was that as this "mission" of conquest and then occupation and rule occurred, the conditions imposed by the various private enterprises, like Leopold's Belgian Free State, resulted in enormous numbers of deaths and horrendous acts of oppression, even what we'd call reigns of terror. Many examples abound, like that of the French in West Cameroon in their repression of independence movements.

7 https://www.amnesty.org/en/latest/news/2016/01/Child-labour-behind-smart-phone-and-electric-car-batteries/

8 "The bourgeoisie, wherever it has got the upper hand, has put an end to all feudal, patriarchal, idyllic relations. It has pitilessly torn asunder the motley

feudal ties that bound man to his 'natural superiors', and has left remaining no other nexus between man and man than naked self-interest, than callous 'cash payment' . . .

The bourgeoisie cannot exist without constantly revolutionising the instruments of production, and thereby the relations of production, and with them the whole relations of society. Conservation of the old modes of production in unaltered form, was, on the contrary, the first condition of existence for all earlier industrial classes. Constant revolutionising of production, uninterrupted disturbance of all social conditions, everlasting uncertainty and agitation distinguish the bourgeois epoch from all earlier ones. All fixed, fast-frozen relations, with their train of ancient and venerable prejudices and opinions, are swept away, all new-formed ones become antiquated before they can ossify. All that is solid melts into air, all that is holy is profaned, and man is at last compelled to face with sober senses his real conditions of life, and his relations with his kind." Karl Marx, *The Communist Manifesto*. (https://www.marxists.org/archive/marx/works/1848/communist-manifesto/ch01.htm)

9 This is presented in the film as a pratfall.

10 The ghost who haunts and drives mad Andy in *Living in Bondage* is another woman, one closest to him in the film: his wife, whom he sacrificed.

11 Portions of these descriptions of Žižek's work in relation to African cinema appeared in Chapter 12 of my study *African Cinema: From the Political to the Postmodern* (2007).

12 Think Mobuto or Mugabe on their last legs—especially Mugabe, whose fall was precipitated by his failed attempt to install his wife as his heir. Zuma has followed a similar trajectory.

13 California Newsreel gives us this summary: "Mory, a troubled Senegalese poet (played by writer/director Moussa Sene Absa himself) living outside Paris with his French wife and their children. We watch his marriage fall apart under crosscultural pressures, specifically his father's demand that he take a second wife in Senegal. Homeless in winter, separated from his children, his poems scattered over a Paris street, Mory returns to Senegal, penniless and with uncertain prospects." (https://newsreel.org/video/AINSI-MEURENT-LES-ANGES)

14 The babalawo in *Ti Oluwa Ni Ile* states, "I can say there is almost no difference between the way Ifa has designed certain things and the things enlightened people do" (125).

15 Haynes: "A story about sacred land being sold to build a gas station might seem to be bluntly opposing tradition and modernity, and Kelani was motivated by an urgent sense of the need for environmental and cultural preservation" (119). The evil conspirators discount the spiritual forces at play, and are ultimately defeated because of that: "The land is said to belong to both the gods and the ancestors, but 'the gods are nothing but fiction. We are the gods. If you hear any strange sound we are behind it. The spot is perfect for a filling station. Any god that trespasses will choke on the fumes'" (119). Obviously this is a set-up to discount the unvarnished acceptance of western secularism; but in my reading the power implied behind the developers is capital, not ideology.

16 Haynes notes, "Abacha died between *Sarowoide*'s writing and its release, relieving the filmmaker of serious anxiety—making a film in which a clear representation of Abacha collapses to general rejoicing was not a safe thing to do" (198).

17 A typical parody of the feminist "New Woman" in Africa comes in Frank Aig-Umoukhuede's well known poem, "One Wife for One Man." It is quite humorous, although the humor is of a time. Here is a sample whose brief references

to the liberated woman, so feared by the poet's narrator, is easily recognizable in the figure of Funmi. (Suppose your wife is born, the poem states, but is educated, can read, but not make dinner.) The punch line of the poem becomes, this culture "no waya O" (Aig-Umoukhuede: 265).

Frank Aig-Umoukhuede, in Moore, Gerald, and Ulli Beier. *The Penguin Book of Modern African Poetry*. Aig-Umoukhuede went to the university in 1955, and this poem is emblematic of the attitudes of those years up to the 1980s when it finally appeared in the famous Penguin collection.

18 In *Looking Awry* (1991), Žižek describes the disorder in the family generated under these circumstances: "The father is absent, the paternal function (the function of the pacifying law, the Name-of-the-Father) is suspended and that vacuum is filled by the 'irrational' maternal superego, arbitrary, wicked, blocking 'normal' sexual relationship (only possible under the sign of the paternal metaphor)" (1999: 99). For Žižek, the mother in *Psycho* (1960) presents such a figure, attesting to the "unresolved tension in intersubjective relations" (99).

19 This is the now conventional argument that Film Noir's emergence after World War II, when the men were away to war and the women supplanted them in the workplace and at home, led to the representation of male anxiety in the form of the fallen, dark world characteristic of Film Noir. The dangerous woman, now out in the world, leads to men's fall, or threatens to do so. Classically this is seen in *The Maltese Falcoln*, *The Big Sleep*, *Double Indemnity*, and many others, where the femme fatale has become the central figure.

20 In this venture, we can say he has come full circle since his start in film was with Nigerian television: "I was employed as a trainee by the former Western Nigerian Television Authority in Ibadan in 1973, I left for London training school in 1976, came back in 1978 and I have been In the industry since then." (http://asirimagazine.com/en/tunde-kelani-launches-online-tv-channel/. Accessed December 21, 2017)

5

MODERNITY, DOMINIQUE LOREAU, AND *LES NOMS N'HABITENT NULLE PART* (1994)

Kenneth W. Harrow

What if it was . . .

> . . . impossible not to mix genres. What if there were, lodged within the heart of the law itself, a law of impurity or a principle of contamination? And suppose the condition for the possibility of the law were the *a priori* of a counter-law, an axiom of impossibility that would confound its sense, order, and reason?
>
> *(Derrida 1980: 57)*

Derrida's "Law of Genre" begins with this question, one that spills over to our positioning of Kenyatta, and Kelani, as belonging to, and being outside of, a world we could call modern, or traditional.

For Gikandi, Kenyatta spans two worlds, embodying the dyadic state of modernity: "[Kenyatta]was a product of the structural ambiguity inherent in the modernity of the African" (Gikandi 2001:374).

It is in that sense that Kelani, too, is a product of the modernity of the African. But what is modernity?

Within the world of Kelani's oeuvre, modernity has often been set against traditionalism. It is ensconced in objects, following a clear path we can read in James Ferguson's (2006) depiction of the Malawian youth in front of computer screens, waiting to join the IT generation. If modernity is located in its technology, we can trace its path via the Western technological devices that brought wealth, cultural capital, power: containers and cargo ships, fast pirate boats off the coast, 419 scams, carscomputersairplanesdataplatformssmartphonesmemorycontentplacement. And movies,

DOI: 10.4324/9781003397595-8

on VHS tapes, then VCDs, and finally digital platforms. A hip language renewed with each new generation: no longer simply that of youth and its music; no longer centered on style and sap, as in clothes, hair, nails, and exposure, but on global tech.

The point of this section on modernity and African cinema is that we have to look inside and outside, using Derrida's "Law of Genre" (1980), which troubles the location of inside and outside, unsettling boundaries because the contents and frame that enable the boundaries to be established participate in the "genre," the location of the film along with its placement. It is instrumental in helping us define the film while functioning within the very definition by marking it.

To disrupt the transparency of standing outside the inside/outside divide, both establishing and being part of what it defines, Derrida resorts to an ambiguous term that denotes something like a Moebius strip that cannot control the placement of an inside: invagination (sometimes also "fold" or "supplement"). Here the term is evoked in his destabilizing attempts to define and fix genre:

> Before going about putting a certain example to the test, I shall attempt to formulate, in a manner as elliptical, economical, and formal as possible, what I shall call the law of the law of genre. It is precisely a principle of contamination, a law of impurity, a parasitical economy. In the code of set theories, if I may use it at least figuratively, I would speak of a sort of participation without belonging—a taking part in without being part of, without having membership in a set. With the inevitable dividing of the trait that marks membership, the boundary of the set comes to form, by invagination, an internal pocket larger than the whole; and the outcome of this division and of this abounding remains as singular as it is limitless.
>
> *(Derrida 1980: 59)*

Derrida's Law claims that the world that is posited simultaneously bears the mark of that which posits it; that belonging to a given universe, or a given genre, carries the trace of having been posited/designated as a particular world, a particular genre. The mark both designates and belongs. The genre cannot subsist by itself: it must be posited by that which doesn't belong to its world, but which not only perceives it but enables us to perceive it as a given world.

Applying the Law of Genre to other categories, we can imagine standing outside Nollywood and asking what would disrupt the definition of films as Nollywood and neo-Nollywood when viewing the marks inside the perspective we take of the films, one that reveals the frame utilized in determining the marks and the categories. Every question that alludes to a mark opens the invagination, like the supplement that is needed within our definition of the film. The category put in question opens a second issue that begins with where we are standing when considering its frame. Those questions might be addressed to the inside/outside division of allogeneity/ autochthon worked through by Geschiere (2013). Instead of defining that binary and seeking to destabilize it so as to escape the limitations of binarism, I want to multiply the procedure by evoking the key concept of modernity I used to access Kelani's films and repeat the question: modernity and traditionalism, modernity versus tradition, modernity/tradition. These are barred terms. If the McGuffin is present and invisible, is it determinant in framing the narrative? Why not seek the McGuffin's placement as the same effect of the Law of Genre? Before proceeding to expand on that Law, here are the complementary pairings to be applied to our binary divisions of cinemas: world/local, global/local; world and professional/local and amateur; world/African; world-African/world-local; African-modern/ African-calabash.

With this multiplication of the simple duality modern/traditional, we would have to begin with the trace or mark used to distinguish the African from the European. The marks abound in African films. Each theme might be an example of a trace, which needs to be read in reaction to what is left out or omitted. We can begin with homecoming: that of Abdallah in *Heremakono*; with the return of Ibrahima in *Moolaadé* (2004), and that of Mory in *Ainsi Meurent les anges* (2001). With the oiseaux, the Eneki bird that learned not to perch,[1] as in Loreau's title, with names that can't take root, *Les Noms n'habitent nulle part* (1994), and can't avoid taking root when traveling from home to abroad. The final story of the griot Sotigui Kouyate in *Les Noms n'habitent nulle part* entails his magically inventing an autochthonous space in Brussels for an African woman whose home and genealogy had to be discovered for her to be healed.[2]

For Derrida, it is not possible for a film not to belong to a genre. Genres are fluid, and change. The definition of a genre, depending on how it is packaged and how it is received, also changes. Yet for all its fluidity, it comes to us, and we read it as a "certain kind of film." The question of its definition, its place in a category—as a mode, with its place in the pharmaceutical cabinet, like the pharmakon—has to be confronted. Here is Derrida's first claim:

> [A]text cannot belong to no genre, it cannot be without or less a genre. Every text participates in one or several genres, there is no genreless text; there is always a genre and genres, yet such participation never

amounts to belonging. And not because of an abundant overflowing or a free, anarchic, and unclassifiable productivity, *but because of the trait of participation itself, because of the effect of the code and of the generic mark*. Making genre its mark, a text demarcates itself.

[*1980: 65, my stresss*]

Now, let's apply this same contention—"a text cannot belong to no genre"—to the same issue of "world" and of "modern." What modernity does African cinema belong to; what world? In asking those two questions of specific films, of Kelani's in contrast to Loreau's and to Sene Absa's, the question I want to pose is "what world" or "what worlds," which modern, which moderns—those of Ferguson or Mbembe—will help guide our thinking on both issues? More importantly, where are we standing when we pose those questions, what is there in our locations that marks our answers?

Gikandi shifts us away from hybridity or Bhabha's play of difference by affirming the African's agency in strategically deploying the elements of both worlds in embracing modernity. Those worlds, identified by Gikandi in reference to Kenyatta's era, the 1930s to the 1960s, as colonial and African—what are they in reference to Kelani? In the world of cinema, by the 1990s the institutions of the colonial had shifted to the institutions of world cinema and of African Cinema, neither of which had existed as such before the 1960s. What is the trait of participation in the modern, and in the world, by the end of the 20th century, and what trace is left on what it marks? That last decade that saw an enormous growth of Nollywood marked one approach to the modern, whose traits I identified chez Kelani as associated with medical and business models,[3] bearing marks that might be evoked in key objects, like McGuffins that despite their absence bring the characters into relations with each other. We might posit a host of other, similar objects to those identified with value like the land or landownership in *Ti Oluwe Ni Ile* (1993). "Modern" diseases like AIDS, Ebola, "African" diseases like Magun, and sickle cell anemia associated with black bodies became marked by contestation over their prevalence and presumed origins in central Africa. With narratives focused on their traveling by airplanes to the US and Europe, with their signifiers of race and racial displacement, their Afrocentrism and Afropolitanism, the marks of modern racial displacement appeared.

In *Dazzling Mirage* (2014) Kelani shifts the focus from Funmi's business office and presentation of the ad campaign with her initial symptoms to her mastery of the corporate environment. She rises within the ranks of the company, borrows the clothes of the professional businesswoman and the community NGO activist, and lends her skills to leading the fight against the disease. As Bayart said, "life itself became a business enterprise" (Bayart 2007: 163).

The mark of the modern, in Kelani's *Abeni* (2006), as in Loreau's *Les Noms n'habitent nulle part* (1994), Safo's *Amsterdam Diary* (2005), Absa Sene's *Ainsi meurent les anges* (2001), and Sissako's *Heremakono* (2002), bears the traces of place and travel. The car in Loreau's second "African" film *Divine Carcass* (1998) is transformed from European *bagnole*, family car, carrying the memory of absent childhood to Africa where, in due deference to Gikandi's model, it acquires the presence of an African god, even as its metal remains the core of its substance. The traces in *Les Noms n'habitent nulle part* are more complicated, with references to airplanes and mock mini-models of the world serving as mediums for the modern African to enter the international "mondes" according to Brussels, with its mini-world fair displays. In contrast, the travelling shots in Dakar are used to evoke the old world pull of home on Sekou, the homesick student.

The slick, shiny car in Safo's *Amsterdam Diary* performs the task of dazzling the young women, luring them to their coyotes who move them by plane and bus to the borders of a Europe, again more marked in its absence, when they arrive, than in any presence. In *Heremakono* (2002), the train is the vehicle for the transport from one modern world to the other in the story dealing with the young boy Khatra. This functions in counterpoint to the taxi that takes the other protagonist, Abdallah, home to Nouadhibou after his arrival in Mauretania from Europe. In *Ainsi meurent les anges* (2001), the car carries out the similar function of transporting Mory across the modern landscape of Paris, followed by planes and travel back to the ferry taking him home to Gorée. These marks and traces, carrying absence with their mark, also function as punctums, conveying unplanned images that prick our feelings as only in relation to being away from or back home.

The modes of transport in the above films denote worlds that are being constructed and whose modernity is always constrained by those representations. Worlds and their modernity are coterminous in cinema. Both terms belong to schemas of representation that purport to organize the physical and mental spaces to which we belong. And they are modern to us, those addressed in cinema, addressed in the movie theatres or on television screens, in mall cinemas or on computer screens, that are presumably marked by the immediate present, i.e., to those present to the showing. At times the act of screening is thematised: Kelani's inclusion of the television in the background of the hospital room in *Dazzling Mirage* (2014) is one example. But there are many ways that cinema presents its self-reflexivity, from Truffaut's classic *Day for Night* (1973) to the Imperfect Cinema of Cuban Solanas's *The Elephant and the Bicycle* (1994) to Teno's postcolonial *Afrique, je te plumerai* (1992), to Bekolo's *Aristotle's Plot* (1996), and Afolayan's *Phone Swap* (2012). From New Wave to Third Cinema, to neo-Nollywood, awakening the audience's consciousness frames the act of looking at the screen with the "modern" awareness of representation.

With the promise of postcolonial modernity, a train appears on the horizon in *Pather Panchali* (1955), and we see it crossing the screen as the children race to approach it. The city is almost within reach, as it passes by the country villagers. With its imposing gleam, the modern railroad engine brings the dotty Carla in Fellini's *8 ½* (1963) to her lover and to the luxurious spa town, and we see Guido (Mastroianni) awaiting her arrival as the other passengers descend. We hang around in the traffic in Godard's *Weekend* (1967), and in one after another of his films race down the autoroutes to the south, watching the gangsters flee, the lovers passing from stolen car to stolen loot, as in *Pierrot le fou* (1965). We wait and watch with Anna on the ocean liner l'Ancreville in *Touki Bouki* (1973). We watch the ships on the horizon, again, in *Heremakono* (2002), passing in and out of Nouadhibou with Abdullah. The coughs and sputters of these moments, as when the steamship's horn sounds for the departure for Anta, as in the myriad shots that cinema has made of trains and cars, and now planes and rockets, move us into a world and a modernity in which each image that highlights the act of transportation, of transporting us, carries an unspoken punctum that conveys our participation in this world of modernity. Simms-Greene aptly dubs it postcolonial automobility (2017).

The cars are there, already performing the familiar work of constructing a world with roads, passengers, motion in a motion picture frame, and especially action in a cinematic world constructed by the act of filming. Automobility drives the action of the frame being moved before the lens, occludes the work of the camera and its mystifications from which the presence of those in the films seems to emerge by itself, as we are watching them. *Confusion Na Wa* (2013) and *Phone Swap* (2012) play on the missing cell phones that contain messages marking their owners when the messages had been exchanged, and those in possession when the stolen cell phones are reclaimed. Every act of watching these films places us in a world whose construction as modern we accept and share, opening us to its dangers and blessings. Seven years of blessings in *The Figurine* followed by seven years of curses, the blessings and curses to come assuredly with the act of participating in the emoluments of modernity.

When the world and its modern features, its wealth and its modes of transportation, are represented in *Hyènes* (1992), Rama's arrival is staged as a dramatic production when she stops the train in mid-route so that her entourage might descend. When Draman tries to flee, it is at the train station. And when the old, disappearing world of yesterday's Africa in *Hyènes* is represented with its replacement by the new, the way is cleared by huge bulldozers that open the spaces for modernity to be framed and staged. Modern time is embodied in the motions and noises of these machines. As they move the dirt they inscribe the genre.

My interest is not simply in how this technology of motion, of transportation, of communication, of projection, functions like a cinema, like a modernity that conveys the contemporary moment, but in how this automobility is used to generate a sense of participation in modernity by the action on the screen that interpellates the audience. The old school patriarchy in *Moolaadé* (2004) wished to resist that act and motion, that European school of modernity, by burning the women's radios. But their failure to impede the movement and temporality of modernity becomes visible in the transformation of the women, as in the establishing shot of *Faat Kine* (2001) where Sembène portrays the new African Woman of today driving her children to school and discussing the exams for the bac they are about to take.

In *Ainsi Meurent les anges* (2001) and *Les Noms n'habitent nulle part* (1994), Moussa Sene Absa and Dominique Loreau thematize the movement between Africa and Europe by presenting us with protagonists who are transported across continents, learning to fly without belonging anywhere—perching provisionally.

While the famous quote from Achebe on Eneke the bird—"Eneke the *bird* was asked why he was always on the wing and he replied: 'Men have *learned* to shoot without missing their mark and I have *learned* to fly without perching on a twig'" (Achebe [1958] 1972: 183)—focuses us on Eneke, simultaneously we are made aware of that speech act that has been generated so as to place the bird, the tree, the hunter, and their world into a frame. What is posting the frames of *Ainsi meurent les anges* (2001) and of *Les Noms n'habitent nulle part* (1994)? I will begin by suggesting a modernity that both films set in motion as their protagonists travel across the two coevally infinitely distant worlds entangling "modern" Europe and "traditional" Africa, only to contaminate each world with the other. And in that visible contamination, in it and hidden from view as the invisible driver of action, the original McGuffin, is the powerful vision of a crossing, an intermixing, an invagination, that compels each of these distant worlds to be entered by the other. My question of contamination asks whether the act of opening the notions of modernity and tradition assumes and affirms the participation of these two films in "world cinema."

If there is a marker that places the film within a world—a world as genre, as geographical space, and as a body of films constituting world cinema—we would have to enter that film via the opening that carries the marker. All film does this with the establishing mise en scène. The opening of *Touki Bouki* (1973) poses the same question that applies to a significant body of films that thematise the crossing of boundaries: *Ainsi meurent les anges* (2001) and *Les Noms n'habitent nulle part* (1994); but also *Rostov-Luanda* (1998), *Bye Bye Africa* (1999), *Little Senegal* (2000), *Frontières* (2001), *Goodbye Solo* (2008), *Des Etoiles* (2013), *Ije* (2015), and *The Figurine* (2009). In each, there is a figure of Eneke the bird.

What set Eneke the bird on his course? What started his film role of "flying without perching," what launched him into the mad course of modernity? The guns men used to shoot had not been there before traders and slave merchants brought them. Eneke had to survive in a new era, in a new way, continually ill at ease. *Touki Bouki* (1973) begins with the sound of the flute, the country image of the boy on a cow, riding before the herd as it heads toward the camera, toward some destination that exists behind the space of the camera's gaze. We arrive there by a cross-cutting that takes us into the scene at the abattoir. Vlad Dima tracks this movement from what he calls the outside—the initial scene of boy and cow with herd, and the subsequent scene in the abattoir that conveys the horror of the arrival in the city. The passage across time and space culminates when the now-grown boy Mory rides his motorcycle alongside the road, the cycle's handlebars mounted by a bull's horns. Here is Dima's take on the opening:

> The film begins with two shots of a herd of cows led by a young boy on an ox. These shots precede a series of images of cows being slayed in a slaughterhouse . . . From the beginning there is a movement from outside to inside, and this back and forth becomes a trademark during the development of the movie. The outside-inside movement is cinematically doubled, and therefore reinforced, because the little boy and the herd are shown in long shots, while for the gory images in the slaughterhouse the camera moves in much closer, into medium shots and even close-ups.
>
> *(Dima 2012: 44)*

Gradually Dima leads the analytical gaze to the inside, crossing the spaces between the former rural ranges for the cattle and the present abattoir in the city, including aural spaces that track the closure of distances, placing the mark of the observer within the observed spaces.

In the first shot, the boy on the ox is framed in a very long shot. On the aural level, Mambety introduces cows' moos that are barely distinguishable. And most prominently, a flute playing. The music is very peaceful and understated, and the choice of the flute leads us to expect a bucolic story . . . In the next shot, the boy is still far away. It is as if he could not quite approach the camera; there is a sense of distancing play in this opening sequence. The boy finally moves ahead of the herd a little, but importantly it is the sound that becomes louder; it is the sound that comes 'closer' to the camera and thus to our 'point of view' (hearing). The oxen and cows are heard more distinctly in the second shot, and as the boy disappears to the right of the frame the moos increase dramatically. At this juncture, Mambety cuts away to an ox being pulled by the horns into a slaughterhouse. Aurally, the moos have now intensified, and they are intercut with the yelling of the men working at the slaughterhouse. The action moves from the outside in the third shot to the inside.

(Dima 2017: 45)

Dima's interest lies in the way sound works in Mambéty's work, and as a result he is able to capture better the notions of closeness and distance without being limited simply to the visual, much less its linear ordering of events. Modernity will work on several levels that mark absences: a "pastoral" flute conveying, along with the landscape, the countryside; the not-yet-urban land which doesn't become a city-scape except through the changes leading to the death of the village, the theme presented exactly at the end of *Hyènes*. Sonically what Dima dubs the sonic rack focus would parallel the way the city comes into focus as the rural backdrop fades.

As the animals are being slaughtered, the sound works mostly with the image, instead of against it. However, the horrible cries of animals dying are slowly muffled, to the point that they become inaudible; one gets the sense of having been thrust into a very chaotic world that is paralleled by a very chaotic noise mixture. As sound comes in and out of focus, a certain "sonic rack focus effect" is created.

(2017: 46)

Mambéty's sentimental evocation of the world of a certain Africa passing away in the face of modernity is captured in the transformation of the cows, normally associated with Fulani herdsmen.[4] The opening shot of the barefoot boy riding the ox, leads to that of a slaughtered bull being converted into beef; and finally into a *jolie bete*, that is, Mory's motorcycle ridden by an outsider, the crazy white boy.

The inside/outside dichotomy continues in this first sequence through one shot of several oxen waiting outside for their fate. The animals are

filmed from inside the slaughterhouse. The visual narrative explores the
outside first, and then, in the next shot it moves completely outside,
back to the young boy. This time he is riding alone and no cows follow
him. . . . On the soundtrack the music of the flute returns triumphantly.
Visually, the film switches perspective from the little boy to Mory's back
shoulder on the motorbike. Mory has attached the horns of an ox to the
bike, and in the first shot over his shoulder only one of the two horns is
visible. The transition from the boy to Mory occurs aurally through a
sound-bridge created by the flute music.

(Dima 2017: 47)

The beginning sequences are all contained within the frame of the opening credits, so that by the time we have gotten to Mory on the motorcycle, we have left not only the "outside" of the pastoral landscape, but
also of the diegesis. The boy and cattle are in the past—the past of the
action, of the story, and the world of the countryside. They are in the
past of the modern film we now gradually enter. We stop talking to our
neighbor seated next to us. We start looking more closely at the character
on the screen. Our semi-averted gaze in the abattoir can return, slowly,
to full focus as we end our half-gazing at the boy, and see the motorcy-
clist from the side and behind, as if riding behind him. Now an adult,
Mory rides like all motorcyclists, weaving on the dirt side of the road,
until he mounts up onto the paved highway that will take us into Dakar,
and zooms off.

Gikandi has often used the notion of Africa's entry into modernity as
being the incomplete project of colonialism (1996: 9). *Touki Bouki* begins
with marginalized figures, from the boy alone on the bull to Mory riding on the dirt alongside the paved street. He has placed the cattle horns
outlandishly onto the handlebars, and his loud motorcycle is chased by
children running in the dirt after him. Dima concludes his description of
this scene that leaves the quartier in the dust by qualifying the space as
modern—a modernity now written in terms made comprehensible by the
"African" modelling:

Murphy contends that 'time and location are fragmented' (2000, 243)
during the transition from the rural to the shots taken from the motorcycle; in other words, atemporal intellectual montage. In his study
with Williams, Murphy returns to this fragmentation and lack of logical narrative to propose that Mambety may be targeting Sembène's
linearity (2007, 26). The fragmentation and the choice of shots push
the audience into 'a tale of modern Africa, complete with motorbikes,
motorways, and machinery' (Murphy 2004, 243). This may be a

modern Africa, but it is one deeply rooted in tradition, and the sound transition emphasizes the connection that still exists between times and locations.

(2017:47)[5]

The connection is central to Loreau's "noms" as she begins with migrating flocks that gradually form a link from the dusty streets of the quartier in Dakar to the paved, cold, wet, and dark pavements of Brussels.

I. Dominique Loreau

Dominique Loreau comes at Africa from another location altogether. Her husband is a psychiatric doctor who worked in Senegal for years, travelling between Belgium and Dakar. The couple eventually bought a home on the Petite Côte, and Loreau made several films set in Africa. Her entry into modern cinema might be described as effortless and aleatoric. She describes hitchhiking in the south of France with a friend when they had finished high school, about to take entrance exams for the university—she for painting, her friend journalism. As they were on a quiet secondary road, no one picked them up. They sat down and started a game of cards. Eventually a young man stopped his car.

> Une voiture s'est arrêtée, un jeune homme en est descendu, a attendu que nous finissions notre partie, puis nous nous sommes mis en route. Il nous a dit qu'il étudiait le cinéma, et pendant les deux jours que nous avons passé à nous balader avec lui, le cinéma a pris le visage humain de cet homme gai et intelligent. Puis nos chemins se sont séparés. C'est alors que nous avons décidé sans réfléchir, par jeu et par défi complice, peut-être pour déjouer un destin tout tracé, peut-être pour que ces vacances s'éternisent, peut-être pour des raisons plus profondes, de passer les examens d'entrée à l'INSAS. Et nous avons réussi. Mais ce n'est que bien plus tard que j'ai réellement éprouvé la nécessité de faire des films, nécessité qui, à chaque film, est remise en question et prend d'autres chemins.
>
> (A car stopped, a young man got out, waiting for us to finish our game, and then we set off. He told us he was studying film, and during the two days we were off wandering with him, film took on a human face, that of this gay and intelligent man. Then our ways parted. It was then we decided, without thinking too hard about it, playfully and with a certain sense of defiance, perhaps to undo a destiny already set in motion, perhaps thinking that these vacations would go on forever, perhaps for deeper reasons, to take the entrance exams for INSAS [film

school]. And we succeeded. However it wasn't until much later that I really felt the need to make films, a need which was put in question with each film, and which led to new directions).

("Dominique Loreau, cinergie.be)

How different might we envision the path of the African students of Loreau's generation (she was born in 1955, so we are talking about the generation of 1970s) seeking entrance into World Cinema, or African Cinema, or simply filmmaking as a vocation, with the job to fall where it may. Mahamat-Saleh Haroun was born in Abéché, Chad, six years after Loreau in 1961, and his parents' occupations led him to Paris where, on completing lycée, he entered the Conservatoire Libre du Cinéma Français. He worked for regional newspapers in France before he was able to make his first short film at the age of thirty. By 1999 he made a feature length film, *Bye Bye Africa* (1999), which launched his world career. His biopic *Sotigui Kouyaté, A Modern Griot* was made in 1995.

In contrast, Loreau's haphazard choice of INSAS, the prestigious Belgian film school, did not lead directly to an easy path into film. She passed three years studying the history of philosophy at l'Université Libre de Brussels. Starting in 1980, at the age of 25, she made three short films : « Départ » (made with Philippe Simon), « Le Saut dans la Vie » and « Zigzags, » all the while making several trips to Africa and earning her living as film editor. Her first feature length film came in 1992 after studies at the Cinémathèque Française with Rouch. (Similarly, Claire Denis learned her craft at IDHEC beginning in 1969 at the age of 23, and from there went to work as assistant with Rivette.)

A third member of their generation—also to become a "world" cinema filmmaker—was Abderrahmane Sissako. He began his studies at the Gerasimov Institute of Cinematography in Moscow from 1983 at the age of 22, following the footsteps of a generation of aspiring African cineastes like Sembène and Souleymane Cissé.[6] He passed six years in Russia, before completing his studies, and coming out with a short film in 1991. In 1998 *Rostov-Luanda* and *La vie sur terre* were completed, and with those films and the ones that followed, he too achieved a certain renown. His origins prior to film school were entirely in Africa: mother Mauretanian, father Malian, growth and schooling in Mali, brief sojourn with mother in Mauretania, and then off to the Gerasimov Institute of Cinematography in Moscow.

Recalling the difficulties of many African filmmakers to obtain access to film schools in the metropole, with the Soviet Union offering an anti-colonialist alternative to France, we can see how the "world" presented these three filmmakers with radically different paths, marked by considerably different obstacles—not least of which would have been the necessity to learn Russian for Sissako, along with living in an alien environment with few ties to African people or lands.[7] All three began to make important films by the early 1990s, just at the moment when celluloid filmmaking became prohibitively costly, when theatrical exhibition became increasingly difficult, when "postcolonial" had begun to turn from its activist origins to more personal film-essays, à la Sissako and Loreau, with self-reflexive or New Wave style narratives, as in Haroun's *Bye Bye Africa* (1999) or Sissako's *La vie sur terre* (1998). Loreau, unlike Claire Denis, never projected herself into her "African" films or conveyed a postmodern meta-cinematic aspect or sensibility. But as the titles of her two African feature length films—*Divine Carcasse* (1998) and *Les Noms n'habitent nulle part* (1994)—convey, a subtle philosophical remainder marked the narratives, bearing the trace that would welcome an identification as "world" for the growing festival circuit where her films succeeded in garnering significant awards.[8]

It might be of interest to explore how her films lead us into their respective worlds. At this point we will explore *Les Noms n'habitent nulle part* (1994) which leads us, like Mambety's *Touki Bouki* (1973), into town, into the quartier of Dakar, to the encounter with the griot and his story that begins with the baptism of a new child.

I.A.

Les Noms n'habitent nulle part (1994) opens with shots of birds flying high in the sky, while their shrill cries are heard. Then a piano motif, a simple melody, accompanies their flight. The title appears, followed by a solitary bird seen in relative close-up. The music carries us immediately into a tracking shot that takes us, like Mory in his opening entry into Dakar, down a dirt road. A handheld camera and a traveling shot bring us into the quartier. We do not see who is moving behind the camera, behind this entry: children wave, the music comes up louder, dominating the shot since we have no face, no body to situate the point of view. The piano continues and is joined by an accordion. And then the name Loreau appears on the screen.

Is she looking, or is someone in her place? The solitary bird, joined to the title and the narrative, would appear to signify the émigré, someone abroad whose place is provisional as long as he is away from his umbilical cord, which the griot soon explains is what anchors him ineluctably to his homeland. He is the autochthon, despite being abroad: separated from the flock, from his flock, but about to be introduced at the baptism where he received his name, his ties, and his real being.

To be autochthon is a temporary stage. If no one can claim originary purity and absoluteness as a basis for identity, everyone can claim a point of tentative origin, a provisional home. Autochthonous is relative to allogenous, to use Fabian's terminology, and for Glissant that difference is inscribed in all Caribbeanness—a state, in fact, that characterizes all people. It is marked differently, with Africa's relationship to European fundamental to its history and troubles; but also to its possibilities and creativities. The key notion for Glissant is "Relation," that turns on this double tie to the Other, where for his use of Caribbeanness I would transpose as an uneven but still relatively pertinent concept for Africanness, also grounded in colonized peoples and their liberations. "Caribbeanness *is* the Other and mixture, not as defiance but as a (potentially) fecund condition that embeds painful memory in the pleasures of expressive life and that transforms through open contact and the refusal of a single root" (Drabinski 2019: 159). There are a multitude of terms used by Glissant to define this condition of the Caribbean, or of the Africans here, and especially those who are moving, travelling, emigrating, leaving home, and assuming allogenous locations. For Glissant, famously, Deleuze's rhizome is seen as marking such subject positions, but he also uses such terms as nomad, and in contrast to single-rootedness or primal origins, chaos and difference. His central concept is "Relation," rather than that which would signal the single being. Relation as tied to a past, a history, and a condition of oppression; but also, contrariwise, to an openness performed in the possibilities of the present, even in the heart of the plantation and its brutalities. In the Caribbean this emerges in figures like repeated islands and archipelagos. In Africa it turns in myriad figures, where we might turn to the "souffles" of Birago Diop, who suggests that such figures as the wind and the water bear the traces of those who had been there before—rather than turn to fixed and archived texts, or Negritude's certainties over identity. The original image of the bird in flight could as easily be captured in Birago's well-rehearsed figures in the classic stanza ordering us to listen more closely to things than beings: to the wind and the breath of ancestors ("Les Souffles" in *Anthologie de la nouvelle poésie nègre et malgache* 1948).

What these familiar verses return us to is the way difference is embodied in the form of what is not fixed, not a fixity, not an ontic substrate, and not an ontological presence. "*Antillanité* recasts Caribbean cultural production as the ecstasy of Relation—the mixture of contraries, opposites, and points of complement and tension without dialectical resolution" (Drabinsky: 161). The tension is bound up in motion, expressed not only as exile or loss, but as anticipating possibilities that only loss can enable by its traces of absence. This trope of the Caribbean rhizome depends on the relation to the Other, expressed in Glissant's thought as a circular no-madism. It conveys uncannily Loreau's tropes of departure and exile that become meaningful when posited in terms of Glissant's notion of Relation, as in the "search for the Other:

> [U]prooting can work toward identity, and exile can be seen as ben-eficial, when these are experienced as a search for the Other (through circular nomadism) rather than as an expansion of territory (an arrow-like nomadism). Totality's imaginary allows the detours that lead away from anything totalitarian.
>
> *(Drabinsky: 163)*

There are two movements in *Les Noms n'habitent nulle part* that are ad-umbrated by the birds' flight. The first is centripetal, with the entry into the community and the family. The community is Senegalese, and the cir-cle of women who dance in the opening scene are celebrating the entry of the new child into the family. This is the autochthonous site offered at the outset as the depiction of home. The bird that wings off on its solo flight takes us outward, to the world abroad. If world cinema means, as Dudley Andrew (2004) awkwardly claimed, an exposure of "our" stu-dents to the world out there which is unfamiliar to them,[9] then this depic-tion of the African quartier—without any signposts to guide us, i.e., titles announcing the location, the language, etc.—represents otherness to the camera, and shows how those "foreigners" generate their own circles of relations, down to the umbilical cord superstitions. The outsider, unseen by the viewer but signalled by the handheld camera motion, holds a cer-tain fascination with what transpires, and in recording that response we can say that the fascination is mixed with a measure of pleasure, if not more. That it is fascination might be read in one small thread of shots in what transpires. The women dance, as is always the case in "Africa," or in the "real" Dakar, for baptêmes with sabir drumming. The dance, now illegal, was commonly known as the "ventilateur," performed by women bent over and rotating their bottoms vigorously. That scene has become a trite one in many representations of Africa, but given that the film was made in 1994, when it was common enough and not really forbidden for public display, one might forgive the camera's fascination with the shapes. Similarly, the scene that immediately precedes our entry into the courtyard where the dancing is taking place is played out with a second obligatory gesture toward home and to the "authentic" African mouthpiece. This is with our introduction to the griot, Sotigui Kouyate. Here he defines his role, hears the drums, and tells us to pay attention. He provides the ticket to the "real Africa."[10]

The subtlety of the title of the film—(the) names have no home—the gentleness of signifying the movement of emigration across the invisible borders of the sky for those who can fly is reduced when we come to earth and must travel to "l'Afrique, mon Afrique," the Africa of ancestors whose voices comes to us in the form of griots. When Sotigui appears in the film he announces his role in life and in the conceptual spaces of "Africa" by identifying himself as the griot.[11] "I am a griot," he says, and no one can be griot without being born griot. "Je suis le maître de la parole, le mémoire, le conservateur, le grenier," and most significantly, in a word, "la bibliothèque de l'Afrique."

It would be tendentious to unpack the conventionality in the usage of these signifiers, except to argue that the camera and its eye are positioned to access, witness, and go beyond the notion of a certain Africa adulated by the outsider. Lindiwe Dovey (2015) has convincingly affirmed the positivity of the curator's love for African film—so that the act of presenting entails a certain closeness and desire. This can be read as nonetheless remaining at a distance from the actual closeness of a family member, which normally would go unsaid, needing no justifications. As Eileen Julien has famously said about the earlier generation of African authors, the works are "extroverted" (2003), or simply not autochthonous. At its limit it is a world cinema's "Africa," but, in the most critical way: not that of an outsider's worldview, but with the lover's embrace of the other's world. And that embrace requires a portraiture infinitely more subtle than the outsider-outsider's worldview, which is found in the world selections of national geography issues. Loreau is, in fact, the outsider-insider as Trinh T. Minh-ha put it, trying on roles for her own work in representations of otherness in *Reassemblage* (1983). The closest she would permit herself was to be "speaking nearby."

The griot tells us about "roots." At the baptism the child's umbilical cord, its double, is buried in the home courtyard, the child receives its name and is inscribed forever into its lineage. For Glissant such is the definition of the "originary," not the monde in "Relation." Glissant would not stop at the griot's moment of baptism or naming, but would unsettle its claims for origins. "Roots are lost, new roots are set, and the task for the theorist is how to appreciate the multiplicity of roots and the entanglements of relationality against compulsions to unify in the one and the single" (169). He goes on to distinguish his Caribbean poetics from the standard postcolonial approaches that resolve differences, often by resorting to identity claims. Drabinski situates this within the frame of creolité.

So much of postolonial theory from the mid-century black Atlantic fled from this puzzle of fragmentation and multiplicity, turning instead to models of unified culture and nation, whether the racial origin (Negritude in Césaire and Senghor) or the radically new born out of revolutionary struggle and its severing of ties to the past (Fanon). Glissant's poetics signals a new beginning in the new World but a sense of the new that is not new at all. There is instead counter-modernity and the life of the Plantation. Creolised cultural forms and composite senses of identity. All of that is set in motion. No notion of dialectics, search for origins, or breaks with the past can account for what has already been made.

(Drabinski 169)

The griot's attachment to roots, like being, like opacity, cannot be denied; but it isn't enough. Initially, that's all this act of naming contains and all he needs to tell us. We follow the figures of the women into the courtyard and the ceremony unfolds. When it is completed, we return to a view of the sky, and the question of the griot hovers over the shots of the birds on the wing: "How do we tell the story and genealogy of those who have left?" Genealogies are attempts to fill in absences. Relation is made possible by them. Thus the griot tells us that usually letters, money, or gifts come from those who have left. And as he often travels abroad, he frequently meets someone from home. The frame is not set for this story: what are we to make of those about whom we hear nothing, those who are lost, but whose traces remain?

The birds now shift in their signification. They change, are changed, perhaps to save themselves, Achebe's proverb again applies: "*Eneke the bird* says that since men have learned to shoot without missing, he has learned to fly without perching." Like the figures of the griot, of tradition, of the ventilateur, the sayings about elders being libraries of African knowledge, and so on, the solidity of home and autochthony begin to dissolve with distance and time, with the stories themselves that might be repeated as tales, but that inevitably change with each telling. Loreau has set up an expectation of The African Story, in whatever location it will be found, but the encounter with its retelling—here the griot's chance sighting of Nar Sène—takes flight and leads by itself, like the trembling of the handheld camera, to an unexpected set of ramifications.

There are two African stories that meet in Brussels, where the griot now appears. We pass to Europe directly after the baptism ceremony, first via the image of birds who are succeeded by an image of an airplane. The voiceover of Sotigui, the real griot character (or *comédien* [actor], as he also calls himself), narrates his concern over those lost to the genealogy (which it is his job to keep track of) when they go abroad. If the names have no home, the homelessness of those who have a name becomes the condition for names to wander, to become separated from their home and lost. The griot is their rescuer. He remembers their stories (French *histoires*), their ties, and thus their real names. He saves two for us. He becomes Loreau's mouthpiece for the lost bits of wood, the *bouts de bois de Dieu*[12] who have become *épaves*.

Nar Sène plays the conventional *épave*—that is, lost bit of driftwood, seaweed, *objet abandoné flottant au gré des flots*—abandoned object floating at the whim of the waves. He is the nomad (functioning closest to Glissant's circular nomadism). He arrives in Brussels walking rapidly and deliberately, like someone who knows his way around. The griot tries to keep up, but cannot. Nar winds up in a girlfriend Mouche's apartment, and their banter leads to her expressing discontent that he isn't committing himself to their relationship sufficiently, and she threatens to break it off. He fends off her complaints like an old *roué*, and as she resigns herself and snuggles close to him, he recounts the story of his father, the chief with many wives, who knows what love potions to distribute when needed. She recoils, as he laughs.

Framing this episode is the griot's visit to Nafi, Nar's daughter in Dakar, who explains that he has been gone for ten years, that the family expected more from him, and are disappointed that his escapades abroad are at their expense. He has become a success in his own romantic terms and with a career as an actor—but not as a "comédien" like Sotigui whose role as griot represents traditional values in their positive aspect. Nar Sène is amiable, attractive to women, easygoing. Not serious, like Sekou Baldé, or like his polygamous patriarchal father. Nafi says he travels a lot and has no fixed address. In the scene with Mouche, we understand he has a girl in every port. He sleeps around, with a woman here, squatting with friends in an abandoned place there. We hear Mouche out, and through Sotigui's narrative and imagination we gain entrance into his life and affairs, and most of all, his character. Through Nafi's eyes he appears inconsequential and lost to the family. And in his scenes with Mouche we find it hard to understand his appeal, given his mocking playfulness, his apparent refusal to become part of her life or to meet her serious needs.

Sekou plays the foil of Nar. He has a girlfriend who importunes him to stay with her in their first exchange. She is unhappy about his intention to complete his medical studies and return to Africa in three days without her having known about it. She and Sekou appear younger than Nar and his Mouche, and yet they seem more serious. She entreats him to come out for a drink, and when he insists that he has to leave, he still gets her to agree to attend a Peul dance with him the next day. Unlike Nar, he seems to have weighty decisions to make and can't determine whether to stay in Belgium with her pursuing a medical career or to return home. At this point we have no idea that he is actually married and has a family in Senegal. When he sees his sponsors who entreat him to stay beyond the six months of his *stage* or brief training for medicine, when he is told that he needs to acquire a serious professional status before returning to his broken down dispensary, we can't imagine him refusing what seems such an obvious choice.

Sekou's story is also framed by one back home. His brother appears annoyed at the prospect that he might stay without first returning home and obtaining permission. We appreciate Sekou's relationship with the young woman; that he is drawn not only to life with her, but to the prospect of accomplishing more important medical work by staying on in Brussels, and acquiring money and training that he could later apply in Dakar. His brother tells us he is Peul (in English Fulani), one from the less developed north, with a serious religious commitment that had to be channelled into development. Both Nar and Sekou have family back home ready to perform whatever rituals, call on whomever they need, to recall back home their relatives. The magic of the family, that which is the strongest and most dangerous (Geschiere 2013) will destroy them if they try to ignore the *appel*, the song of family. The distance from Africa exacerbates tensions over power and control. Nar's account of the love potions irritates Mouche, who laughs but expresses her annoyance, no doubt due to her not being in a position to control the relation. The same is true of Sekou's brother whose irritation is expressed in threats to use magic in proportion to his helplessness to actually bring Sekou home.

The space covered between these locations, home in Africa versus abroad in Europe, appears aleatoric, that is, an open expanse of air that birds have no difficulty in traversing. In Belgium the landmarks shrink in proportion to the seriousness of the question put to both emigres about commitment—commitment to home, family, girlfriends, careers, social obligations, life, to themselves, and especially to the question put to them by the griot, that is, who are you and where do you belong. The dark night scene on the cold streets of Brussels stages the reflections of the griot about those who left for a few months, and didn't return until a few, or even several years later. There is no joy or liberation implied in this question, but something like work involved in getting accustomed to a cold and alien climate where small communities or a few friends provide a shelter. The openness and warmth of home in Dakar is lined with resentment of those who abandoned them. The sexual appeal of the women abroad remains couched in terms of loneliness as they are not offered to the men as part of a new, embracing family. Even when the couples are formed, and children arrive, the isolation remains, as in *Ainsi meurent les anges* (2001) where Mory is married and has children, but with not enough of a real family in a Senegalese sense. His in-laws are alienating, and when he returns home to Gorée, the family comes at him with a vengeance, and he fails to find a complete life there as well.

We have well traced paths for these two stories to follow. Nar should somehow get his comeuppance and learn to treat Mouche with respect, commit to her, and raise the metis-children he joked about, following the path of his father to have as many children as he can. Perhaps he will keep his women in Brussels and Paris, return to Nafi and his family in Dakar. The genre's conventions would have him confront some shock, overcome some contrived obstacle, and learn his ways. The world cinema formulae might impose that obstacle from left field, unexpectedly, in a crossing with Sekou where each acquires what is needed to turn from the other, and Sekou would become the model that had eluded Nar for his years of living in exile. The birds would turn again, but there would have to be an end to exile, and a home-coming, as we have at the end of *Guelwaar* (1992) where the acculturated son would find his father, his fatherland, his mother tongue, and assume his responsibilities. That would be a Third Worldist ending, a *Moolaadé* (2004) ending leaving us feeling that right has been done, even at the cost of risking one's skin. Not an ending that conforms with Glissant's Relation, however.

The scale of such a hypothetical world cinema today, with its virtual universe of globalized digital film, requires a different measure from that deployed by Loreau. At every point she is painting a scene that gestures more to the noir night urban scapes that films of a neo-Nollywood variety might favor: films like Daniel Oriahi's urban *Taxi Driver: Oko Ashewo* (2015); Kenneth Gyang's darker *Confusion Na Wa* (2013) or truly dark *Oloture* (2019); or Andy Amadi Okoroafor's gritty *Relentless* (2010). The repeated scenes of Sekou walking the dark, cold, wet streets of Brussels echo the freezing streets of NYC in *Des Etoiles* (2013), the dark mise-en-scene in *Ije: The Journey* (2010), or *Relentless*'s noir scenes of Lagos, and reframe Loreau's lighter crossing narratives of Africans and their love lives abroad. The griot's pursuit of the main characters' genealogies to save them from more permanent loss is haunted by these scenes of darkness whose ominous traces linger. In *Des Etoiles*, Mame Amy's return to Senegal is compelled by her husband's death. At the end of *Les Noms*, a similarly bleak scenario of death is averted by the griot's imagination. There are two compelling scenes that lead us to this ending where he meets a disoriented woman and sees the need to recognize what she herself has lost.

In the first the griot gives an account of a certain Mamadou Ba's brother, lost to the family. Samba Ba, Mamadou's brother, is adrift in Europe. Samba has disappeared, after spending his university years abroad. His mother pronounces proverbs affirming that he can't hide from his own, and ultimately Mamadou sets out to track him down. The griot's account pauses as we see the women back in Senegal holding the newly baptized baby, while the drums are drumming and the women dance. There are women dressed elaborately for the event; the music carries us into their circle. The griot pauses for effect, highlighting the proverb about not being able to hide from one's own so as to allow it to sink in. Loreau has brought us into close contiguity with the sounds, odors, rhythms, look, and feel of the women and children whom the voyagers have abandoned. She leaves far behind the cold dark streets of the North where the griot is speaking. The griot's story provides the occasion for Loreau to evoke images of Senegal for those who are far away, lost, or dying. That can echo, for example, the account of the anguished Sekou whose world is escaping him. It might also be seen as a judgment on Nar, who has almost left for good, according to the griot. Except that the griot can't catch up with Nar, as the camera does when he reaches Mouche's apartment. We have to ask whether something escapes the griot. Sekou's story seems to turn into one of unadulterated loss. But Nar's loss is uncertain, and perhaps more gain than loss, despite Nafi's anger, and despite the griot's predilection to provide judgment on these cases.

The griot continues with Samba's account: he was seen by a seller of bags in Berlin, had married a white woman, began a small business, and carried on without concern for his people back home. The mother is told to go to a fetishist, who tells her to gather a leaf from her courtyard, and have it given to the lost Samba. Mamadou, his brother tracking him down, brings a leaf from the tree in their courtyard. When Samba sees the leaf, he reacts with fear and says, isn't that from our courtyard? On hearing the affirmative answer he says mothers always want to keep their sons by their sides. He runs off and then slips on a leaf, hurting himself. Finding no cure in Europe, he returns home to be cured. He makes a sacrifice at the location where his umbilical cord was buried. The griot concludes their mother had buried a magical substance in the cemetery, there where it is well known: *les morts ne s'en vont pas* (the dead do not go). The wandering brother never left again.

The griot smiles, sings that one's troubles never cease if one is alive, and walks off into the night. Shots of Brussels at night, tall buildings without grace, traffic without any edge of modernity. Europe in its soulless complexion, the frame for emptiness. The griot's story of the brothers, its lesson that home had won that time, undercut by the son's bitter recognition of the family's inescapable power over him Not the colors, rhythms, dancing, and beauties of the women, charm of the children imitating their dances, but the dead who, as Birago Diop famously had it, are not dead. Here Loreau's griot Sotigui, changes it to the dead who do not leave. As such, the story suggests a haunting of those who shrug off their responsibilities when seeking a new life with new families abroad. The magic and ghosts are set against Brussels at night without need for commentary because once we begin to let go of the initial simple dualism that sets Sekou against Nar, or the temptation of modernity against the pull of tradition and home, we can begin to sense that the haunting will unsettle the frame, disturb the proportions of the familiar narrative about the foolish one who leaves home, only to learn his lesson at the end.[13] The constant interplay of shots from Senegal with this account of the griot, at night, on the wet streets of Brussels, reinforces Derrida's sense of the genre where the sign of its identity marks the account like an outside impurity: "a participation without belonging—a taking part in without being part of, without having membership in a set." (1959: 80). The allochron informs the circle, "without belonging," yet creates by invagination an internal pocket within the newly bounded circle: "an internal pocket larger than the whole; and the outcome of this division and of this abounding remains as singular as it is limitless" (Derrida 1980: 59). The Peul dances and gatherings, like the griot's account of Samba's recall, and the other endless stories of the African abroad, form the pocket within Brussels or mini-Europe or Paris, Berlin, each reiterating the same trajectory of the previous one. When will you come home?

The return of those fatally departed, for Mati Diop in *Atlantiques* (2019), is as zombies.

Sekou gives his account of his life while on a train as he returns to his lodgings in Brussels. The scene shifts back to another train he had taken, prior to deciding to accept the scholarship and go to Europe. He travelled up north in Senegal to consult with the family, the marabouts, and the spirits of his dead parents at the cemetery. At the end of his telling, we understand the pull from the magic of home as he gave markers to his children when he left, with bits of his clothes for their arms, while he himself followed the instructions of the marabouts to give cola nuts to the workers at the airport. Like Abdallah's mother in *Heremakono* (2002), when she gathered up the sand that her son had stepped on as he left her home in Nouadhibou for Europe, Sekou distributed the markers needed to protect himself, not simply for the voyage, but so that the ties to home would not be dissolved. He is pulling against these markers when we first encounter him, as he seems to be viewing with some favor the appeals made to him by his Belgian sponsors and female companion. Now on the train it isn't the dance that he remembers, but the seriousness of his departure, his own account that is evoked and re-evoked on the train he is taking back to Brussels, and the memory of the train he had taken at home when deciding to depart.

The traces become visible markers of his absence: we see the train, hear his voice remembering, reflecting, recalling home, and the ties he himself placed, like the mother burying the umbilical cord in the ground, under the tree, or those of the parents in the cemetery. These are the traces transmogrified in Belgium's commerce with Africa, its famous Royal Museum for the Congo at Tervuren when Leopold's masks and statues were displayed. None of this is made explicitly visible in the film. The griot's stories are the counterweight to that heavy historical record that would have sunk the lighter accounts of Nar and Sekou. It is striking how the scenery that passes before Sekou's gaze on the Belgian commuter train is that of the most ordinary, unspectacular view of Europe imaginable, just as the train in Senegal is old and decrepit, in contrast to a TGV for instance. The Europe that frames the setting for his reflections, this moment of decision, holds no obvious advantage over the Senegalese scene, especially if this is to be the city in which he will eventually be living. Just as in the earlier story about the brother Samba Ba who wound up in Berlin and Czechoslovakia, it is a small shop, not a glorious footballer's career, that awaits him as the *nègre à* Paris or New York, or elsewhere. The direction of the narrative is now set for the critical events to unfold, and Loreau crafts an extraordinary conceit just at this moment to shift the direction beyond that created by the appeals from home.

Sekou bumps into Nar at a phone booth, and Nar offers to take Sekou to "France, to Europe," without visas. They establish their relationship—both having been at Diourbel for family and upbringing, and for origins, both now speaking in Wolof, the home language, if not the native tongue of Sekou. Both now easily fall into that relationship of brothers abroad, if strangers at home. Nar, the experienced traveller, guides Sekou, the newcomer to this world, as if through the stretches of life he had known in his earlier days. They set out to visit what turns out to be a mini-world's fair exposition, what appears initially to be almost a joke located in the heart of the city.

The first facsimile in the mini-Europe they encounter on their "trip" is that of the Arc de Triomphe. Here is the image of what colonization had to seduce us, Nar intones, as if to mock that great force that had induced them to come to Belgium. Sekou asks what the Arc represents, and Nar responds, I have no idea, it is just there like that. Like the Eiffel Tower, he says: *très beau*, but no more than that. They deposit flowers for the unknown soldier. The world of this world's fair, with Loreau's gently magical evocation of Europe, lies slyly adjacent to the modernity of Brussels' center, like the World Fairs of the past where the exoticized worlds of the colonies were exhibited. It appears as a parody of the great European power. At night, in the darkness, cold, and wet, trams and trains run past the ordinary buildings of the metropole that purports to form its Africans into adequately modern citizens to perform their proper duties in their home countries. Sekou will return as a correctly trained medical specialist. But Sekou and his story, ensconced in the magic of a ritual, marked by the buried umbilical cord, are old-fashioned, and he tells his Belgian girlfriend that European women are too emancipated, that he doesn't like that, doesn't like to be told he must stay for more training.

Modernity has shrunk to the point where its magic is reduced to the comic image of a Santa figure. Sekou and Nar encounter such a man that night, as his shift as Santa Claus is almost over. They buy their chips, and munch on them sitting on a bench. Their day has come to an end. They had travelled to the mini-world of "Europe" where the world's fair had housed the ultimate symbol of modern science with an enormous sculpture of the atom towering over the mini-Europe models. As the two discuss sorcery in Europe, as well as in Africa, the figure of the atom appears, and Nar explains it is a sculpted version of the Atomium from the 1958 World Fair. Nar calls it fantastic, playing the tour guide, and Sekou says wow, wow (yes, yes), voicing the mild appreciation of the tourist at the sight. There is no weight to the atomic reconstruction, to the science of knowledge in this heart of the metropole, where the conversations about Africa and its magical hold over its sons becomes flattened into the same experience as the encounter with the atomium and with the Santa figure—*père noel*.

As in the apparently off-hand style of Jean Rouch, or New Wave cinema, or even the Left Bank nonchalance of Chris Marker's *Sans Soleil* or Varga's more personal essay-films, we see in the editing that element of intellectual montage that lends equal weight to the silliness of the magic and sleight of hand, from mini-Europe to Santa to an outsized atom, the world that beckons to Sekou, to stay, to advance, to become one of them.

Sekou meets his girlfriend at the Peul dance and we hear, repeatedly, the rhythms, and see the ventilateur now re-enacted by the expat Africans living in Brussels. Sekou sees his friend, goes up to her, and they exchange *bises*. The sounds of the drumming, the feel of the dance, the circle of young Africans and their friends watching—it is the same, but now transplanted, and we are carried from one world to another, as we were at the beginning with the birds circling in the sky. Africa is being performed, just as Europe had been earlier in the day at the mini-world's fair. The cross-cutting increasingly brings out Fabian's focus on the non-coeval temporalities as being at the core of colonial discourse. Loreau's juxtapositions of both scenes encountering the dimensions of the family and the world simultaneously undercut the claims of superiority on which the non-coeval finds its basis. Thus the immediate transitions through quick cross-cutting allow Loreau to speak alongside, but not for Nar or Sekou, and to give Sotigui his voice that carries us simultaneously to Berlin and Dakar.

We pass from the Peul dance immediately back to Nar Sene, in close-up, a slightly canted shot, his big eyes half closed as he lies in bed, listening across the distance, the time. His thoughts: "We dance in a circle, and if you leave you marginalize yourself." However, there is no regret here; not the hesitations of Sekou who is wondering if he should stay or leave. As Sekou and his girlfriend chat outside the dance, he tells her he loves her, which makes him want to stay. She responds, don't stay because of me. His four kids and wife back home, whom he had only recently left, seem not to have a very firm grip on him, or on us, as we haven't encountered them directly, only heard him make passing reference to them when he first met Nar. Now, Nar appears less flighty than this seemingly serious student.

Nar in bed: "If you marginalize yourself, often," he thinks, it's madness" (*c'est la folie*). Nar. He has his woman in every port, his children back home, but also newer ones in Paris; and his Brussels girlfriend wanting to settle down with him, not recognizing in him the nomad who can circle back, but never settle down. His mind returns to the circle, which he says is affective—emotional. Then the key reflection: "la cercle est extensible. A la limite, l'élasticité est trop rude. On ne peut pas même parler de l'élasticité. C'est plus fluide que le gaz" (the circle is extensible. At its limit, the elasticity is too strong. One can't even speak of elasticity; it is more fluid than gas).

> With the inevitable dividing of the trait that marks membership, the boundary of the set comes to form, by invagination, an internal pocket larger than the whole; and the outcome of this division and of this abounding remains as singular as it is limitless.
>
> *(Derrida 1980: 59)*

Immediately the dance returns, more vibrant than before. Nar Sene is like a voyeur now. Although the transition is made through cross-cutting, its effect is to create a focalization through Nar's reflections and visions, as though he is seeing the Peul dance and especially hearing the circle of the audience clapping enthusiastically. The dancer leaves and returns as the drums urge her on. Her force, the sexuality of her movements, the power of the call from home reaches to Nar through the images of this dance that

Nar's compatriot Sekou also is hearing: both from Diourbel, both communicating to each other in the shared languages of Wolof and French—the circle has stretched to include both of them.

The image of whites and blacks also persists through the traces and absences, and carries to the subsequent scene when Sekou and his girlfriend leave the dance. As in a chiasmus now it is he asking her if she loves him, rather than she urging him to stay as at the beginning. He is lost, despite his brother's assurances. We need a story to resolve this tension between Nar, now our guide to reflecting about the dance, the community, the family, and Sekou who needs Nar to help him see his way in this foreign land.

The extensible nature of the circle is all that Nar remarks upon. Those who have been away a long time become more attached to home and held within the circle than those who recently left. He seems to dream. He speaks about distance and closeness, as if we hear his

FIGURE 5.1   Nar in bed, reflecting

thoughts, while seeing what he sees: a woman in a courtyard back home, with other women and children, while she pours thé à la menthe. The mundanity of the scene brings us to ordinary life, which his words and even tone convey. "Quand tu es loin comme ça comme moi, pendant longtemps, comme ça, aussi longue, je pense pas que ça t'éloigne, ça te rapproche." (When you are far away like that, like me, for a long time, like that, as long as that, I don't think you are more distanced; rather you approach more.) He goes on to say there are those who don't know where they are going, and should return to their roots, but have lost both paths.

His closed eyes, transported back in his dreams and thoughts, re-evoke the children left behind, who sing and dance and become infinitely compelling. His distance from home, under his colorful blanket, does not disappear, but rather shapes his participation in the extensible community that memory and attraction compel. He becomes an irreproachable witness that enables us to see what he reaches out to rejoin, and what reaches to him. He is, in fact, the marker or trace that makes the dance into the occasion of the community. This is as close to something like an identity that the film permits itself, a phantasm of a memory. In the immediacy of the dance, as at the beginning of the film, the name of the baptized child is whispered to the baby by the marabout. We are witnesses to the naming. But here, we reach the dance across the ineffable, behind the closed eyes of the voyager, Nar Sene the son of the Chief Sene who founded a village. He closes his eyes, as if both hearing and remembering, and the close-up of his face is extraordinary, as if transformed into a mask. His recollection gives presence to the absent people back home. His tension between being absent and re-creating presence is what gives a vestige of closure to the circle. He is the mark from without which defines what we can then witness and close within the meaning of being, perceived and constructed behind the mask.

In short, this is the "contamination" of Derrida's law of the genre:

[T]he law of genre . . . is precisely a principle of contamination, a law of impurity, a parasitical economy. In the code of set theories, if I may use it at least figuratively, I would speak of a sort of participation without belonging-a taking part in without being part of, without having membership in a set. With the inevitable dividing of the trait that marks membership, the boundary of the set comes to form, by invagination, an internal pocket . . ."

(Derrida 1980: 59)

The way Loreau chooses to open our reach to this notion of the extensible circle whose external pocket, now encompassed within it, is with another, final story, recounted by the griot. What the story will provide is the griot's means of stretching the extensible circle of memory so as to restore the lost attachment to the identity of the wanderer, the absent and missing African, lost somewhere in Europe, far from home.

This is the story he tells: "I knew a woman," he says, "who maintained no link to the circle of her people." Sotigui gives us this story as a recollection, but we can say, this is the griot now speaking—the griot as liar, as *bonimenteur* who both flatters and remembers for the great families— and of course for the larger *verité*. He meets a woman sitting alone on a bench in a train station in Paris. Having come to the metropole without the consent of her family, pregnant, dropped by her husband, she is now alone. Sotigui looks directly at the camera, holding an umbrella behind his head to protect himself from the rain, to frame himself now so as to shut out the rest of the world around him, to enter into the recollection and reconstruct the memory of this encounter, and to transmit it to us. We become the host of the gaze, lost in Europe, lost in the foolish images of modern Europe, its modern life imagined as the location where the world, the real world of the dream, can be met, if not conquered. Or dismantled. We need a story to enter into the inevitable space of the genre, its law to be knowledge of how a circle, for even the most distant figures of loss, is to be reconstructed.

The story is simple. A pregnant Senegalese woman has a child who speaks a word that provides the clue to Sotigui that the child is a water spirit. But as they are in Europe, where there are no spirits, where they have been banished, no longer to be recognized, no longer to be taken seriously, the mother cannot recognize what her son really is. When Sotigui inquires about her ancestry, she responds that it has no importance. His reflection takes the form of a proverb, that when one is in the country of the mad, the sane person is taken to be crazy. When Nar recounted to his friend Chretien his story about almost diving into sacred ponds in Kedougou—a location where tourists throw chickens to the crocodiles, but which Nar Sene evokes in terms of local animist beliefs—he credits them with being truthful. It was a question of a water divinity that took the form of a white animal that came out at night. Had he jumped into the pool, he would have died. Chretien mocks his beliefs in the superstitions about the beings inhabiting the pools. I wouldn't have died, Chretien says, but, Nar responds, you'd be the one out of place . . . The one out of place, like matter out of place, trash according to Mary Douglas. It is the same out of place comment that Loreau uses in concluding the final account of the griot when he recounts how the child of an African woman he encounters, and who had been visited with a series of problems, had its spirit taken over by a water genie, causing the child to speak in tongues. Chretien's being out of place in Kedougou as a white man complements the African child's being out of place in Paris, and in both cases it is the encounter with magic that "trashes" any realist account of the situation of the outsider, the emigrant or traveler who is abroad, away from home, the other to the autochthons.

Matter out of place defines the circle to which one belongs, because it is being out of place that provides the location from which one can view the circle—or the genre. And when the one who is out of place enters into the space, the extensible circle, this performs the act that makes visible the external contours of the circle—the mark that makes visible the genre, following Derrida. The end of Sotigui's account performs that action. He closes his umbrella after walking past a wall marked with trashy graffiti and enters into the memory that provides the lost woman with her past. He recognizes—as in recollects or re-collects—the fragments of the histoire-story of *Sundiata*. This is the greatest of all fabulist histories-epic stories of the region, and he places her family in one of the camps, blacksmiths. He toys with this idea, and then the opposite, placing her ancestor with the *horon* or nobles, which he identifies as that of the great ruler himself. As Sotigui turns the words over in his account, speculating, we hear sounds of birds overhead, which we can't see but can hear. They provide his backdrop. As he walks off, to an outsider he would appear like a crazy man talking to himself.

In re-creating the African woman's lineage through this recital, this recollection, Sotigui restores her to the world. He appears like the water spirit that haunted the woman's infant son, and which only those with magical eyes can perceive. He haunts our African in Europe like a foolish figure babbling about the most trite of African epic accounts, and like the dance transposed overseas, allows his performance as griot to take hold, like the vision lying behind Nar's eyes—creating a scene for us.

These visions and stories spin out an Africa that is made up, but that expands the circle like the mark that is needed for the genre to come into being, and using all the myths and fables, like Negritude itself, constructs a truth from the fabric of cinematic invention, extending beyond every conception of "world" or "modern" into the impossibility glimpsed in the film's poetic neorealism, like the spirits that rise with the umbrellas at the end of De Sica's *Miracle in Milan* (1951), or the magic of Souleymane Démé's dancing in *Grigris* (2013). Or simply the quiet scenes in the courtyard filled with women and children in Dakar, where a whispered word of a baby's name takes flight.

Notes

1 "*Eneke the bird* says that since men have learned to shoot without missing, he has learned to fly without perching." (20, *Things Fall Apart*)
2 That healing is the work of the Law of Genre, too, since it leads to the magical permutations of the word Jour employed by Derrida in his discourse on the law Derrida does an extended riff on the law of genre with Blanchot's *La Folie du jour* in "The Law of Genre."
3 Bayart describes the neoliberal period of globalization (1980–2004) in these terms: "Certainly the *Ordoliberalen* and Alexander von Rüstow, argued for a *Vitalpolitik* of a kind that modeled the individual in accordance with the ethos and the structure of a business. In their writings, the spirit of enterprise was

transmogrified into a total project of subjectivication, and *life itself became a business enterprise*" (Bayart, 2007: 163, my stress).

4 I am using "Fulani" poetically. Mori as he appears as an adult, speaks and appears as a Wolof city dweller. But the pastoral image of cattle in Senegal evokes the northerners, typically Fulani, who are pastoralists and who represent a certain non-"modernized" population.

5 Dima's take on modernity is worth citing: "The two main characters of *Touki Bouki* thus oscillate between modernity and tradition. I disagree with Sada Niang's assessment that Mambety does not use that opposition to define his characters: *Touki Bouki* makes us vibrate through this ambivalence: a fascination for elsewhere and an integration of the origin. Some have wanted to see an opposition between tradition and modernity. Mambety has always escaped this dichotomy. To him, modernity was in marginality, in challenging the power and indiscipline, in rebellion, in the force to say 'I' while integrating 'us,' not the 'us' of social constraints but the one of essential values brought on by the origin, transmitted by the story and the myth" (2002, 7). ["*Touki-Bouki* nous fait vibrer de cette ambivalence: fascination pour l'ailleurs et intégration de l'origine. Certains ont voulu y voir une opposition entre tradition et modernité. Mambety a toujours échappé à ce manichéisme. Pour lui, la modernité était dans la marginalité, dans l'irrévérence et l'indiscipline, dans l'indocilité, dans la force de dire "je" tout en intégrant le "nous," non pas le "nous" des contraintes sociales mais celui des valeurs essentielle portées par l'origine, transmises par le conte et le mythe. 17 (Niang 7).] On the contrary the character of Mory encompasses both traditional elements (his very strong connection to the land), and modern ones (like his passion for the motorcycle). These elements help us define Mory as a postcolonial, hybrid subject; he has a split identity, with which he attempts to come to terms throughout the film—and really even beyond, because incarnations of Mory resurface in later films. (See Dima 2017: 42.)

6 From 1962 to 1963, Sembène studied filmmaking for a year at Gorky Film Studio, Moscow, under Soviet director Mark Donskoy. Other renowned African directors who studied in Russia include Sarah Maldoror, Souleymane Cissé. A closer look at the relationship between the filmmakers and Donskoy and others whose approach to filmmaking privileged socialist realism can be found in Monica Popescu's monumental work on the Cold War and Africa, *At Penpoint* (2020).

7 A good account of African students learning filmmaking in Russia during the Cold War is provided by Monica Popescu in her study *At Penpoint* (2020).

8 Public information on her life and work can be gleaning from her website http://www.dominiqueloreau.be/.

9 "Any study of World Cinema, however, should instead be ready to travel more than to oversee, should put students inside unfamiliar conditions of viewing rather than bringing the unfamiliar handily to them" (2004: 9).

10 Sotigui becomes quite famous during his career for playing griots as voices of tradition; see especially *Keita: L'Héritage du griot* (Kouyaté, 1995).

11 I will attempt to reduce or minimalize the scare quotes that would have to be placed around these usages of the term "Afrique" that evidently signifies the so-called Africa of an outsider's imaginary. The outsider here, in this film, is not naively posited as in commercial cinema, but played at to open space for the drama of being both autochthone at home and allothone abroad. The film is played continually as located in one of these spaces in confrontation with the other.

12 Sembène draws on this expression, which means children, for the title of his first major novel dealing with the railroad strikers in Senegal. For us the significance lies in the indirect way in which Wolof, from which the French expression is directly taken, refers to children—protecting them thus from malevolent forces. This take us back to Sekou for whose more traditional family his exile is gradually translating into his being lost to them.

13 One of the common—commonplace—stories of the gentleman who turns out to be a demon, a spirit, a warning tale for women not to be easily seduced by strangers.

https://sites.pitt.edu/~dash/skull.html

Dayrell, Elphinstone. *Folk Stories from Southern Nigeria, West Africa* (London: Longmans, Green, and Co., 1910), no. 8, 38–41.

6

TWO FILMS OF SOTIGUI KOUYATÉ, A MODERN GRIOT

Mahamat-Saleh Haroun, *Sotigui Kouyaté* (1995);
Rachid Bouchareb, *Little Senegal* (2000)

Kenneth W. Harrow

Part One: Mahamat-Saleh Haroun, *Sotigui Kouyaté: Un griot moderne* (1995)

At the beginning of Haroun's film *Sotigui Kouyaté: Un griot moderne* (1995), Sotigui says he has the word griot on his calling card: "Je suis griot avant tout." It's like the tree beginning with its roots. "Griot, ça fait mon identité."

The figure of the griot has become romanticized, rendered one of the common, almost painful clichés about Africa. As a result, one's first reaction to Sotigui's introduction of himself in *Les Noms n'habitent nulle part* (1994), as in this Haroun film about him, is to recoil, to refuse the interpellation as a false presentation of his role, or identity, played for the gullible tourist. It returns us to Eileen Julien's use of the term "extroverted," or worse, the designation "calabash cinema," with contrived images of "real," "authentic" Africans in the bush, etc (Diawara, 2010).

When Sotigui uses it in Haroun's film, it is to bring us into Peter Brook and Jean-Claude Carrière's presentation of Sotigui as uniquely special, his genuineness a piece of his semi-magical qualities as healer. Brook's introduction to him is the most interesting in a way. He states that there are people like himself incapable of acting. Then there are "professional" actors, who are skilled, but not genuine. They learn to put on the mask and do it well. Their implied failures to reach inside to any authenticity leaves us space for the third category to which Sotigui belongs, those who assume their role naturally by getting in touch with and deeply engaging their inner being. This language echoes strongly Lee Strasberg's take on Method

DOI: 10.4324/9781003397595-9

acting, and might be best characterized as pre-postmodernist in its assumptions about inner being and authenticity. Brook's own predilections for the more extreme aspects of the theatrical experience with the non-Western or theatre of cruelty are not really pronounced here, except with the mystification of Africans, whence the embrace of "griots" and spiritual depths. For instance, at one point in the film Carrière mentions he had a splinter in his foot that Sotigui was able to remove, after the recitation of the proper chants. Sotigui is able to carry a certain aura around himself, which no doubt proved irresistible to many who encountered him and worked with him in the theatre.

The imagery used to convey their impressions of Sotigui is familiar. They reiterate their initial impression of him as being tall and thin like an African tree—and Haroun bizarrely evokes that with a distant baobab! As Lindiwe Dovey puts it so well, Sotigui is the Other for them,[1] and that sense of his Otherness was no doubt what Brook was looking for in having him play Bhishma in his Mahabharata. With his stature, dreadlocks, striking Malinke features, Kouyate lineage, and embrace of the djeli role as synecdoche for "the African," he easily conveys his otherness within the theatrical world of Paris as well as of Belgium. But not that of Ouagadougou or Bamako. And as soon as the mise-en-scène shifts us back to his homeland, first in Bamako and then in Burkina, the entire distinction between him and those around him falls away, beginning in the airport of Bamako, and then in the respective homecomings he is given in his mother's and father's family compounds. There another kind of otherness manifests itself, that of the successful been-to, or rather lost son who has returned after 26 years, in the case of his mother's side of the family, and 30 on the side of his father.

The details of his enormously long absences are only hinted at in the film.[2] We learn he was a few months away from having earned his retirement pension when he quit the public service job he had held to join Brook's company, recognizing this as a once in a lifetime chance. Sotigui was born in 1936 and joined Brook's troupe in 1983, making his claim to be that close to having a pension difficult to parse, but he is very precise about the dates of his absence from the Africa he claims to represent in his roles and his status as griot. When Haroun filmed *Sotigui Kouyate* in 1996, Sotigui had turned 60. His return after all that time evokes something of Moussa Sene Absa's *Ainsi meurent les anges* (2001) made five years later. In Sene Absa's film, Mory, played by Absa himself, returns home to Gorée after having lived long enough in Paris to have started a family and settled in. Ultimately, Mory fails to find his way in Paris, and returns empty handed, his marriage apparently ending despite having two children.

Sotigui himself returns with his European wife and two children, and the film prominently displays his young son whose striking métis features, and almost blond curly hair, create a noticeable visual effect as the whole family is seen being welcomed in the family compounds. There Sotigui no longer needs to proclaim his identity, his inheritance as griot, his embrace of the role as the African. He is now the long-lost son, brother, child—lost like those stolen, sold children of the diaspora whom he will track down in New York in his next prominent role as Alioune in Bouchareb's *Little Senegal* (2000).

In reviewing Haroun's film of this distinguished actor, with the personal details of his life and career taking us between an Africa where he had learned to perform and a Europe where he made a career and settled down to earn a living, it is striking how the films about the diaspora from Africa shift, settle, and unsettle our readings. An account of Sotigui's career after 1990 must include his stint as promoter of the "authentic" griot figure. His son, the director Dany Kouyaté, made two films in which Sotigui played key roles (*Sia, le rêve du python* [2001] and *Keita: l'héritage du griot* [1995]). Notably, in the 1990s he played the role of storyteller in a play created by Sotigui: "Between 1990 and 1996 [Dany Kouyaté] was on tour in Europe and the U.S. as a storyteller, part of 'La Voix du Griot'('Voice of the Griot'), a theater show created by his father, the gifted actor, artist, and griot Sotigui Kouyaté."[3] In Cynthia Guttman's interview with him, Sotigui presented the quintessential vision of himself as inhabiting this role:

> Let's be modest. Africa is vast, and it would be pretentious to speak in its name. I'm fighting the battle with words because I'm a storyteller, a griot. Rightly or wrongly, they call us masters of the spoken word. Our duty is to encourage the West to appreciate Africa more. It's also true that many Africans don't really know their own continent. And if you forget your culture, you lose sight of yourself. It is said that "the day you no longer know where you're going, just remember where you came from." Our strength lies in our culture. Everything I do as a storyteller, a griot, stems from this rooting and openness.
>
> *(2001: 51)*

The dilemma of Sekou in *Les Noms n'habitent nulle part* (1994) about whether to return to his native Senegal or stay and study medicine further in Bruxelles, his attraction to his beautiful Belgian girlfriend, and his profession of love, all are rendered complicated and less attractive as we learn what she apparently doesn't know, that he is already married and has children back home. Sotigui alludes to his own past, his own having been married with children, when he came to Paris and ultimately decided to settle down, marry, and have children there. In that regard, he resembles all the more the second African protagonist in *Les Noms n'habitent nulle part* (1994), Nar Sene, with his references to multiple lives, families, and children, moving between his grown daughter in Dakar, and his many homes and women in Paris and Bruxelles. When Mouche complains and wants him to settle down, he says, I am here, I love you now, that should be enough.

Les Noms ends with the griot Sotigui inventing a history for a lost African, a woman, who can't remember her origins. He sings the same song Samaguera, as if reciting *Sundiata*, to remind us that she/he is on one side or the other, Keita or Kouyaté, and embodies the epic figure of the past. He gives his one eternal truth, that one's being is rooted in the past, and to know oneself is to know that past. Why the film ends with the griot and not the other two main characters might seem to make no sense. But the shift back to a history that gives definition to the present becomes clearer when it is the figure of the griot's creative act of remembering that takes central stage. These are uncontested as "African truths."[4]

The griot in *Les Noms*, and his two subjects, Sekou and Nar Sene, appear as lost nomads. The griot hunts down the stories of the lost children of Africa, adrift in the spaces up North and alienated from home. Sekou pulls away from his kin and family, so easily forgets his obligations to them when trying to forge a relationship with the Belgian girlfriend who herself says she is not ready. Nar in bed, eyes half closed, hearing the sounds of home, the drums, the dancing, the children, "so close, so far," as Wenders would have it. Sekou and Nar Sene are facets of Sotigui, the griot who can make a living as an actor and perform as the griot only abroad since it has long been the case that the role of the griot at home as it had once been is long since over, and now many have reconfigured their roles with new generations of musicians and performers.

The function of memory in this order of the New, that of the griot abroad, the griot in the diaspora, is not to restore a lost identity, one always reinvented with each historical shift anyway, but to play the role of the *lieux de mémoire* (Nora 1984) that recreate historical memories that function so as to create the nation. The national identity that is forged here takes the form given by Negritude, and is called, plainly, "Africa." The *lieux* where this memory situates itself are evoked, humorously, with the mini-Europe monuments visited by Sekou and Nar Sene—monuments of the colonial metropoles—set over against the human, living *lieux* that reattach the wandering African. These include those of the home courtyard, the great trees under which the umbilical cords are buried, sites where the mothers and brothers anchor the wandering child to his home—*lieux* in the dreams of the Sekou-Nar figures brought to life in in the imaginary-memory of the griot.

For Nora the past has slipped, is displaced, disappears, and in its disappearance weakens our adherence to the identity as citizens of a nation (Nora 1989). We function in a turning point in history and require the work of re-creating the lost past to anchor ourselves in our present roles. The role of griot in Bruxelles and Paris shapes the figure of Sotigui Kouyate and the form of the great historical epic in which he locates his life, as well as that of the woman who cannot remember her past in Paris. In its diaspora, it recreated that of the American "Negro" woman in Harlem in *Little Senegal* (2000), and that of the Sotigui character's lost nephew killed in New York. The setting is close to a neighborhood called Little Senegal. The Hudson River setting where the Sotigui character loses his nephew becomes the archives for the griot—the current lieu de memoire that Bouchareb chooses in his attempt to track the lost ties of the family.

In making the connection to home, the fragile line between a fictional and an historical account is often infiltrated. Nar Sene plays the role of someone called Nar Sene. Sotigui Kouyaté does the same, as if playing himself. Narrator and protagonist evoking griot and historian in *Little Senegal* (2000) are ensconced in a work of contemporary social realism that opens the genres of diaspora historical fiction to the work of historical recuperation and reinvention. The imaginary performs the work of memory, and is taken as seriously as the performance of the griot. That is why the ending of the film *Sotigui Kouyaté* (1995) is so remarkable. Having repeated the clichéd words about his identity at the beginning, Sotigui comes to perform the role at the end when he sings in praise of Miriam Touré. Just as Nar Sene returns to the courtyard of his family in his dreams at the end of *Les Noms n'habitent nulle part* (1994), so does Sotigui return to his family courtyard at the end of Haroun's film, where he successfully reinvents himself. Sene Absa does the same in *Ainsi Meurent les anges* (2001), rescripting the former "been-to" narratives.

We see the Africa Sotigui wants us to see, with children trying to get on a bicycle. He returns to the family courtyard in Ouaga where he tells us, "Mon âme est ce cours." With a certain humility he is able to say to the camera that he sees himself as speaking "au nom de l'Afrique," and not in the name of the griot Sotigui. Even if it is pretentious on his part, he says, "l'Afrique vient avant de Sotigui." He thinks in the first instance that he is conveying an image of Africa (while Mariam is singing praises of him). His honor, minimal though it may be, risks spreading like a *tache d'huile*. Wishing to be an example for others, like a wind, *un vent porteur*, he dreams of stronger winds to follow. Others better than himself. There is no hint of conceit here, but what Brook signals as his admirable, interior self. He then sings back as griot to Mariam Touré who has herself sung his praises. His qualities that had so impressed Brook and Carrière, and that were lost in their evocations of his African Otherness, become simple, direct, and thoroughly winning when we see and hear him singing in praise of Mariam Touré at the end. He no longer needs to be the griot, but simply Sotigui, another whose name has no home, or, if it has no home, takes root wherever it lands. Loreau's poetic figure in *Les Noms* is completed in Haroun's film where the ending provides some sense to Sotigui's role.

Pierra Nora begins his famous exposition on *lieux de mémoire* with this statement:

> An increasingly rapid slippage of the present into a historical past that is gone for good, a general perception that anything and everything may disappear—these indicate a rupture of equilibrium. The remnants of experience still lived in the warmth of tradition, in the silence of custom, in the repetition of the ancestral, have been displaced under the pressure of a fundamentally historical sensibility. Self-consciousness emerges under the sign of that which has already happened, as the fulfillment of something always already begun. We speak so much of memory because there is so little of it left.
>
> Our interest in *lieux de mémoire* where memory crystallizes and secretes itself has occurred at a particular historical moment, a turning point where consciousness of a break with the past is bound up with the sense that memory has been torn—but torn in such a way as to pose the problem of the embodiment of memory in certain sites where a sense of historical continuity persists. There are *lieux de mémoire*, sites of memory, because there are no longer *milieux de mémoire*, real environments of memory.
>
> *(Nora 1989: 7)*

Nora references the change from peasant societies to contemporary industrial societies, but lest we think his point of reference is purely European, he switches immediately to those nations recently having experienced decolonization:

> Among the new nations, independence has swept into history societies newly awakened from their ethnological slumbers by colonial violation. Similarly, a process of interior decolonization has affected ethnic minorities, families, and groups that until now have possessed reserves of memory but little or no historical capital. We have seen the end of societies that had long assured the transmission and conservation of collectively remembered values, whether through churches or schools, the family or the state.
>
> *(Nora 1989: 7)*

He doesn't mention griots among those charged with remembering the past or processing it. They are, in fact, not historians in the academic disciplinary sense. However, they are, themselves sites of memory, *lieux de mémoire*, and as such move from a position behind the camera—as narrators in a film—to one in front of the camera, like Sotigui, the object of the camera's gaze. Objects, but also performers in a scenario. The collective heritage is gone, according to Nora, replaced by "the ephemeral film of current events" (1989: 8). Collective memory has been eradicated, and replaced by a notion of history with an ephemeral duration. What is imagined as the griot's memory might fit closely into this description he has of the older social mechanism of earlier societies: "On the one hand, we find an integrated, dictatorial memory—unself-conscious, commanding, all-powerful, spontaneously actualizing, a memory without a past that ceaselessly reinvents tradition, linking the history of its ancestors to the undifferentiated time of heroes, origins, and myth" (Nora: 8). The contemporary replacement entails the loss of that approach to the past, as memory has become "nothing more in fact than sifted and sorted historical traces" (Nora: 8). Change has replaced continuity. History has replaced memory, leaving the "ancient bond of memory and history" broken, and in need of replacement, which accounts for the erection of such monuments of the past, *lieux de mémoire*, to capture what is already gone. *Sundiata* is one such site.

What if we now reconstitute that past in the figure of the griot himself? He functions within the realm of historical epistemology, and thus is reconstituted as a trace of the past: "With the appearance of the trace, of mediation, of distance, we are not in the realm of true memory but of history" (Nora: 8). My original disparagement of the figure of the griot has now to be reconfigured when he is considered as an object of mediation, and specifically one mediated by the camera's lens. Sotigui passes from the person he wants us to identify with the ancestor, whose courtyard bears his name to the actor's personage he embodies in film after film, each time he sits in front of the lens and intones, "je suis griot," and explains yet again who he is. His functioning within this new realm of history is set, according to Nora, not by his living, or being a griot, but by performing the role of the griot. "History, on the other hand, is the reconstruction, always problematic and incomplete, of what is no longer" (Nora: 8).

In contrast to history, Nora sees memory as an attribute of the present, and his claim resonates closely with the functioning of the griot's memory moments in the three films under consideration, *Les Noms n'habitent nulle part* (1994), *Sotigui Kouyate: un griot moderne* (1995), and *Little Senegal* (2000). "Memory is a perpetually actual phenomenon, a bond tying us to the eternal present; history is a representation of the past" (Nora: 8). The "eternal present" in each film is *capitonné* in Lacan's sense, that is, nailed down to a signification, an act of signification, that endows the performance of an "African" past with an aura of authenticity, what Brook and company purported to have recognized in the figure of Sotigui—what Glissant identifies as originary, that is, constructed in compensation for the losses of history. At every point I am now tempted to write "Sotigui" for Sotigui since he inhabits, for them, his Otherness, which he conveniently defines for them as "griot," the term conveniently appended to his name in Haroun's film title.

Nora continues to describe memory as affective and, best of all, magical. As such the past it resurrects is suited to its "griotic" nature as "nourish[ing] recollections that may be out of focus or telescopic" (Nora: 8). In film terms, this action is performed by camerawork and editing, especially with the selective use of rack focusing; and rather than debasing the authenticity or value of the shot, it can be called creative constructing, or film-making. At the heart of the film it is not its *verité* that matters, but the joining of mise-en-scènes with *lieux de mémoire*.

The work of memory, and its sites, is open, and can function in a broad range of milieux, with a range of objects: "Memory takes root in the concrete, in spaces, gestures, images, and objects" (Nora: 9). Here we are locating it in the person, and words, of Sotigui: that is, in his performance. We turn to that performance in this decade of the 1990s and early 2000s at a moment precisely when the nation—served by history and its sites to couple society to the nation—has become increasingly supplanted by the global and the local. The social tension exacerbated by a past that no longer can be mobilized in the work of nation-building or development, supplanted by the dominance of NGOs (cf. Comaroffs, Piot, Bayart) and global economic forces (SAP, World Bank, IMF), requires the figure of a non-threatening, comforting tradition that works through the performance of a mythic act of remembering. Griots that comfort rather than historians that disrupt; memories of a fog, joined to the ethnic dance performance in the courtyard. Extremities of violence and sexuality are avoided by Sotigui; rather it is family and affection that bind the central figure and his family courtyards. His songs entrance us, as does the image of the chain of griots, rather than the violence of history his performance is conventionally thought to retain. His is the cinematic griot, not the historic griot performance.

Whereas Nora might see an Arc de Triomphe as the barest remnant of a past recalled by acts of memory, Loreau presents the Arc now in a theme park setting where the camaraderie of Sekou and Nar Sene can be forged. The miniature nation *lieux* become globalized entertainment settings, as shrunken on the screen, proportionally, as the Santa Claus figure's is enlarged, his face filling the screen at one point. Under these conditions, the *lieux de mémoire* are the result of defensive gestures intended to ward off the threat of history:

> *Lieux de memoire* originate with the sense that there is no spontaneous memory, that we must deliberately create archives, maintain anniversaries, organize celebrations, pronounce eulogies, and notarize bills because such activities no longer occur naturally. The defense, by certain minorities, of a privileged memory that has retreated to jealously protected enclaves in this sense intensely illuminates the truth of *lieux de memoire*—that without commemorative vigilance, history would soon sweep them away.
>
> *(Nora: 12)*

The *raison-d'etre* for the creation of these *lieux* is risky: as an act of defense it defers to the framing by what has threatened its identity. As Nora puts it, why create them unless one feels under threat? "We buttress our identities upon such bastions, but if what they defended were not threatened, there would be no need to build them" (Nora: 12).

What must unsettle this reduction of the past to the folkloric will be the transposition of the griot's location to the world of the diaspora. Recalling the scene of the encounter of the borom sarret and the griot in Sembène's first short film, we can reconstruct that scene along the boardwalk in Cannes where he shot scenes for *La noire de . . .* to conceive of that performance as a defensive action taken to ward off the threat still posed by the colonial frame. The New York City setting of *Little Senegal* distances us from the threat and the defense; the African setting continually represents it in its renewed forms of SAPs and IMF loans, as in Sissako's *Bamako* (2006). To manage the threat, we must succeed in making the transition from home to abroad, cross the difficult middle passage, now represented increasingly by the horrors faced by migrants, with refugees seeking to make it up north.

Mostefa Djadjam represents this in *Frontières* (2001), his film about a group of such migrants/refugees, as does Moussa Toure in *La Pirogue* (2012). In Bouchareb's *Little Senegal* (2000) we begin with the *lieux de mémoire* closest to the imaginative reconstruction of the past, the "slave fort" on Gorée—a location most recognizably identified with the slave trade, with the door of no return typically figured as the site symbolizing the greatest threat of loss of freedom. That this is memory and not history is perhaps most clearly seen with Philip Curtin's claim that this building was probably not a slave fort but a private house. He has been largely ignored in favor of the curators' desire to maintain its attraction to tourists.[5] However, despite Curtin's claim, the fort functions perfectly as a *lieux de mémoire*, to launch us on the return voyage to the past, taking us, via the character of the newly reformulated griot Sotigui, now appearing as the historian Alioune, back to the past. We track his passage through the American South, the plantation in South Carolina, following the traces of the passage of his ancestor's slave itinerary. In South Carolina he continues the performance as one who can reconstitute the past, i.e., as historian, by consulting the archives, tracking down the ship's manifest and the name of his ancestor, as in *Roots* (1976), until he can locate his distant relatives in New York. There the passage by train completes the transformation, relocating us in a present in which the griot Alioune will reattach himself to the black community so as to communally ward off the threat to their family.[6]

In *Little Senegal* (2000), Harlem becomes the destination, not Bruxelles or the family homestead. In that regard, we have a completion of the journeys initially figured in the earlier Sotigui films. In *Les Noms* the journey to Bruxelles is given as a flight, like that of the birds, without borders. In *Sotigui Kouyaté* (1995), we have the pieces of the journey, as in the scene in the airport of Bamako, when he arrives back home. But the most compelling journey there is the train ride from his maternal to his paternal family's city, from Mali to Ouagoho. The train ride takes us, via a long tracking shot, along the platform, as the camera turns slowly back onto the increasingly distant location, emphasizing the act of looking back, of departing. The past and the family become the sites of a lost heritage, now increasingly inhabited in the wreckage of that long colonial encounter and postcolonial demolition. The Benjaminian angel of history is located in the point of view of the camera.

In the entry into New York, on the train that runs through Harlem to 125th street, Alioune makes his entry. He is still Sotigui Kouyaté, but soon to become someone quite new, as he encounters, with some slight of hand, his long lost relative. Where this story will take the griot is the subject of the next section, *Little Senegal* (2000).

Part Two: Rachid Bouchareb, *Little Senegal* (2000)

Little Senegal (2000) begins with a shot out of the "Door of No Return" from the slave fort on Gorée. The soundtrack is that of a sad Negro Spiritual lament over the loss of being sold. The action then opens with Alloune going over the logs of the ships headed for North and South Carolina. He plays the role of the curator and a tour guide at the museum who addresses a crowd of tourists whom we see arriving on the ferry. He holds up the chain, explains the details of the enslaved people's experiences and of settings in the museum. In the *New York Times* obituary of Ndiaye, this is the image employed:

FIGURE 6.1   Boubacar Joseph Ndiaye, in a 2007 documentary *Return to Gorée*, at the House of Slaves in Senegal

Pierre Nora writes, "Memory takes root in the concrete," whereas history is relative (1989: 9) and it aspires to the status of science that would change its account with the discovery of more evidence. The historian Philip Curtin sees no problem in relativizing the claim that the slave fort in Gorée was only a personal house, not a slave fort; the curator, both the actual Joseph Ndiaye,[7] who served in that function for years and turned it into a shrine, and Alloune in the film, deal with the concrete. Alloune picks up a ball and chain, demonstrating its materiality, its weight, its function in impeding the enslaved people's movement. If history would want the audience to acquire knowledge, Alloune is more interested in motivating them by the encounter with these *lieux de mémoire* that animate their right to mourn because of their ties to those who had been captured, forced to wear the chains, and were transported across the ocean.

Alloune follows their passage, in his body, not simply in his readings of their experiences. He relives their experiences, down to the point of coming to Harlem where his life is changed, and where the original purpose, to rediscover his relatives, passes far beyond that into his redis-covery of his own self in the life he recreates in the diaspora. And not only in diaspora, which might have also been in Paris or Amsterdam, but especially in Harlem, the Harlem Senghor had discovered shortly after World War II, where something new, something black, something creative had emerged, not bound to the past but to its own present. "New York! I say New York, Let the black blood flow into your blood" (Senghor 1975: "Harlem").

I. Making Connections

Why does Alloune need to forge a relationship with Ida (played by Sharon Hope)? The film functions on two distinct levels. On the first, Alloune seems driven to track down the passage of an enslaved ancestor taken from Gorée to America. As in *Roots*, the historical mystery is fashioned like a procedural, with African history and "traditions" like scarification used to track the passage of the man. Alloune dresses in an overcoat and fedora, even in the heat of the Carolinas, carries a briefcase, and is seen as an edu-cated man who can work through the archives in Gorée and the American South. The archivists and librarians give him the help and respect denied him by the plantation owners, and he succeeded in tracing his ancestor's descendants to New York.

But when he arrives in New York, and establishes his presence with his nephew Hassan, he shifts from the scholarly researcher to someone whose mission to find his long-lost relatives takes on another, uncertain quality. We don't know at this point why he feels so driven to find living relatives, except perhaps for the pleasure a genealogist takes in uncovering the unknown traces of one's ancestors, despite all the obstacles. He has overcome the greatest of all impediments to American Black people, that of the loss occasioned by the middle passage and the subsequent renam-ing of the enslaved by their owners. Renaming, along with forbidding the use of African languages, and the conversion to Christianity worked to change free African subjects into American enslaved people, and in par-ticular into the plantation's enslaved laborers, insuring the break from the past, the culture, the family.

The movement across time and space from the early 18th century South-ern plantation to 20th century New York takes us through the history of the enslaved people's past world to that of the current generation, with Blacks now living in a ghetto, not the plantation. The change in habitus is thus from an African slave-trading past to that of Harlem, the Black quartier of New York, the location for the mise-en-scène for most of the rest of the film. When the train pulls into the station at 125th Street, the diegesis switches to a world that evokes radical difference, one in which black identity and urban modernity frame all of the action.

Alloune meets his long lost relative Ida, and unaccountably withholds the key information that he is a distant member of her original family. This reticence continues even after he has already won Ida over, and has passed the night in bed with her. At this point, the notion that their meeting holds a special meaning because of a shared loss due to slavery and the Middle Passage shifts focus. We leave the historical charge of *Roots*, the need to overcome the trauma of slavery, the abuses of the masters and the system they had set in motion, and another set of issues emerges whose burden is less historical and more personal. It too is centered on loss, on both sides of the Atlantic, and a determination to repair the loss.

Dispossession is inscribed in the concepts of race and Blackness, according to Mbembe in his *Critique of Black Reason* (2017). At the heart of that loss is slavery, and at the base of slave-owning and -trading cultures is the figure of the Black Man presented as the site of a less than fully human being. The slave trade preceded the Atlantic slave trade by hundreds of years, and its actual practices varied considerably depending on where and when it was practiced. But the creation of notions of race and of the figure of the Black Man provided the ideological positioning of Europe vis-à-vis Africa, marking the dominant feature of modernism and of the subsequent humanist work of the 17th and 18th centuries.[8] In the universalizing theories of the Enlightenment were the seeds for the structures of globalization, not only in the notions of rational thought and science, but in the burgeoning capitalist economic order that undergirded the enormous expansion of European production, wealth, and power. At one end, the pen of Voltaire, and at the other end, the plantation and the Black enslaved person producing wealth for the French nation. Between them, as Gikandi has shown in his monumental work on slavery, *Slavery and the Culture of Taste* (2011), the creation of a European system of values dependent on the figure of the Black: lost in the corners of the paintings, the figure who served her master in the boudoir, intimate, close to, but to the side of, the central object of the artist's desire.

What was Alloune searching for when he looked out of the Porte du Voyage Sans Retour, when the ship left with its human cargo, and returned months later, empty, to pick up the next load? There is a point where Philip Curtin's critique[9] of the mistake in attributing genuineness to the fort doesn't matter: with or without attribution, that door, that building, with its curved staircase leading upstairs to the masters' quarters, and down to the enslaved people's dark cellars functions for the visitors as a slave fort, a *lieu de mémoire*. Its "minstrelsy" (Reid, *Redefining Black Film*, 1993) is as real as the performance of Black identity, of white overlordship.

Something began at that point, for the enslaved held in similar quarters, if not necessarily for those who held them in confinement until the next ship returned to pick them up.

There is an echo or ghostly reminder that somehow worked in Alloune's imaginary when he saw the ferry bringing its tourists from the dock in Dakar to the landing in Gorée, day after day. Sotigui Kouyate played the role of Joseph Ndiaye, the tour guide/curator, who displayed the chain and ball, leading the tourists up the stairs to the fancy suites where the air would dissipate the odors from the prisons below, and then over and over onto the door of no return.

The connection was made every time: Black tourists, often women who wept at the reminders, opened in Alloune the need to understand that loss, something he couldn't have done without himself repeating the same journey into hell that their ancestors had made. Another film that closely embraced that same journey is Haile Gerima's *Sankofa*, made in 1993, eight years before *Little Senegal*. In that film Mona, a contemporary Black American model, undergoes time travel back into the past where she has become an enslaved woman forced to go through the Middle Passage and live as enslaved on a plantation. Alloune's road journey leads him into the present, to the life of the African diaspora in New York, where Africa has effectively disappeared. In this Sotigui Kouyate film the figure of the sage griot disappears and any ancestral privilege and status goes unnoticed. The family is adrift, the dignity lost, the comforts of the African compound and its generations all lost in Harlem where Hassan, his nephew, is now driving a cab for a living.

What is Alloune searching for when he traces his ancestors' path down to the door of the news stand owner, Ida Robinson? The difference he encounters, along with her own experiences of precarity, would seem to have nothing to do with those imagined by Alloune when looking out of the door of no return on the empty horizon of the Atlantic. But in bringing the African and the African American together, Benchareb makes possible a deeper inscription of dispossession than either of them had known in their own separate worlds.

It takes a convoluted plot to bring us to the point, with the forming of a relationship between them, and their ultimate separation following the death of Hassan, that makes visible their own precarity we had only sensed at the outset. That precarity is not one of isolated individuals, but of figures caught up in the web of violence that the life of the diaspora community experienced in the New World. The precarity of dispossession is described by Judith Butler and Athena Athanasiou in their key study *Dispossession* (2013). Its link to race is fundamental, as Mbembe claims: "[T]he systematic risks experienced specifically by Black slaves during early capitalism have now become the norm for, or at least the lot of, all of subaltern humanity" (2017: 4). He elaborates on this association for the term "Black":

> Across early capitalism, the term 'Black' referred only to the condition imposed on peoples of African origin (different forms of depredation, dispossession of all power of self-determination, and, most of all, dispossession of the future and of time, the two matrices of the possible).
>
> *(217: 5–6)*

Mbembe makes a point of distinguishing race thinking from colorism. Importantly, both are historicized, placed into relation with the institutions of slavery. Whereas early American slavery did not particularly distinguish the color of the enslaved person's skin, the conditions of plantation slavery, which came to be the dominant factor driving the Atlantic Slave Trade, marked a shift.[10] The early enslaved populations of the United States in the 17th century were heterogeneous, and slavery itself was but one of a number of conditions of subordination, including indentured servitude, which was of a limited time period, and touched such notables as Benjamin Franklin. With time the legalization and formalization of the category of enslavement insured that only Blacks were generally assigned to that category. It took about a century, from 1619 to 1720, for this process to be completed (Mbembe 2017: 16).

The process of transformation of Blacks from African enslaved people to a race of Black people occurred as the rise of scientism accompanied the transformations of the economy from mercantilism to liberal capitalism, and eventually industrial capitalism. In each period the need for servile labor drove the categorization of people, and the notion of what constituted a people. The initial period of capitalism, termed "early capitalism" by Mbembe, was marked by the usage of the term "Black" for people of African origin, and it was they who experienced the conditions of loss. The long duration of plantation and then industrial capitalism requiring the exploitation of servile physical labor begins to end with the rise of the neoliberal global economy and its digitization and outsourcing of labor. The term "Black" for Mbembe now extends to populations throughout the world; he calls this the "Becoming Black of the World."

The association of "Blacks" with Africans began before the diaspora became significant, i.e., the 17th and 18th centuries. With the development of plantation slavery in the New World (first Brazil, then the Caribbean islands, and subsequently the United States) came the transformation of Blacks from Africans to enslaved populations. That shift meant a gap grew between Africa and the Black population in the New World—some being free, most being enslaved; some being part of the mechanisms of maintaining slavery; some being part of the resistance; some policing the enslaved themselves, or, as freemen, owning enslaved persons; some joining the Union Army, or assisting abolitionists. Throughout the 19th century abolitionism and resistance, beginning in Haiti, and ending with abolition throughout the New World by the end of the century, meant that Africa's role in serving the servile laboring needs of the New World economy ended.

For Europe, colonialization during that century created new relations of dependency and dispossession, but also generated movements of resistance to occupation and new concepts of self-rule fostered by opposition to colonialism. Throughout the 20th century, resistance to colonial rule, like that of abolitionism in the previous century, was joined to resistance to the attributes of an economic order that entailed the exploitation of African resources, including African labor.

All of this is to signal that the "Black Man" embodied in the African character Alloune at the beginning of *Little Senegal* was radically different from the "Black Woman" played in the role of African American Ida in the film. Alloune's passage through the door of no return was that of an African Black Man. In New York he had to encounter a world described by his nephew Hassan as one in which New York Blacks hated Africans, had nothing to do with them, and would happily stab them in the hand. As Hassan saw it, they "take us for monkeys, we are too black, they would stab us and rob us given the chance." When he is killed at the end, it is in a fight which he has provoked, based on his anger against those he accuses without proof of having robbed him.

When we first encounter him working in a garage in Harlem, Hassan winds up in a fight with an African American man who unjustly accuses him of malfeasance and who calumniates him using the term monkey. If there are two worlds in New York, for him it is African and African American, not Black and white. His girlfriend is African, his roommate is also African, albeit Algerian, and they speak French, not English, in his apartment. When his uncle comes, they use Wolof and French to communicate. Alloune has come to re-establish ties with the long-broken, forgotten family, but for Hassan they are not cousins or relatives, but more enemies, as he accuses Eileen (Ida's granddaughter) and her friends of having robbed him.

Alloune's transition from Gorée to New York, via the American South, is not a Middle Passage in reverse; not an overcoming of the Middle Passage, like that of Achille in Walcott's *Omeros* who returns to Africa in a fantasized journey, traveling back in space and time. Rather, it is in the wake of his nephew's own migration doubled by that of his ancestors in the past who passed from being Dioulas of Senegal to being the Robinson family in New York, their graves now located in the cemetery in Queens.

The great distance he had experienced from his long-lost family was transformed into the intimate closeness of a lover when he wound up in bed with Ida. He begins to "take care of family business," including when Ida's granddaughter Eileen becomes pregnant and goes off on her own, angry at Ida. He takes care of Eileen, bringing her back home for the birth; takes care of ensuring that the child, when born, is not lost to the family again as Eileen initially refuses to accept it.

After coming from another world which Ida thinks hates her and rejects her own people, he moves in with her. They come from two worlds, which he decides to bridge, bringing Ida across the same chasm. Distance and closeness; being away, being a stranger, being at home, being indigenous; the fears and apprehensions of the foreigner versus the acceptance of the autochthonous. Although there are no whites in their lives in Harlem, the TV brings in stories of the killings in Tyler, Texas of a gay man, and the killing of Amadou Diallo in an apartment doorway in New York. The violence of exclusion and inclusion join the twin figures of the fossil and the monster, the two sides of the Black man that Mbembe sees as produced over time (2017: 17–18).[11] The fossil retains the closeness of identity, despite time and obscurity; the monster reproduces the emotional charge required to remove the all too familiar features of the human from the proximate presence of the Black man.

The monkey, in its difference, is implanted onto the "monstrous features," the broad noses of Alloune and Ida, as they say when laughing at their resemblances. The "monstrosity" of the African features includes the scarifications that help Alloune identify their ancestors, the Diallos, of Guinea. Distances are created and recreated as race and "Black Man" identities get reforged in each new iteration of the capitalist order, the plantation order, and now the neoliberal, global order. There is no family or race without the impulse to mark an identity, and that impulse morphs enormously as we see Alloune marching through the plantations of the south, with the ghostly reminders of slavery, the slave houses and cemeteries, and the reticence of the descendants of the slave owners who seem hesitant about extending "Southern hospitality" to the distant African relative when he shows up at their door.

"To produce Blackness," Mbembe writes, "is to produce a social link of subjection and a *body of extraction*, that is, a body entirely exposed to the will of the master, a body from which great effort is made to extract maximum profit." He adds the whip to the conjuration of the body: "An exploitable object, the Black Man is also the name of a wound, the symbol of a person at the mercy of the whip and suffering in a field of struggle" (2017: 18). When Alloune asks Ida for a job as a pretext to approaching her, he enters into that relationship of boss and worker—master, servant. He starts on the process of becoming a "Black Man" in America, like Amadou Diallo, exposed to the risks of being taken for a monster, and not recognized as a fossil. The question left posed and unanswered in the film is what kind of Black Man he is in Africa, or if he was a Black Man at all. His only position as Slave Fort curator did not present him as subject to the White Man or the whip, they having long since departed; did not represent him within the state or any other institution of the global economy. He was, in fact, a guide to the mostly Black Americans who had come to him in search of their past, in an effort of recovery. He presented them with the images of the ball and chain—in fact duplicates and not originals—in order to lead them through the emotional field of pain experienced by the enslaved, and to the door that gave on to their final departure, the passage as he called it.

His need for undertaking that passage was marked by their death. He had already shown the tourists the suffering figure of an enslaved man in revolt being bound up and hung. In North Carolina he paused at the slave cemetery on the plantation. Even the archives he consulted were about enslaved persons who had long since died; and the last thread he followed led to the cemetery where Ida's daughter was buried. The end of the film comes with the death of Hassan, and Alloune's repatriation of the body for its burial at Gorée. He returns to the door of no return and looks out on the ocean, across which now Ida can be seen as back at work in her newsstand; both in the shadow of death.

The haunted presence of the whip in both worlds, its trace, is framed in two worlds of Blackness[12]—not two races, white and Black, but an Africa's independent population, and African Americans working for themselves in NYC: those selling goods in the slave fort and those on 125th Street, hawking to Black people who pass by; those who run the taxi service, who staff the cemetery, repair cars, staff the restaurants, and finally those who aid Alloune in tracing his relatives. In each world, race and Blackness is now reproduced radically differently, despite the fossilized remains of the traces of the past that continue to haunt the denizens of the present. "But blackness does not exist as such. It is constantly produced. To produce Blackness is to produce a social link of subjection and a *body of extraction*" (Mbembe 2017: 18).

Blackness not as a source of unity, but strife. "An exploitable object, the Black Man is also the name of a wound, the symbol of a person at the mercy of the whip and suffering in a *field of struggle that opposes socioracially segmented groups and factions*" (2017: 18, my stress). Where could Benchareb find a bridge between these groups in this new staging of difference? Certainly not in the past when Arab slavers carted millions of sub-Saharan Africans across the desert, and carried with them all the attributes of racial difference and hatred as well.[13]

Rather it is in the forging of a new American Blackness, comprising a subaltern set of figures including those outside the sphere of the white world, represented by the police seen on TV carrying out their murderous duties in shooting Diallo. These figures include Hassan's roommate Karim, who can speak French to Alloune when he arrives, and has set up a false marriage with the Black American woman Amaralis, in order to qualify for American citizenship. The subplot on which this Black-white couple turns focuses not on their race—they are both non-white in the new America. They both work within the economic order in Harlem, and need to bridge the huge gap between them, with Amaralis as autochthonous and Karim the foreigner. Both are familiar with the pains of distance and dispossession; both live with an apparent measure of precarity, concerned over and again about money, payments, and the struggle to meet their needs. But if the film ends with the rupture of Alloune, who leaves Ida, despite her pleas, in order to return home and bury Hassan, it is also simultaneously marked by the moment when Karim and Amaralis make a new start, leaving the finances of their old relationship aside and going off together. They will give definition to a new world of "Blackness" in America as their children, métis, will certainly be known as "Black," if not as the same Black Man understood as fossil and monster in the terms of the old racial order (Mbembe: 17–18). Notions of diversity and multiculturalism will disrupt the order of loss that Alloune had to deal with on Gorée, with its museum of the ugly history of the slave trade—a fossil, if ever. And they will disrupt Hassan's assurances of the hatred for Africans felt by African Americans, since Karim is not only not-"white," but light; also African, but not Black African. And Amaralis, who begins their relationship by showing him the tattoo on her buttock, will also expose her losses to him, in order that they might forge a new bridge, a new future.

The underside of the city, its trash, its detritus, its televised stories of death and difference, present what Hannah Arendt would see as also offering a new moment (*The Human Condition* 1958), creating the positive possibilities of confronting time. Time in Africa meets time in New York, and anticipates not a repetition of loss, but a possibility of resistance to its order. Globalization from below reinscribes modernity with a reconfiguration of difference that takes its distance from the dead plantations and their inhuman order.

II. Loss

Loss in *Little Senegal* is a function of the past, the historical account of slavery and its haunting of the present (Parham 2009). And it is a function of a present that has become detached from the past, as in the lives of people who have migrated abroad, gradually losing touch with their homeland, and suffering abuse from the local people. They are forced to focus on merely surviving, often reduced to the circumstances of bare life; if not as *homo sacer*, nonetheless reduced in circumstance to bare existence (Weheliye 2014). What sense would it make to ask the inmates of the concentration camps about their past, the times when their lives had been reduced to such minimal elements? To view life in the ghetto, for Jew or for Black Man, as bare life would be to remove from the survivors any possibility for a future—for an experience of time.

Carol Reed ends *The Third Man* (1949) with a final long tracking shot of Anna, who never breaks stride and walks past Holly Martins. Vienna after the war had become the state of exception, home for those whose lives were so reduced they could not even be sacrificed, but merely die. The reference point for Agamben's *homo sacer* is the concentration camp; for Alloune it is the plantation.

Little Senegal doesn't erase the possibility of such loss because when Alloune shows up after his long trip across the ocean, passing through the stages that take him up north, we have tracked the historical path and carried its weight with him to the doorstep of Ida Robinson, who is now living close to the margins of an empty existence. Her daughter has died. Her granddaughter has run away. The shop provides her with a minimal existence; even the doorstep to her basement apartment has garbage strewn on the ground when she awakens in the morning and sets out to work. The question of loss, for her as for Hassan, is confronted in the immediacy of getting through the day and trying to earn enough to make it to the next one.

The life of the American Black is no longer circumscribed by the master of the plantation, or even by Mr. Charlie. In the Harlem of *Little Senegal*, no whites in any significant position appear on the streets to control the Black population. Rather, it is the everyday, banal, more distant reach of the television news that evokes the violent features built into the habitus. Two news reports provide answers to Ida's question to Alloune, after he has entered into her life and recounted the amazing story of their relationship and past history. "What's the use of the past?" she asks, as if playing the role of the modern father in *Keita, The Heritage of the Griot* (1995) who not only doesn't know the meaning of his name, but has no sense that his indifference to his great ancestors matters much in his urban setting. The griot's response would seem to inform every film in which Sotigui Kouyate plays his role; the role not only of the griot, the wise old figure of Afrique itself,[14] but more importantly, Sotigui Kouyaté himself, the tall, thin Black man in dreadlocks whose voice and stature transform his role into that of a supra-persona that signifies "a certain Africa." Even more, the roles continue to signify

Sotigui himself, his figure created across dozens of films, from *Les Noms n'habitent nulle part* to *London River* (2009) to Brook's *Mahabharata*, in which he played Bhishma as "the conduit of wisdom and memory who uses his power to choose the time of his own death to manipulate the outcome of the *Mahabharata's* great war" (Todd, 2010).[15]

No one has described better than his wife Esther Marty-Kouyaté the "Sotigui" he created for the screen and stage, his family, and the world. He embodies *une certaine Afrique* because in every generation the figures of Tierno Bokar return, that is, *les vieux* or elders in whose death a "veritable library" is lost. These are clichés, as is often the case with the very term "griot"[16] itself. But in his person, Sotigui managed to transform the cliché. Often seen carrying a briefcase, whose contents are never disclosed, it is, in fact, as if he is guardian of the elder's library that he will render periodically in saying or song. His wife paints that familiar picture in his obituary:

> Pour Sotigui l'art et la vie sont indissociables. Il vivait ainsi sa vie familiale et professionnelle. Les griots ont tant de connaissances dans un monde spirituel, dans celui des ancêtres et dans le monde concret que, pour eux il est naturel des tisser ces liens. C'est un enrichissement extraordinaire qu'ils nous transmettent alors. Sotigui, en sus de la tradition familiale des griots, était un "initié" de la nature qu'il considérait comme un maître.
>
> (For Sotigui art and life are indistinguishable. He lived this way as a family man and as a professional. The griots know so many in the spiritual world, in the world of the ancestors and in the concrete world, that for them it is natural to draw them together. It is an extraordinary enrichment that they transmit to us, thus. Sotigui, beyond his family tradition of griots, was an "initiate" into nature which he considered as a master).
>
> La rencontre avec Sotigui a changé ma vie. J'ignorais tout de l'Afrique que j'ai appris à connaître et à aimer au fil des ans. Quant à lui, sa formation dans la brousse le rapprochait de ce contact avec les éléments naturels que possèdent les montagnards suisses. C'est là, au bord d'un torrent, qu'il a ramassé les galets de Prospéro. Voir au-delà des apparences était l'une de ses facultés. Être disponible à accueillir ce qui se présente à nous chaque jour était sa devise. Je l'ai faite mienne.
>
> (The meeting with Sotigui changed my life. I was ignorant about everything concerning Africa, which I learned to know and love over the years. As for him, his training in the bush brought him into closer contact with natural elements, like Swiss mountain people. It is there, on the edge of a torrent, that he gathered the pebbles of Prospero [the wine of life]. Seeing beyond appearances was one of his faculties. To be available and gather up what each day offered us was his motto. I made it my own).

Her conclusion to this encomium demonstrates how she views his life as spanning two worlds:

> 'Sötigi' dans ma langue maternelle désigne des êtres exceptionnels et insaisissables qui proviennent d'un 'ailleurs' mal défini. Sotigui, pour qui le hasard n'existait pas, m'a dénommée Siraba : 'le grand Baobab', arbre sacré auprès duquel il a attaché ses racines en Europe. Nos enfants Mabô 'celui qui est sans pareil' et Yagaré 'l'adorée.'
>
> ('Sotigui' in my mother tongue designates exceptional individuals who cannot be categorized, and who come from an indefinable elsewhere. Sotigui, for whom chance did not exist, named me Siraba: 'the great baobab tree,' sacred tree to which he attached his roots in Europe. Our children Mabô 'he who is without parallel' and Yagaré 'the adored one').[17]

Ida Robinson might have penned the same words, in her own way—if he had stayed. The meeting with Sotigui—Alloune in this version—changed her life, as it was supposed to. But the change to her life had to be set against what encompassed her world, and the key moments that we saw being mediated by the TV accounts of the deaths of Amadou Diallo and James Byrd.

On February 4th, 1999, Diallo was fired at 41 times by four New York policemen. The insignificance of the figure he cut—a poor African, reduced in his circumstances, trying to survive on street hawking, and finally killed as he held out a black wallet in the dark doorway entrance to a Bronx apartment—ensured that the four policemen who killed him would not be held accountable for his murder. The television on which this report was made is placed against the wall, appearing between Alloune and Ida as they sit at their dinner table.

FIGURE 6.2 TV report on death of Amadou Diallo

As the camera cuts to Ida's face and then Alloune's, we hear the plain reporting in the background as she looks at him. He looks down. She, "You're sad." A pause. He, rising, "I have to go home." She looks at him with some alarm as he leaves without another word.

The narrative focus on the slave ship, the plantations, the ancestors, the cemetery, the sleuthing leading to the details of their distant family tie, the sense of an amazing discovery of a long lost relative, all of that is lost in Harlem as the immediacy of the threat faced by Blacks in the U.S. comes to the fore. This loss, a refocusing, is repeated later in the film when Alloune is looking for Hassan, who has died in a confrontation with Eileen's friends along the Riverside Drive underpass.

In a second news report Alloune intently watches the story about the killing of James Byrd, another Black man, by three white racists. The report shows prosecutors holding up the chain that held Byrd as he was dragged behind a pickup to his death.

FIGURE 6.3   TV report on death of James Byrd

The account of Byrd's horrific brutal death is conveyed in the reporter's flat words as the TV is seen in the foreground, centered, demanding his full attention. The image on the screen shows a man holding up the chain used to hold Byrd. Alloune sees the chain, and behind the screen the railing to the street, like bars.

The role Alloune had been playing as guide to the horrors of the past is now returned to him as he watches the screen. His unease could be seen as arising from his having minimized the violence and racism of the present in his obsession with a griotic construction of the past. The present returns to him like a trauma that he had felt as if at a distance—as if it haunted the past. His growing proximity to his relatives, finding Eileen for Ida, intervening in their family and finally joining it, is all dropped as he leaves Ida to go "home." He sets out presumably to reestablish his contact with Hassan, and failing that, with his home in Africa, taking the body of his nephew with him.

The main players, Alloune and Ida, remain in Harlem for the moment, but the moment can't hold. With Hassan's death Alloune relegates his relationship with Ida and her family to the background, and tells her he must return home. Home is no longer with the distant family, but with the present one: with all those in Dakar for whom Hassan would have been a son, lost son, distant son.

The shift in narrative focus generates a tension in changing this story from the improbable love tale to one of a violent street killing. We pass from joining two worlds together to one that again separates the Dioula family from distant relatives—restoring the distance, once again, through violence. Thus Blackness and Race are displaced to some location where the control over the narrative slips out of the hands of the principal narrator, passing from the words of the griot, the curator, the archivist, now to those of the reporter: he died, a terrible death, far from his family—the story of those like Diallo, Byrd, and Hassan.

If anything, now, Alloune has become prepared to actually understand the responses of the Black American women in the fort in Gorée who had reacted so emotionally in the face of his demonstration of the same instruments of torture. From the slave fort to the plantations to the streets of New York, and finally back to Gorée where we see the mound of dirt under which Hassan lies buried—Alloune has moved from confronting death and pain in the past to the iteration of racial hatred and violence in the present. Africa no longer meets America in this sequence, but rather racialized violence takes charge of the narrative, pushing the rest to the background.

The question at the outset of this analysis was what did it mean that Alloune set out to reconnect with his long-lost relatives; that he sought to reunite the broken ties, broken by the forces of slavery and the Middle Passage, and then to reknot those ties with a loving relationship with Ida. But the death of Hassan made his project appear illusory, and force him to rethink what constituted his world. The key moment where we see that return to confronting the immediacy of loss is in the morgue that contains the remains of Hassan.

Karim comes to Alloune immediately after Alloune has seen the television report on Byrd, to inform Alloune of Hassan's death. In the sequence that follows one might argue that Alloune shifts into the figure of "Sotigui." Alloune appears in the morgue watching the body of Hassan on the metal table, covered with a sheet. Behind him there are dark spaces; to his right, with more than half of the shot, is a brightly lit wall containing plastic containers. The antiseptic scene of death in the modern hospital is placed against the darkness underlying the scene of the death of a relative, one who had said to his uncle, I am your family, not her; and, in his bitterness, you are not my family any more. As Alloune slowly places his hand on Hassan's head, standing quietly while he looks down, he carries with him all the weight of the tale of misery he had recounted about the runaway slaves, as if from a distance, in the slave fort. We might have expected a tight close-up, dramatic music, but instead there is stillness. We cut immediately to a shot that evokes the transformation of Alloune, not unlike that moment that conveys the fall of El Hadj in *Xala*, when he learns of his financial crash at the bank and descends with the elevator.

Here the elevators' walls are bare and plain. The flat noise of its mechanism encases Alloune whom we now see in a medium shot, looking off slightly to the side. The texture of the elevator walls, marked by coats of paint in the dim light, frames his desolation as if holding him painfully in place, conveying all that this trip back to the United States, to its violence and now conveyances of death, implies, leaving us face to face with Sotigui Kouyate. Not the griot who always tells us that "les morts ne sont pas morts," but rather that another one of us is lost, and maybe he could have done more to stop it. The shot in that elevator lasts about 21 seconds, and the sound lasts for what seems like an eternity with the small audible effects of its clanging, jarring movements and stopping. He looks off. Cut to a framed window in a doorway, behind which Eileen is seen being questioned by the police as Ida comes hurrying up. The framed shot echoes the framed door of no return, and the twin movements of both stories, both families, Alloune's and Ida's, seem to lead us to a final rupture.

FIGURE 6.4 Eileen being questioned

Ida doesn't appear at Hassan's funeral. Rather it is Karim and Amaralis for whom this occasion will lead to a fresh start after Alloune leaves in the hearse. The words to the Negro spiritual intone "wounded and still" as we see Hassan's African girlfriend Biram in black walking off alone. The hearse pulls up at the newsstand and Alloune gets out. Ida looks up at him, sighs, "You're leaving me? Why do you have to leave me?" He responds, "I'm taking my nephew home." Eileen appears, he puts his hand on her cheek. We cut to the ferry boat, Sotigui sitting on its white plastic benches, alone in the interior of that tourist boat. The break between the two shots is made immediate, restoring the immense distance with which the film began when we looked out across the ocean.

Back in Gorée, Alloune appears at Hassan's grave, and then inside the fort. Looking through a rectangular window, like the frame of the door and window through which Eileen had appeared at the police station, Alloune watches another guide give the same spiel he had given before about the ball and chain. He stands against a dark brown wall, rough in texture, speckled with bits of light, appearing somber, and turns to look out the door of no return. We look out at the sea, the boat, and then at a dark brown wall and door that opens. Ida comes through to open her shop, rubbing her hands in the cold. In close up we see Alloune staring as if seeing her. Then the boat, the door giving on to the empty sea, and the griot is gone.

Sotigui has disappeared into this story, finally. Leaving us, not with a happy knotting of the past and the present, but with the fuller sense of loss he alone knew how to carry in his expression and gestures, in the deepening of his role that required infinite sadness, and infinite invention, to combat the work of racializing bodies and compelling them to become enslaved persons. At the end of one film we might find him rejoicing in how his stories will save some lost soul. In another, he presents a worn figure of care that has to face death on the screen, in the hard city streets, in the family. Brook had seen in him something extraordinary—we can say something special, but not in its difference. His gestures, in placing his hand on Eileen's face, on Hassan's grave, are completed with the last shot of his face looking out at the sea, across the sea.

FIGURE 6.5 Alloune/Sotigue Kouyaté

Notes

1 Lindiwe Dovey gave me permission to print this affirmation based on my memory of her comment. Sotigui is an "icon" for many. Here is Josef Gugler's statement: "[*Little Senegal*] features Sotigui Kouyaté, a veritable African icon now lost to us, who previously gave body and life to Dani Kouyaté 's *Keïta! The Heritage of the Griot* (1995) in the role of a griot who introduces a boy to the *Sundjata*" (Gugler 2010: 5).

In example after example, the trope of the griot as representing "authenticity" is repeated. Another example: "The griot character symbolizes African traditions and customs and the continent's rich cultural heritage. His role is played by the famous Sotigui Kouyaté; a real Malian-Burkinabé griot, who during his life was hailed as one of the most significant contributors to West African cultural heritage (Guttman, 2001)" (Lensu 2016: 17).

Another example of the "authenticating" approach: "Through selecting him as his [sic] film griot, director Loreau both acknowledges and addresses the lack of meaningful exchange between Africa and Europe in terms of economy, culture, social realities, and of course migration. Furthermore, by situating the griot in the location of Brussels, Loreau allows for a traveler who is not blinded by stereotypes and able to carry back the messages into the South that otherwise never get out or get di storted along the way. With the inclusion of *a real life griot, rather than letting an actor perform the part,* Loreau furthermore acknowledges her limited access to the cultural context of her film" (Hoffman 2010: 37, my italics).

2 Also see Guttman 2001.

3 http://spot.pcc.edu/~mdembrow/sia.htm.

4 For Glissant or Stuart Hall this adherence to a foundational or originary past represents a closed notion of being that eschews the openness of becoming. Any subjectivity is composed of both sides to the ontology of "Afrticanness," or better still for Glissant, Caribbean identity—*L'Antillantité*.

5 "While many visitors to Africa have been to Gorée Island in Senegal, described as a site where as many as 20 million Africans were fattened for shipment across the Atlantic Ocean from the Slave House after being shackled there in dank cells, Curtin debunked the traditional account, stating that "[t]he whole story is phony". Curtin stated that the Slave House, one of the most beautiful houses on the island, would not have been used for storing slaves, that the rocks near the shore would make docking boats perilous and estimated that a total of no more than 50,000 slaves had passed through the island. Senegalese academics criticized Curtin's statement, stating that he was guilty of "stealing their history" (https://military-history.fandom.com/wiki/Philip_D._Curtin). See Murphy, John. "Senegal Slave House's past questioned", *The Seattle Times*, July 17, 2004. Accessed June 16, 2009.

6 This restoration of the family and community is a major theme of Dyana Gaye's *Des Etoiles* (2013), where the contemporary diaspora covers three continents.

7 This chapter was originally being penned in 2018 when I learned Ndiaye had died in 2009 (https://www.nytimes.com/2009/02/19/world/africa/19ndiaye.html).

8 "Although this fact has always been denied, Euro-American discourse on man depends on the two central figures of Blackness and Race" (Mbembe 2017: 6).

9 http://www.telegraph.co.uk/news/obituaries/5837059/Philip-Curtin.html; http://articles.chicagotribune.com/2004-07-27/news/0407270330_1_senegal-region-slave-trade-goree-island

"Curtin's assessment is widely shared by historians, including Abdoulaye Camara, curator of the Goree Island Historical Museum, a 10-minute walk from the House of Slaves. The House of Slaves, said Camara, offers a distorted account of the island's history and was created with tourists in mind. No one is quite sure where the House of Slaves got its name, but Camara and Curtin credit Boubacar Joseph Ndiaye, the House of Slaves' curator since the 1960s, with promoting it as a tourist attraction.

Boubacar Joseph Ndiaye is famous in Senegal for offering thousands of visitors chilling details of the squalid conditions of the slaves' holding cells, the chains used to shackle them and the walk through the door of no return.

Tour guide vs. historian

'Joseph Ndiaye offers a strong, powerful, sentimental history. I am a historian. I am not allowed to be sentimental,' Camara said.

But Camara said he thinks Ndiaye has played an important role in offering the descendents of slaves an emotional shrine to commemorate the sacrifices of their ancestors.

'The slaves did not pour through that door. The door is a symbol. The history and memory needs to have a strong symbol,' he said. 'You either accept it or you don't accept it. It's difficult to interpret a symbol.'"

10 This is the subject of Toni Morrison's wonderful novel *A Mercy* (2008).

11 Mbembe quotes Foucault on these two terms. "If the fossil is 'what permits resemblances to subsist throughout all the deviations traversed by nature," and functions primarily "as a distant and approximative form of identity," the monster, in contrast "provides an account, as though in caricature, of the genesis of differences" (cited in Mbembe 2017: 18). Mbembe claims that "Blackness" represented a "synthesis of these two figures" (2017: 18).

12 Mbembe on how the term "nègre" was taken up by Senghor and Césaire, and the work it was intended to perform. In writing about this, he turns to the term Black, which, along with race, is the focus on his book *A Critique of Black Reason* (2017)—the title of which is a writing back to Kant, Hegel, and Spivak.

> Some of those who were enclosed in the nickname [Black, and implicitly in this paragraph nègre]—and who, in consequence, were placed *apart* or to the side—have, at certain moments in history, ended up inhabiting it. The name 'Black' (Nègre) has passed into common use. But does that make it more authentic? Some, in a conscious gesture of reversal that at times is poetic and carnivalesque, inhabit this name only to rebel against its inventors and its reviled heritage as a symbol of abjection. They instead transform the name into a symbol of beauty and pride and use it as a sign of radical defiance, a call to revolt, desertion, or insurrection. As a historical category, Blackness exists only within these three moments: of attribution, of return and internalization, and of reversal or overthrow. The latter inaugurates the full and unconditional recuperation of the status of the human, which irons and the whip had long denied.
>
> *(47)*

13 This history is reproduced in Mostefa Djadjam's *Frontières* (2001).

14 In David Diop's poem "Afrique mon Afrique," he sings of the proud warriors from the ancestral savana, and most of all of that which his grandmother sings.

15 "His 18 films included collaborations with the directors Thomas Gilou (*Black Mic Mac*, 1986), Cheick Oumar Sissoko (*La Genèse*, 1999), Amos Gitai (*Golem, Spirit of Exile*, 1992), Stephen Frears (*Dirty Pretty Things*, 2002) and Kouyaté's son Dani (*Keita, Heritage of the Griot*, 1994). He was the subject of the documentary film *Sotigui Kouyaté, a Modern Griot* by Mahamat-Saleh Haroun (1996), which followed him on a journey back to Burkina Faso. In *London River* (his second film with Rachid Bouchareb, after 2001's *Little Senegal*) he played a French Muslim father seeking his son, who is missing after the July 2005 terror attacks in London. He described the film as being 'made by love'. The performance earned him the best actor prize at the 2009 Berlin film festival" (Todd, 2010).

See also http://lavoixdugriot.blogspot.com/2011/12/sotigui-kouyate-raconte-par-son-epouse.html

16 Sometimes clichés are grounded in real figures, as griots continue to exist in various caste roles in society; but their functions and the societies for which they were formed are gone, so griots are not mutated forms of their previous roles. Some can play this role for a public, as we see in the very first African film to incorporate the figure of that praise-singer who profits from those whose praises he sings ("Borom Sarret"). In others like *Keita, The Heritage of the Griot* we have a figure playing for an extroverted public, as Eileen Julien might have put it. See Cornelia Panzacchi, "The Livelihoods of Traditional Griots in Modern Senegal," *Africa* 64, no. 2, 1994: 190–210.

17 http://lavoixdugriot.blogspot.com/2011/12/sotigui-kouyate-raconte-par-son-epouse.html Accessed February 29, 2018.

7

FRAMING MODERNITY ABROAD

Ije: the Journey (2010) and *Mother of George* (2013)

Kenneth W. Harrow

Modern cinema. To take us into the current period of African cinema in a global age, we can carry on the earlier comparison of the auteur film *Chocolat* (1988) with the Nollywood film *Living in Bondage* (1992) by considering two Nigerian films, *Ije: The Journey* (2010) and *Mother of George* (2013), which both appeared in the second decade of the 21st century. Their appearance has to be framed by the new digital universe created by major platforms: "As of March 31, 2022, Netflix had over 221.6 million subscribers worldwide, including 74.6 million in the United States and Canada, 74.0 million in Europe, the Middle East and Africa, 39.9 million in Latin America and 32.7 million in Asia-Pacific" (CEO: North America 2022).

Netflix's expansion into the international market, beginning with Canada in 2010, rapidly grew in September of 2011 as it reached to over 40 countries in Latin America and the Caribbean regions. By the end of 2012 it was streaming in the United Kingdom, Ireland, Denmark, Finland, Norway, and Sweden, and the following year the Netherlands. More of Europe followed in 2014, and Australia and New Zealand were included in March of 2015. Then East Asia began in the fall of 2015 with Japan. By 2017 it was operating in over 190 countries (Brennan, "How Netflix Expanded to 190 Countries in 7 years"),[1] including much of Africa. The growth was vertiginous, the changes monumental for cinema.

As of May 29, 2022, *Ije: the Journey* was streaming on Amazon Prime and Netflix. *Mother of George* was streaming on a dozen platforms, including Amazon Prime, Hulu, Apple TV, etc.

Genevieve Nnaji's *Ije* (2010) intrigued me in my attempt to ask how framing in cinema can be linked to framing in special relativity. Special

DOI: 10.4324/9781003397595-10

relativity posits the notion that the measurement of time and mass change with motion. If we designate a train station as the inertial location and the train as the moving object, from the point of view of the observer on the station platform as the train speeds up the length of objects on the train contracts and the mass becomes denser while the clock measuring time on the platform shows more time elapsing than does the clock on the train. On the train that moves, the speed creates "dilation" of time and "contraction of length." We cannot observe these changes without fairly subtle instruments, although when traveling by airplane there are clocks now with adequate precision to note the dilation of time.

Similarly, the issue of spacetime being four-dimensional (time being the fourth dimension, when added to our normally perceived three dimensions of space) again precludes our physical ability to perceive its dimensionality. Our thinking about space and time can no longer be what it was before 1905 when Einstein published his first papers on relativity and changed our thinking about space and time. The common "classical" notion since Newton was that space and time were objective entities whose reality exists independent of our locations, movement, or observations. With Einstein we begin to think of our location as the point where a frame of reference is constructed. Our observations do not correspond to those whose frames of reference are in motion relative to ours. Any question of frames—in cinema as in physics—must begin with this question of how they are relative to other frames. What is our motion with relation to theirs, our measurement of time with relation to theirs, our point of reference with respect to theirs?

For this section there are at least two intersecting frames to consider in *Ije*, and to compare with those of *Mother of George* (Dosunmu 2013). A relativity approach would entail placing each frame in relation to another. The first two frames that present themselves to us in *Ije: The Journey* (2010) are the African and the Western, specifically those of the Nigerian Igbo and the Southern Californian American setting. In *Mother of George* an attempt to construct a reading of the characters along similar lines will depend on the category of modernity, so that we can place Ayodele's mother into a familiar location of one with the "traditional" perspective, and her daughter-in-law Adenike (Nike) and especially her friend Sade as marked by the "modern," although it might be better to say that Sade is closest to the modern figure and that Nike moves in her direction. Similarly, if Ma Ayo is traditional, Ayo moves gradually in the direction of modernity, slowly following after the path of his wife.[2]

I. *Ije* (2010)

The two central locations of Africa and the U.S. in *Ije* are relatively vexed, as are any that purport to inhabit a place called modern, perhaps the most illegitimate of terms popularly used in the West. I will continue to use these two terms as if under erasure, and understood as having been grounded in colonial discourse: "traditional" and "modern" function as broadly as opposing perspectives that are used to construct some "world" or universe, or horizon of expectations. They inevitably are intended to normalize an order, and that order and its codes can be read in the ways the characters and readers perceive and structure their physical and moral universes.

The African scenes are relatively few and brief in *Ije*. They function with clear purposes, and create cinematic worlds that are familiar and relatively stereotypical. The film opens with the two sisters Chioma and Anya running through a field that bears little resemblance to the tropical location of eastern Nigeria dubbed Igboland where they hail from. Their "foreignness"—or indigeneity, depending on your frame—is established by their use of Igbo, and by the drums and music that awaken in Anya the desire to become a singer. Verisimilitude is not a terribly important issue, especially as the Western audience would not notice any discrepancies (at the time of my original writing about it, 2018, the film was accessible on Netflix, whose audience was predominantly Western). The elements of the frame appear with Anya's desire to be a singer from her earliest days despite the opposition of her father who wants her simply to be a farmer like him. The images of the "peasant" African village are built around her singing and her domineering father.

The village is invaded by a crazed militia, in the style of *Blood Diamonds* (2006). Anya is about to be raped when her father saves her and kills her aggressor. These scenes really don't deepen conventional portrayals of the pastoralism of "natural" Africa and the brutal violence of the men wielding machetes.

We jump fairly quickly to Los Angeles, where the setting is equally reductive. We learn Anya has become the wife of a white music producer Michael who is managing her career. The one key scene in their home involves two young men who are gambling with Michael, an occasion marked by drugs, alcohol, and violence. If Africa is constructed from the distance of Hollywoodian cliches, California is equally constructed from Global or African TV cliches, and the violent, misogynist, macho images of dispossession and domination in both locales, intended to convey "Africa" and "America," override their superficial difference.

Crossing the gap between these two cine-scapes is Anya's banker sister, Chioma, who has now become an adult, no longer ensconced in the village, and who conveys the image of the successful modern African woman. She is forced to travel to Los Angeles to save her sister when Anya is arrested for killing three men, including Michael and his two musician friends. Our first sight of the adult Chioma, coming to the rescue, is in an airplane as the flight attendant instructs her to bring her seat up for landing. On the ground, she is singled out by the customs officials, ostensibly because she appears African, despite her passport and visa all being in order.

When she visits Anya in prison, they speak Igbo, and pretend to carry out rituals before the wary eyes of the guard so as to be able to get close to each other. But despite their role-playing as "traditional Africans," Anya also embodies the attributes of modernity and the power it confers. She has enough money to pay for a hotel, has enough psychological command of her relations with her lawyer and the district attorney to manage them. She deals capably with a mugging, an ugly scene of American street violence, and manages to ward off racist attacks to which she is subjected from her first encounters in the airport in the States. She is the bridge between the two cinematic worlds of Nollywood and Hollywood, and further to the point, is herself played by the Nigerian star Genevieve Nnaji. In the film she is a banker from Lagos now, not a girl from the village. In Nollywood terms she is "modern."

That axis of Africa/America,[3] or even Black/white, is crossed by another meeting between Africa and the United States, which is the African American dimension. Chioma's lawyer is a handsome young African American Jalen (Larry Ulrich), who is suave and heartfelt. He periodically speaks on the phone with his mother from the South. He and Chioma soon develop a relationship, and both are seen as subject to varying degrees of racism, like that which Chioma experiences from her Korean hotel proprietor and her son, who actually mugs her. Jalen meanwhile is subject to the scornful barbs of his firm's partner, a white female attorney whose "worldwise" attitude is marked by her gratuitous denigrations of him.

Jalen agrees to take Anya's case and, helped by Anya's own eloquent self-defense, wins her release. If there had been no African component or scenes in the film, the American racial axis would have overdetermined all of the meanings that emphasize white supremacism, demonstrated throughout by signs of wealth and its influence in the judicial system, and by black struggles for equity. There is really no larger context within which to set the action or characters: they are relatively stock figures whose dialogue is predictable. Yet, when set against the African scenes, they change the contours of the genre in unpredictable ways.

When Chioma first goes to the Los Angeles mansion that George and Anya lived in, the music and camera create a spooky setting so that when the inquisitive little girl from next door is flushed out and flees, the scene edges on the esoteric corners of Nollywood horror films. Later the neighbor's Mexican domestic helper is introduced, first as a mysterious presence unseen during the night of the murders, and then as extra help at Michael's parties. She is working in the States without papers and is thus the double of Anya's and Chioma's presence as foreigners working in the

States. She testifies to Anya's participation in Michael's parties, with her having sex with his guests, drinking or sniffing cocaine. These depictions of Hollywood wealth and corruption work as counterpoints to the scene of destruction of Anya and Chioma's village by the half-mad armed militia. The forced attempts to create equivalencies, such as the imprisonment of Anya and her treatment in prison with the racist treatment Chioma receives on arriving in the States, seen in cross-cutting scenes, generates a set of frames with no effective differences in motions within the frames or between them. The cast of ethnic characters, the commenting on accents and hair-scarf styles, the correction of spelling of names, and so on create a sense of multinational and multiethnic presences, we could say for "world cinema-lite," but the weakness of the script pulls us away from any meaningful engagement between competing frames. Africa's construction as Other is artificially pressed, so that the pressing more than the frame moves to the fore.

After being mugged, Chioma leaves the Korean hotel where she first lodged and spends the night at Jalen's. That night she dreams her sister enters the room. The coloring and lighting create an eerie atmosphere. Anya points a gun at Chioma who then wakes up. In the following scene Jalen is going through the police report, a phone to his ear, papers and books on the table in front of him. Nighttime Nollywoodian drama; daytime LA murder trial movie. Melodramatic Nollywood images abound, as when Anya reconstitutes the scene of the murder.

- I didn't want him to die.

FIGURE 7.1 Anya in *Ije*

The question of how we are to understand the creation of cinematic time under these circumstances seems tied directly to the question of genres, and particular to the meta-generic question of how the genre itself is being framed. There are numerous moments where the representation of the act of reportage, as with the TV scenes witnessed by Anya in prison or by Chioma and Jalen, create a meta-frame level. These are complemented with photos of Michael and Anya, and scenes based on memories of the two Nigerian girls in the past. We continually hold to both the time frame of the acts that led to Anya shooting the men, and then to her imprisonment and trial; and then to Chioma's arrival and intervention to save her sister. The breaks in setting and temporality never interfere with the "arrow of time," where we know what happens and when and where. The linear direction of time passing is never lost. The world of this film is so heavily overdetermined by the generic features that the pressures of relativity to construct meaningful relations around difference are never realized. *Ije, the Journey* remains static.

Modernity and tradition are familiar cinematic constructs in African cinema. The tropes used in Hollywood or Western spectacles are not the same as those used in Nollywood, or its commercial equivalents elsewhere on the continent. In *Ije* they generate a soap opera feel, which supplants the conventional temporalities associated with modernity and tradition. Where we have sophisticated representations of the encounter between Africa and African-America, America, or Europe, as in the films with Sotigui Kouyate, like *Little Senegal* (2000) or *Les Noms n'habitent nulle part* (1994), *Des Etoiles* (Dyana Gaye, 2013), or *Mother of George* (2013), *Ije* provides a foil to their dialectical constructions of time and space. Despite the settings in different continents, *Ije* remains in the inertial frame of the station, with no train setting out. It constructs and belongs to a cinematic time generated by its commercial genre qualities, reducing all notions of difference to external, cliched qualities, tropes ultimately of sameness. Although *Mother of George* is set entirely in Brooklyn, it successfully constructs the differences of modernity and tradition that *Ije* failed to build upon, and as a result can pose questions about temporality.

The linearity of temporality is overdetermined by genre in *Ije*, despite the inclusion of racial concerns. In that regard, it can be said not to function with Epiphenomenal time (Wright 2015: 4) but rather the "arrow of time" in which the trajectory of time from the past to the present to the future is linear. Blackness is slotted into non-coeval temporality, where the past means underdeveloped, and where the present means modern. These are the conventions of racial parameters that determine Wright's distinction between spacetime when placed into a linear progress narrative. That is the narrative that underlies Chioma's transportation from Igboland to Southern California. We don't escape the present, determined by the plot that moves all the action into the framework of the trial, its uncovering of evidence and actions in the past, and the outcome when the trial is completed. The present, the "now," is cinematically determined, both in Africa where the girls' past is presented so as to explain how they arrived at the present, and in the United States where the movement of the trial is joined to Jalen's intervention. We are always made aware of the present by the unfolding of the past. In that sense, we do not stand in a present moment outside of these two frames, "Africa" and "America," to unsettle the linearity. In contrast, an epiphenomenal perspective would disrupt the logic of modernity by the introjection of the black historical spacetime.

"'Epiphenomenal' time denotes the current moment, a moment that is *not* directly borne out of another (i.e., causally created)" (Wright: 4). More specifically Wright argues that:

> Epiphenomenal time does not preclude any and all causality: only a *direct*, or *linear*, causality. In other words, the current moment, or 'now,' can certainly correlate with other moments, but one cannot argue that it is always already the effect of a specific, previous moment.
>
> *(Wright: 4)*

The definition of race that drives *Ije* is as straightforward as the crosscutting scenes that situate Chioma within the gaze of the customs officials while her sister is incarcerated: a certain definition of black guilt is attributed in all cases. They conform to the collective identity that Western spacetime narratives assume. It limits Blackness to a direct identity that emerges from a determined past. That precludes Epiphenomenal time. Thus, Wright writes:

> While the linear progress narrative is an invaluable tool for located Blackness, when used alone its very spaciotemporal properties preclude a wholly *inclusive* definition of Blackness, yielding one that is necessarily inaccurate. By contrast, Epiphenomenal time enables a wholly inclusive definition (appropriate to any moment at which one is defining Blackness.
>
> *(Wright: 4)*

The linearity will be disrupted by the moment of interpretation of Epiphenomenal space time (Wright: 5). The disruptions of *Mother of George* (201) can serve as the foil to the linearity of *Ije*.

II. *Mother of George* (2013)

Mother of George (Dosunmu 2013) carries the motifs of "Borom Sarret" to a considerably higher, more complex level than *Ije*, but the "coordinates" that define the frame within which the action is carried out can be tracked back to Sembène's "ur-film," not to mention Fanon's division of colonial space between those of the colonizer and the colonized—the Plateau and the quartier (*Wretched of the Earth*, 1961).

There are many ways to build an analysis of this film, but if we stay within the major perimeters of "Borom Sarret" and *Ije*, we could begin with a notion of an Old Africa and a New Africa, terms that actually do date to the colonial period when the New African Woman and New African Man appeared in the discourses of the times.[4] The colonialists found the "New" in models they sought to lay out for their subjects who undertook the paths of assimilation (Mbembe 2017: 87–88). Although there were many paths, many variants, one fundamental feature of the "New" was "modernity." The parameters of modernity are too familiar to require any detailed enumeration: speaking the European language, dressing and eating in a European manner, working in an occupation that would fit into the colonial economy. Images and concepts of motion were also common, with life in the city moving more quickly than in the village. This goal is realized by Hampaté Bâ's Wangrin, who buys a fast sedan and races down the country roads. Time was measured in the coffee spoonfuls of a moneyed economy, and the slim possibilities of having recourse to the colonial legal system. Pushing back with the master's own tools (see Birago Diop's *La Plume raboutée* [1978]). A look, an accent. Markers of power, and increased means of control over one's life: an agency inseparable from Frenchness or Englishness.[5]

Mbembe's definition of the historical origins of modernity was succinct. Following the struggle for life, it emerges from the (European colonial) principle of "elimination, segregation, and purification within society" (2017: 54). He continues, "'Modernity' is in reality just another name for the European project of unlimited expansion undertaken in the final years of the eighteenth century" (54). With this expansion, conquest, and occupation that followed came the ideological complement: European liberalism, underlying "such questions as universalism, individual rights, the freedom of exchange, the relationship between ends and means, the national community and political capacity, international justice," and most tellingly, "the nature of the relationship between Europe and extra-European worlds" (54). From the colonial notions of that relationship emerged the "non-coeval" temporalities that Fabian attacks in his critique of anthropology.

Set within the narrow world of Brooklyn, *Mother of George* (2013) frames its drama around the emergence of a wife, Nike, who fails to become pregnant after marrying Ayodele. What unfolds bears the consequences of the "entry into modernity" that carries with it all the weight of its historical framing, visible at the outset of African cinema with Sembène's "Borom Sarret."

In "Borom Sarret" the cartman lives on the periphery of the "European" world in the quartier (which he calls mon village). He is paid in coin, but loses his livelihood when he comes too close to the neighborhood of the white man, the Plateau. This is the spatial division in Dakar, and is replicated throughout colonial Africa. In *Ije* Anya appears on the TV screen, is married to a music agent, and lives in a mansion—but, like the "Borom Sarret," is endangered as when she comes too close to the European "Plateau." Her accent remains. She sees her role as that of the migrant who hopes to make it big, but who misreads her husband's intents towards her, and fails to enter autonomously into the world of the rich and powerful white entrepreneurs. In fact, her story is marked by her degradation, due largely to her willingness to serve her husband's commands. She has no community of support, only one sister in Nigeria who must travel a great distance to California to help. When Anya is put on trial for murdering her husband, she is incapable of defending herself, until her African American lawyer gives her voice so that she could appeal to an American jury for sympathy. She presents herself as a poor African girl who barely escaped from African militia rapists, only to fall into the wrong hands in the States.

In both "Borom Sarret" and *Ije*, the lines delineating the Old Africa and the New World are starkly cast, especially as the "modern" and powerful world of California is used to as the site of the New. The past appears in an indefinite spacetime located back in Anya's and Chioma's childhood. There is no present moment for Africa in *Ije*. Or rather, the present begins as Chioma disembarks from the airplane in LAX, and encounters the various airport guards, who treat her as a suspect. Modernity is thus a gated community with its guards at the border who treat Black people largely with disdain throughout.[6]

As Mbembe puts it, in explicating this forging of a "modern" world, it is the role that race plays that provides the basis for its superstructure:

In many ways our world remains a 'world of races,' whether we admit it or not. Although this fact is often denied, the racial signifier is still in many ways the inescapable language for the stories people tell about themselves, about their relationships with the Other, about memory, and about power. Our critique of modernity will remain incomplete if we fail to grasp that the coming of modernity coincided with the appearance of the *principle of race* and the latter's slow transformation into the privileged matrix for techniques of domination, yesterday as today.

(55)

The workings of this transformation depend upon the body, on embodiment, which is where *Mother of George* begins. "In order to reproduce itself, the principle of race depends on an assemblage of practices whose immediate and direct target is the body of the Other and whose scope is life in general" (Mbembe: 55). Mbembe continues, stating that the pregnant body multiplies this targeting, this "transcription of race" (Mbembe: 55). The Black body as modern encounters the whiteness of culture and style when set against the traditional/old/authentic. Africa returns this framing, even in the diaspora, when the notion of a traditional culture, with its images of the Igbo woman, the Yoruba man, the traditional marriage, etc., are imported. The techniques of domination are always more powerful when implicit, and modernity's implicit presence permeates the scenes set in Los Angeles or Brooklyn, just as Africa's traces are continually interlaced into the culturalized settings. Even the languages play this function, as if the history of the *civilisés* and their mastery of the European tongue were inescapable.

Colonialism provides terribly limited frames of separation on which to build a plot involving the old and the new, change, and biopower. The colonial imaginary was bounded by the geographical no-man's-land that separated the "quartier" or the village from the city, the "Plateau." The same space divided the white man from the black man, the white woman from the black woman. The language, the economic order, the crude abusive policemen or racist figures of authority offer no opening for trajectories outside those constrained by the colonial context. And that includes those regions between the two geographical centers, like that between the "African" Medina in Dakar and the white Plateau, where the Cap Verdians came to live, a space that became known for its semi-legal status and prostitutes.

In *Mother of George* there are no race scenes: no whites, no police or judges, doctors, or lawyers whose skin color defines the roles as conveying superiority, or who are racially abusive. The setting is, in fact, Brooklyn, Norstrand Avenue, near the A and C lines that connect the local neighborhood with Manhattan.[7] When the rare white face appears, the cinematographer uses tone painting so as to largely match the skin shades of the Black figures, and the latter are almost entirely Nigerians. The story on which the film builds is an old, familiar one in the "Old Africa."[8] But the characters are immigrants; they work hard and live in New York, and share none of the complexes of those who come for the American dream, none of Adichie's "Americana" or *Ije*'s West Coast music business.

Ayo and his family run an African restaurant, which appears to be jammed with black clients. The restaurant is run by two brothers, Ayodele and Biyi, whose family is headed by their mother, Ma Ayo. As the story goes "at home," sometimes a wife cannot conceive, and when it appears that the woman is not the one "at fault," a substitute for the husband must be found. In this case the substitute is Biyi, thus keeping the child "within the family" whose "blood" is shared. Ayo, unaware of his mother's plan to resolve his wife's childless state in this way, has refused to accede to his wife's request to be tested in order to see who is the infertile one. He can't face the unpleasant possibility that he might be responsible for their failure to conceive. If that sterility were to be ascertained, he would gain nothing by taking a second wife; and he'd have no reason to refuse adoption. He would also face the kinds of pressures conventionally imagined as coming from "home" to allow another man to fill in for him.

"Home" here is associated with Yoruba ways, and the film's opening scenes of a traditional wedding frame the plot and the diegesis thus, despite the establishing shot being one of the subway stop, which places the location as Brooklyn. This is the home of a transplanted community, and as it code-switches between the native Englishes of Brooklyn, and Yoruba, we have a mélange of the two worlds—"mélange" more than "hybridity." When "home" values or sayings are needed, they tend to be voiced in Yoruba. When the immigrant's need is to stress what he or she is saying, it is usually in English, with a strong Nigerian accent. In fact, of all the major characters, only one, Nike's friend Sade, speaks without the Nigerian accent.[9] At no point is the Nigerian identity directly played off against an American White Otherness. The Black community contains all the Otherness, and its appearance arises not in identity difference but in the turn to the New, the Modern for difference—the world inhabited commonly by all New Yorkers who can have their own cultural ways without sacrificing the benefits of "modern medicine" or "modern" commerce. Whiteness is thus naturalized as modernity, and can function without any white characters or actors.

The failure of Adenike to conceive provides the plot with its drivers. When the problem first manifests itself, she is compelled to drink Ma Ayo's brews, but to no avail. She goes to a doctor, and is then faced with needing to pay for testing. As her husband balks at the expense, and the inevitably painful consequences, she feels forced to accept her mother-in-law's urging to procreate with her brother-in-law, Biyi. Biyi is the secret partner of Sade who is Adenike's best friend, and ultimately the solution advocated by her mother-in-law destroys the Biyi-Sade couple, the brothers' partnership, and almost wrecks Adenike and Ayo's marriage.

The men, Ayo and Biyi, are reduced to pitiful figures, while their women partners Sade and Adenike grow in stature and command. The men cannot resolve Ayo's impotence, and rather than a ritualized return to "traditional" cures for impotence, as we see at the end of *Xala* (1975), the old ways are seen as disastrous, while the ascendancy of the "New Woman" appears to indicate the right track needed for life in the New World—as in *Faat Kine* (2001). Ayo's mother belongs to another time and place—one that is outdated and distant.

The framing of Old and New has shifted here, with respect to "Borom Sarret" or *Ije*. It is as if another train, besides that constructed under the white man's whip in the Old Africa of colonial days, has taken off. The New York subway opened in 1904, and the BMT brought Brooklyn and Manhattan together. It grew enormously in the first part of the 20th century, a period during which Britain also consolidated its control over colonial North and South Nigeria. In 1901 Nigeria became a British protectorate. Lugard conquered and united the North and South during the years that the New York subway emerged into that of a large mass-transit system associated with modernity and great engineering feats. From 1895 to 1900 the British built the rail line from Ibadan to Lagos, opening it in 1901.[10] Telegraph lines appeared; a large harbor was created; the lineaments of a modern commercial center took shape: a state subject to governmentality along with extractive industries was created. As Lugard was endeavoring to take steps to usher in the modern colonial state, New York City became "modern":

> In 1895 New York City annexed the eastern Bronx. On January 1, 1898, the City of Brooklyn, Long Island City, and the towns and villages of western Queens and all of Richmond were replaced by the Boroughs of Brooklyn (Kings County), Queens (Queens County), and Richmond (Richmond County). With the Boroughs of Manhattan and The Bronx (New York County) they formed a new City of New York, briefly called "Greater New York." (Macy, "Before the Five-Borough City: The Old Cities, Towns, and Villages that Camer Together to Form 'Greater New York.')[11]

The comparison of the two worlds along the lines of music, styles of dress, and the construction of infrastructure, along with an urban landscape and new buildings, allows us to define the "civilized" aspect of modernity in both Lagos and New York. Worlds apart, they still followed the same trajectories of growth that would lead them each to become

FIGURE 7.2   New York, then. Source: Library of Congress, Prints & Photographs Division, Detroit Publishing Company Collection

FIGURE 7.3   Lagos, then. Balogun Ali Street, Lagos Island. Circa: 1900s. Source: *ASIRI Magazine* and Delcampe.Net

FIGURE 7.4 Nigeria, now. Contemporary street scene of Lagos. Photograph by Zouzou Wizman

FIGURE 7.5 2009 Atlantic Antic, at Atlantic Avenue and Court Street in Brooklyn, New York

megalopolises. It wasn't simply that their modernity was coeval, but that the pressures to form urban infrastructures would follow similar courses. Economic growth and social reproduction obeyed a logic that would lead each to recognize a certain compatibility of purpose and style, so that once the political exigencies of conquest were no longer dominant, the less militant aspects of cultural expression would find the spaces to emerge. Some were easily open to compatibility, like music. Some retained more local flavors, like food. Some responded to the basics, like having children, caring for parents, making a living, and satisfying sexual desires. Two different frames, but brought into a relationship when viewed through this optic of modernity.

From colonial picture postcards of naked African women, to postcard images of exotica in Africa, we pass to those wearing "traditional" dress compared with "hybrid" dress or "modern" dress—from colonial films of ethnographic peoples to Africa on the move to a changing Africa—from point O in the originary framing of Africa to point P of "how far Africa has come." All these images of change were figured in terms of motion, of advancing, of significations of modernity, just like the train from Lagos to Ibadan, or in New York the subway line from Brooklyn to Manhattan.[12] Modernity in the age of relativity is figured in motion as well as time: modern means of locomotion (Green-Simms, *Postcolonial Automobility*, 2017); modern infrastructure (Larkin, *Signal and Noise: Media, Infrastructure, and Urban Culture in Nigeria*, 2008); modernity and tradition (Comaroff and Comaroff, *Modernity and Its Malcontents*, 1993); and modern times (Fabian, *Time and the Other: How Anthropology Makes Its Object*, 1983; Chatterjee, *Our Modernity*, 1997).

In both locations modernity and its offers of access to power and profit engendered assimilation. When it was completed, when we have the models in Sade in *Mother of George* (2013), or Chioma in *Ije: the Journey* (2010), the passage from the native child to fully endowed adult is completed. Mbembe tracks this passage as seen in light of colonial thought:

> Once the condition was met, the *assimilated* became full individuals, no longer subject to custom. They could receive and enjoy rights, not by virtue of belonging to a particular ethnic group, but because of their status as autonomous subjects capable of thinking for themselves and exercising that particular human faculty that is reason. The *assimilated* signaled the possibility that the Black Man could, under certain conditions, become—if not equal or similar to us—at least our alter ego.

Difference could be abolished, erased, or reabsorbed. Thus, the essence of the politics of assimilation consisted in desubstantializing and aestheticizing difference, at least for the subset of natives co-opted into the space of modernity by being 'converted' or 'cultivated,' made apt for citizenship and the enjoyment of civil rights.

(2017: 87)

Those rights could include wearing modern clothes, or choosing to have or not have children, basic components of how European non-coeval temporalities were understood (Fabian 1983).

Cinema's representation always refers to time and motion for images that convey modernity. A simple sample of Adenike's change in attire conveys this. When she meets, on the street, her "modern" friend Sade, she is taken to a store to buy a blouse. We see her (fig.7.6; back to us) dressed in an African outfit—one associated with Nigerian women. Coeval modernity here is seen directly in the African style worn by Adenike, and its New York counterpart with the red blouse worn by Sade:

FIGURE 7.6   "Modern" and "traditional" dress

We could read each of these women's outfits purely by themselves, but when placed in relation to each other, they communicate two frames of style as well as times. Sade is telling her, "We're going to get you a new shirt," and Adenike demurs. "I don't need a new shirt." As she is saying this, we, like her, are seeing Sade's look, which goes with her own way of being-in-the-world.

FIGURE 7.7 Focus on the outfits

But in the next scene, Adenike is trying one on, changing her look, as Sade calls out, "You doin' all right in there?" (Fig.7.8)

FIGURE 7.8 "You doin' all right in there?"

Finally, Adenike returns to the restaurant, garnering looks at her daring "transparent" shirt with her bra showing beneath. Ayo, the conservative, perhaps insecure, older husband, does not respond as she had hoped. He questions her judgment, and she has to defend herself: "I thought that you would like it."

FIGURE 7.9   "I thought you would like it"

At every point the cinematographer Bradford Young interposes shots that disorient the realist gaze, so that we see only portions of the figures, or see them in reflections where the glass or mirror announces its own presence, or where the figures are placed off-center, at the edges of the frames. The framing and visual effects become prominent; and in the process, make apparent the modernist stylistics of the shots. The subjects themselves lose their centrality, while the shots become highlighted as aesthetic moments. That contrast: an ordinary perception vs. an altered state conforms entirely to the contrast I am suggesting between the framings of old vs new, Africa vs America, Lagos vs Brooklyn.

After Ayo's negative reaction, Adenike returns to the conventional, more modest apparel she had formerly worn. Ayo won't be ready to accept the "modern" wife who sees a fertility expert when they can't conceive, until after they have fully worked through the traumatic experience of having recourse to the substitute fathering by his brother Biyi. Ayo and Biyi are essentially broken as Adenike decides not to maintain the secrecy of this solution imposed by Ayo's mother. By the end, the two women, Sade and Adenike, have assumed the positions of power and agency denied to Adenike at the outset when she had understood her role as serving her husband, his mother, and his family demands.

Time and motion become visible as relative only when we leave the one frame and observe the motion and time in the other.[13] Each is relatively fast, though the directions are different according to the observer. On a train, the station is seen as retreating. On the platform, the train is seen as departing. We identify with the observer and her gaze when the camera aligns with the observer's point of view. And even if it is from the point of view of the camera, it still imposes its frame on the shot.

There is no place to stand, in *Mother of George*, outside of these two frames confronting each other. Sade calls out, "You doin' all right in there?" Adenike emerges as the New Woman ready to bring her new self to the restaurant. The men are not ready. They are waiting on some platform that appears to be retreating as the train has left the station with the two women on it. At the end, Biyi stands in the corner, looking depleted; and Ayo, the handsome Isaac de Bankole, has retreated from his wounded pride and the position of rejecting his wife, and goes to see her in the hospital. But she has already left on the gurney, has given birth without him being with her, and I suppose we are to imagine his slow motion walk, his gaze at the camera, is to convey his pitifulness in attempting to catch up.

FIGURE 7.10 *Ayo following Dr. Greene*

All these are metaphorical readings of how a quest to impose a meaning on this old story can be translated into a modern version with Africans living in the diaspora. But the reading has to be haunted by another level of approach, one in which the notion of traditional and modern times, or coeval modernity, cannot be read in a stationary manner any more. The relativity imposed by post-Newtonian physics is grounded in a revision of the absolute time that Newton or Kant had assumed in constructing their notions of a world. The new frame is not simply jangled by the changes in motion or in the measurement of time, but is unreadable when taken by itself. It is missing the crucial confrontation of the observer outside calling out, You doin' all right in there? The metaphor stops our hermeneutical reading; but the relativity of the shot demands a response that changes the perspective of the spectator from that of one with an assurance of rightness being located in one frame to being dislodged in the other. Just as speed is a characteristic of the frame only when observed from the other, so too is meaning constructed only in relation, and relation in film can be figured by an image of one who is looking across a screen at the other. Not only a call and response, then, but a look and returned gaze—a shot and countershot now juxtaposed so as to open the question: which is the shot? And which is the countershot?

Epilogue

Special relativity is "modern" not only because it dislodges the absolute-ness of location—no inertial standpoint exists on its own—but because it adds a fourth dimension to our experience of the world. We can see and feel our place in the world in three dimensions. But the motions of the world, of particles and planets, is governed by the dimension of time along with space, and we cannot perceive four dimensional objects. What dimension to the dilemmas of modernity is provided by time as the missing feature needed for spacetime? The helical motion of the earth around the sun, or of any planetary or solar object in relation to others, needs to be set against the cyclical motions of detectable three-dimensional objects. The earth moves around the sun in a cycle, with minor corrections; but with spacetime the earth never returns to the point of origin, does not move in cycles, but simultaneously cycles around while displacing over, resulting in a return and movement. Over time, the path of a helix is traced.

The helix circles around and moves out, moves "forward." It lends itself so much to conventions of progress and modernity that it retains history as a context and moves forward in advancing, ironically without a goal. The "mother of George"—Adenike—does not deliver before the film ends, but moves out of sight, wheeled away by Dr. Greene who reassures Adenike that everything will be all right. We lose sight of Adenike, and just then our focus turns to the two fathers. Biyi is hovering in a corner, excluded from the seated presence of Sade and Ma Ado. Dr. Greene comes out, and calls for someone to follow her in. She reaches to shake his hand, and from the previous shot of Biyi, we assume he is the one being called back. He is pre-sumably the father, after all. But as Dr. Greene walks back to her patient, she is followed by another figure whom we recognize as being Ayo. The shot is out of focus, we can't see the features of Dr. Greene and the man who follows her, but the general demeanor and gait of Isaac de Bankole are easily discernable. He moves closer to the camera, his face moving in and out of darkness. The final shot leaves his face in darkness.

FIGURE 7.11   Ayo, face obscured, following Dr. Greene into Adenike's room

There is no single frame in which his motion can be tracked as a path toward enlightenment. We don't see Adenike anymore. Dr. Greene has moved on ahead, and at the angle of Ayo's motion, she is lost to any inertial frame of reference. We know that as they move, they are no longer occupying coordinates that provide them with definite identities of time and place. Ayo had wanted to be the father, the one who provided his mother with the reincarnation of her lost husband, the father who could bring the cycle of birth and death around to where "George" could return. Cycles of time past, time present, time to come, with ancestors, parents, unborn children, all leave out the fourth dimension of spacetime that moves the trajectory of motion off center, making any return impossible. Indeed, as Ayo saunters after Dr. Greene, the angle of his motion shifts slightly from a diagonal to one that moves directly toward the camera, a rectilinear shot. Ayo's face comes to fill most of the screen, and his gaze comes directly into the lens, toward us. A gaze that becomes obscured in the darkness of the interval where the overhead lights are not illuminating his features.

The unperceived dimension of time is restored with his motions, until the final freeze frame, with the blacked-out screen ending the motion, the time, the film, and Ayo's journey. He is not the father whose presence gives the story its definition. It is Nike the mother whose name will be repeated to Dr. Greene and who will be the parent of George. Adenike is located behind the camera, where Dr. Greene has gone, leading Ayo. She then moves, in cinematic time, outside the frame which is always in the present, as long as the film is moving. But at this point it stops; it freezes; the image of Ayo turns to a black screen. That is the present moment he, and we, can never reach, can only gesture toward, while following she who went before. The Mother of George is only a reach away, but can never be caught. It is appropriate that this asymptotic moment is the one that ends this diaspora drama, where the arrivants are never able to finally say, we are here.

Notes

1 https://hbr.org/2018/10/how-netflix-expanded-to-190-countries-in-7-years
2 The reader will have (hopefully) seen how this dichotomy of modern-traditional lies at the heart of Johannes Fabian's well-known distinction of non-coeval time, which underlay the fundamental Eurocentric character of anthropological science, at least till Fabian and others' critiques forced a reevaluation of the field's practices. See Introduction, and see Fabian's *Time and the Other: How Anthropology Makes Its Object* (1983). Similarly, Mbembe addresses this binary modern/traditional in similar fashion in his *Critique of Black Reason* (2017).
3 Terms like "Africa" and "America" have to be taken discursively as connoting the cultural or social environs and especially the framing that is cinematic, that is constructed for our imaginary. A horizon of expectations, not a snapshot of anything mimetically realist.
4 For instance, see Mariama Bâ's *Une si longue lettre* (1979) for the portrayal of the New African Woman dating back to the late colonial period in Senegal, or Hampaté Ba's *Wangrin* (1973) for the New African Man figure.
5 Modernity of this sort we could call colonial modernity. It had its history, originating in late 19th century colonialism, notions of Frenchness or Europeanness, or Englishness, and developed over the course of the 20th century into an image of chic moneyed Africans, to one where stylishness, as in Congolese sapeurs, demanded passing beyond such dated fashions. In the end, what money buys became a global preoccupation, and "modern" Français Africans were replaced by their children in the period of late independence and growing globalization with Ghana Must Go bags and Versace whose style was measured in cost.
6 Two models of time present themselves here. The world-line of a particle that carries all the marks/impressions of its past along the lines of its trajectory—a model that does not include a break from the past, but whose present is ever in motion. The second carries the past with the block of time carved out as it moves "forward": the growing block view in which time is always being created as the past is never discarded.
7 Like the colonial geography, Nostrand Avenue also has functioned to divide wealthier and poorer, ethnically separate communities. My Brooklyn friends, Stephen Zacks and Steven Thomas, have provided this description of that area of Nostrand Avenue where the establishing shot of *Mother of George* sets the action.
   Zacks: "Depending on which side of the train stop it's the edge of a part of Bed-Stuy that is a rapidly changing Black neighborhood with beautiful historic

brownstones becoming increasingly converted into apartments, condos, and townhouses for middle-class professionals or a part of Crown Heights that has a strong Jamaican flavor becoming populated with college kids and lower-income earning college-educated professionals or bohemians, as well as, in other parts of the neighborhood, a Hasidic/orthodox Jewish enclave.

Changing much more moderately than the other side of Atlantic Ave, there are lots of Senegalese places, a Ghanaian place, and a Nigerian place especially in the direction of Prospect Heights from Nostrand." (Facebook, October 5, 2021)

Thomas: "Basically north of the A-C subway line (which runs east across Brooklyn from Manhattan) is Bed Stuy and south is Crown Heights. You might recall *Do the Right Thing* is set in the heart of Bed Stuy. The neighborhood around those subway stations has been gentrifying a lot the past 15 years and is becoming 'hip.' I see new bars and restaurants opening up all the time. The Nostrand is prime real estate because it's an express stop—the A train is the express, the C train local. Why this matters is that it's faster to get to Manhattan or up town on the express train. Also, a lot of the old architecture in that area is pre-WW-1, and is really lovely. Before gentrification, it was mostly African-American and Caribbean around those stations. The Hasidic Jewish neighborhood starts south of Eastern Parkway (which is also the 2, 3, 4, and 5 train line, which parallels the A and C line.) So, Eastern Pkwy is like the invisible dividing line . . . .

There is also a large Nigerian-Ghanaian community nearby, but they're more famously located in the Flatbush neighborhood slightly southeast of the Brooklyn museum and east of Prospect Park, basically adjacent to the Caribbean neighborhood in Crowne Heights. Flatbush is also where Medgar Evers college is—the historically black campus of CUNY." (Facebook, October 5, 2021)

8 Couple marry, wife cannot conceive, husband is responsible, a solution must be found, while insuring the lineage stays within the family . . .

9 Well, to be more accurate and honest about it, the characters speaking with the Yoruba account are supposed to be taken as Yoruba. Isaac de Bankolé is originally Ivoirian, though of Yoruba parents. His accent sounds Francophone to me, not Nigerian. He grew up in Côte d'Ivoire and completed his studies in France. For our study he opens the bookend of this book as Protée in *Chocolat*, and spent many years making films and acting in the theatre in France.

10 Beginning in March 1896, a railway was constructed running from Lagos to Ibadan. It opened in March 1901 (Francis 1997). This line connected with another starting in the north of Nigeria in 1907–1911, running as far north as Kano (Carland 1985, 135–153).

According to Ken Swindell, some of these public work projects were accomplished with the help of forced labour, referred to as "Political Labour". Village Heads were paid 10 shillings for conscripts, and fined £50 if they failed to supply. Individuals could be fined or jailed for refusing to comply. (Ken Swindell, "The Commercial Development of the North: Company and Government Relations, 1900–1906," 149–162; Ken Swindell, "The Commercial Development of the North: Company and Government Relations, 1900–1906," *Paideuma* 40, 1994, 149–162.

11 https://www.newyorkfamilyhistory.org/blog/five-borough-city-old-cities-towns-and-villages-came-together-form-greater-new-york Accessed February 8, 2023.

12 In the entry on technology on subways on Wikipedia, titled "Technology of the New York City Subway," there is a subsection called "Modernization." Interestingly, the features of "modernity" include the introduction of technologies, as in the signal system; posting of arrival times with digital clocks; improvements in the train stock; facilitation of payment; and increased speed. We learn about the introduction of block signal systems, automation programs in the 2000s, "countdown clocks" allowing passengers to see train arrival times, Bluetooth clock systems, the presence of wireless access, and finally the use of credit cards.

PART THREE

African Cinema in an Age of Globalism

Prologue to Part Three: Time and the End: Cheah's Normativity and Teleological Time

At the end of Kentridge's *Refusal of Time* (2012), we are back where we started. Throughout the various pieces of the installation he refuses to allow the Arrow of Time to dictate the direction of the narrative. A familiar story of an affair, where the husband leaves, his wife then lets her lover in, they kiss, the husband unexpectedly returns and finds the lover hiding under the table, etc., is upended; The *Refusal* reverses the order of events, saves the lover, throws the fallen plates and silverware, tablecloth, back on the table, undoes what time had done to the lovers. In another gif-like performance we see Kentridge approaching a chair, stepping on it, moving forward, only to have the action repeated and repeated. He is one of the few filmmakers to make reference to the colonial establishment of Western temporality by referring to GMT as imposing an order on the global South, on Africans whose own constructions of temporality had to be sorted out under colonial strictures, under the rule of clocks with hour hands and minute hands and second hands all coordinating motions, work, rendez-vous, life.

At the end, says T.S.Eliot in *Little Gidding*, however you came on the journey, at night "like a broken king," or by day without knowing what you came for, it ends with the tombstone.

Pheng Cheah sees time as featuring in the ends of two principal features of worlding: teleological ending and normativity—endings that impact the readers, the audience, that affirm values: "the normative force that literature can exert in the world, the ethicopolitical horizon it opens for the existing

DOI: 10.4324/9781003397595-11

world" (2016: 5). Normativity for him entails values that transform reality "in the image of human ends or as principles imminent to collective human experience that will unfold and actualize themselves" (6). To arrive at this conclusion requires time, like the arrow, moving purposefully to its end—teleologically. Cheah runs against the tide in proposing this. However, instead of reading this as unidirectional, as time unfolds, he sees it as time returning to an end already implicit in the beginning, as in the famous T.S. Eliot quote, "time present and time past," indeed all time is seen as being eternally present.

This quote has become a cliché with its mystic Buddhist overtones, with Eliot's own religious proclivities matching a period of declining faith in the rationalism of the Enlightenment after the War. But it works for Cheah, who limns Hegel's—and Aristotle's—teleological thinking, seeing the normalization of values as fulfilling the implicit impulses that set the direction of time in motion. This defines "teleological time," Cheah's core concept, accompanying that of normalization:

> Teleological time is the time of incarnation in which national ends are actualized in the empirical world. It functions to bridge the mechanical natural world and the realm of freedom, defined as a sphere of rational spontaneity that characterizes the rational human being's power of self-determination. As distinguished from the linear time of mechanical causality that governs nature, where cause and effect follow each other in an irreversible sequence of succession, teleological time is circular and self-returning. Final causality is the actualization of a rational end in existence. In a teleological history, the end or final cause is not external but originally immanent to its effect. Its effect is the unfolding of, the return to, and completion of an immanent end.
>
> *(6–7)*

Cheah accompanies the notion of teleological time with the force of normalization, the choice of actions over time, that affirm human ends. But the context for that affirmation is the world created by the construction of an understanding of reality along lines that sustain the distribution of power, the validation of knowledge that normalizes existing power. This requires another sense of time—not circular or entelechal—that marks the human insertion into reality, shaping it but opening it for change, for new developments, as Arendt posited in her *Human Condition* (1958). Unlike the force of normalization of what is implicit in the human material reality, worlding in time, through time, is transcendental:

> . . .the prevailing of a world that follows from the sheer persistence of time. The world is linked to transcendence. But unlike teleological

accounts, the world is not generated by the transcendence of finitude. Instead, time itself is the force of transcendence that opens a world. Better yet, temporalization constitutes the openness of a world, the opening that is world.

(Cheah: 9)

Most significantly, Cheah defines this working of time, this temporalization of worlding, as disrupting and resisting (9) the work of globalization, extending Spivak's use of worlding to an oppositional usage. The temporalization that moves this process requires worlding that brings people into relation, where world is now "a meaningful whole that brings all beings into relation" (9).

Paradoxically I see this process along lines similar to that employed by Heidegger where death provides us with the conditions where meaning can be evoked. I am not reaching for authenticity versus false value, but rather a temporality that requires an ending of a process that can only emerge through encounters, through relations. This enables us to deploy the necessity of viewing time as existing only in relationality, that is, time as viewed in special relativity. And as time is viewed, in quantum conditions, as emerging only when forces or matter are engaged in encounters (Rovelli 2017), as being constructed through encounters, we need to amend Cheah's older fashioned classical notion of time as moving, as directional, as measurable, yet see his formulation as going beyond its function as an objective feature of reality existing outside the material realm—the Newtonian classical view. When he states that temporalization "constitutes the opening of the world," this posits a force that affords human action possibilities. This "force of worlding" makes possible the creation of normative value only "if we exist in the world with other beings and have access to them. The unifying power of temporalization is precisely a force of worlding, the precipitous ushering into a world, a meaningful whole that brings all beings into relation" (9). Being in relation enables us to affirm or create values, to effect "normalization," the condition for the formation of norms and values (9–10).

In quantum mechanics relations can disrupt or put an end to values simply by putting an observer into contact with an object being observed. This is the "uncertainty principle," where observation changes the nature of the particle. An electron whose location is marked by the "wave-function," that shows its location in a number of places to be associated with a certain probability for each one, changes when it is measured or observed, resolving its location into one and dissolving the probabilities for the others. All is "air," that is, uncertain until a definite place is determined and assigned to the particle. The relations between objects cannot always respond to Cheah's understanding of causality, as in the case of entanglement where two particles seem to be able to "communicate," despite no known laws of physics that would account for this being possible. Quantum particles are in relations that physicists are attempting continually to understand in "macro" terms, not just on the level of atomic particles.

It is not reasonable to configure our concepts of ending in terms that exclude those of particle physics, relativity, or quantum mechanics; and yet the best we can say for now is that time, temporality, change, and the nature of material being and forces seem to emerge when there are encounters, relations, and all being is in relationship, necessarily, at all moments. For instance, the force of gravity is always working on all elements of the universe, though the nature and extent of that force might be increasingly distant. If we are to carry the logic of encounters into our reading of film, we need to have some sense of beginnings and endings, moments when encounters have meaning within the context of a fixed entity, like a film's diegesis.

And that encounter would make sense to us if we could view its ending as death, even if death, in a larger sense than that limited to human life or other creatures' lives, is a limited way of defining ending. With or without death, our material existence continues to be in relation with other forces and matter. But our story, our narratives, our diegeses are marked by limited temporalities, and for them to have some completion, we need to evoke the impact of death.

This is precisely what Cheah does when comparing the function of character and narrator in a text. The narrator, standing outside the character, always running after the time scheme in which the character is placed and acting, can never bring completion to the story unless there is death, or its equivalent, an ending.

> In the act of narrating, the narrator is the *present* self, and as character, she is the past self. However, a narrator-character cannot give a convincing or 'natural' ending to her story while she is alive, because her life's meaning will not be clear until after her death, when she can no longer recount what happened to her.
>
> *(307)*

The persistence of time enables us to give unity and identity to the character.[1]

At the point where this unity is perceived, a world is constituted. Under colonialism, globalization, that identity is closed; the world is not constituted anew, but reaffirmed as a fixed value, all the more as the colonized subjects are denied the openness of time. Cheah calls this a world in a "state of receptivity, ready to be given and to receive its own story again and again" (309). For him, this is not an "ethical action in an already constituted world" (309). Here is where the Spivak notion of worlding suggests a closed entity lacking the "propulsive force" of an opening. In contrast, for Cheah a "postcolonial world literature" has the normative task of "enact[ing] the unending opening of a world as a condition for the emergence of new subjects in spite of capitalist globalization" (309). For him, "quivering beneath the surface of the existing world are other worlds to come" (309).

The function of the old and their encounter with death provides us with the moment where we can discern the new and the opening to this quivering. Especially the ending for the old woman as witch, as we see in a swath of African films, from *Yaaba* (1989) to *The Witches of Gambaga* (2011), *I Am Not A Witch* (2017) and *The Letter* (2019) can be seen to affirm or to disrupt an already constituted world as the possibilities for her death are both foreseen and unforeseen.

The undoing of time à la Kentridge might be seen as working in the contrasting endings of *Hyènes* (1992) and *I am Not a Witch* (2017). Ramatou's descent into the dark at the end brings an end to her place in the story of seeking justice for Dramaan's and the town's rejection of her. It brings the past into the present, but ends the present as well with a return to the past, as she predicts her return to Dramaan, their coming back together, with their deaths. As if the time between could be cancelled by her power, force of will, and money. She is the example of a global worlding that freezes the opening of time.

The bulldozing of the earth, the appearance of Dakar at the end, and especially the song—"get up and work"—require her presence to end. Not that the films do not predict a happy future, but rather that this offers a grim reminder of the impossibility of a worlding outside the heavy equipment needed to flatten and replow the earth.

Note

1 Note how this resembles the crystal image of Deleueze's time-image: "The crystal-image, which forms the cornerstone of Deleuze's time-image, is a shot that fuses the pastness of the recorded event with the presentness of its viewing. The crystal-image is the indivisible unity of the virtual image and the actual image. The virtual image is subjective, in the past, and recollected. The virtual image as 'pure recollection' exists outside of consciousness, in time. It is always somewhere in the temporal past, but still alive and ready to be 'recalled' by an actual image. The actual image is objective, in the present, and perceived. The crystal-image always lives at the limit of an indiscernible actual and virtual image" (Totaro, 1999).

8

ALAIN GOMIS, *TEY* (2012)

Being Toward Death

Kenneth W. Harrow

We don't know why Satché (Saul Williams) is going to die when the movie opens. He wakens to rather mystic images, patting his body as if to make sure he is still there. In re-viewing the film, we know from the outset what he appears to know already, that this will be his last day on earth. As he leaves his bedroom, the whole family is there, and from his mother on to the others, he is wept over and hugged, as if making farewells. We would normally be confused by this since there is no clear indication what is happening, but it all transpires as if this were Soyinka's *Strong Breed*, where Eman, the one designated for the sacrifice, wakes, knowing what is about to take place.

In Derrida's *The Gift of Death* (1996) he examines the secret that underlies God's actions toward Abraham. Abraham is called to God, and responds, "Here I am." The call becomes linked to the sacrifices he is told to make, and then to the covenant that will join him—an *alliance* in French—to God, ensuring that he will be given "the land," Canaan, and the progeny, the descendants more numerous than the sands and the stars. Too numerous to be counted, if still less than infinity—for Derrida part of the realm of the secret (*The Gift of Death*). But still, like infinity because uncountable, and ultimately, not like the set of real numbers.[1] It is closer to the mystery, and thus the secret of the covenant, which Abraham accepts without question.

In a famous line in *Deuteronomy* (29:29), God tells Moses that secret things belong to God; the laws given in the Torah are for people, accessible, knowable, and closer to them than their hearts. The secret

DOI: 10.4324/9781003397595-12

underscores the promise of the covenant, and it is sealed in magical acts, like sacrifices, repeatedly. For instance, when all living beings, except for those on Noah's ark, are drowned. Or when the lamb is slaughtered and its blood placed on the lintels of the doors in order that the angel of death might pass over the Israelite homes and make its deathly visits only to the firstborn of the Egyptians. Or, most importantly for Derrida, when Abraham is told to sacrifice his son, his favorite son, Isaac. The reasons are kept secret from Abraham, as are the trials of Job; but the reader of the passage in Vayeira reads that "God tested Abraham" (Genesis 22:1). Isaac becomes the sacrifice. Verse 2: "Please take your son, your only one, whom you love, yea, Isaac, and go away to the land of Moriah and bring him up there for a burnt offering on one of the mountains, of which I will tell you."

After this, we learn no more. Abraham doesn't speak of it. Derrida sees in his silence the consequence of the pact with its secret, and in French *pacte* also means covenant, so that Abraham's tie to God—Adonai—remains preeminent in his life. It carries with it the price of Isaac, who might have escaped being killed by the substitution of the ram as the sacrifice, but still submitted to the knife before being saved at the last minute. In short, his father held the knife over him: "And Abraham stretched forth his hand and took the knife, to slaughter his son" (22:10).

Abraham satisfies God, passes the test, but at the price of creating a distance between himself, his wife Sarah, and his son Isaac, the heir intended to carry on the lineage to be fulfilled with the covenant. He is placed in the impossible position of denying the promise of the covenant in order to prove himself worthy of the covenant. The sacrifice must be faced, death must be faced, for this outcome to be achieved.

That is the position of Satché at the beginning. To die, for no reason, so as to satisfy the secret requirement which he alone can accomplish with his death. Like Isaac, the moment of his death confronts him, unlike everyone else who does not know when they will die. Isaac lives the after-sacrifice time when he has to reconcile himself to the moment when his father stood over him with the knife. Thereafter, for Derrida, the question of forgiveness has to be considered, along with the quandary of forgiving for something about which nothing could be known, and about which his father never spoke again.

There is no exactly equivalent moment in *Tey*. However, Satché must have experienced the same being-toward-death because he wakens, when the film begins, apparently knowing, as did everyone else, that he is to die that day. All the events in the film are framed around that common knowledge, his exceptional status as the one-to-die seen by all, as if written on his face.

For Heidegger an inauthentic confrontation with death would be conceived as the perception of deaths of others, which becomes conventionalized as well as cliched with stock phrases ("Oh, he went quickly, thank god, he didn't suffer for long; he went bravely; it was a real tragedy," etc.), and is ultimately something that can't be shared except at a distance. "Inauthentic" is a strange word nowadays in evoking that failure of the individual to come to terms with their own experience of death, not only because the death of others can never be experienced within ourselves, only our grief, but because even our own death ends the encounter with death, with what we face imagining a world without ourselves. For an African encounter with death, it is no different, except the "they-ness" is inauthentically rendered as the community, as if it rose somehow above individuality as a Western construction, and survived the impress of colonialism and postcolonialism. The call to they-ness in *Death and the King's Horseman* is precisely given as Yoruba, not as the work of an individual king, as if the king were a vehicle, not an agent for his own death.

Satché's status as a retournee renders the encounter all the more doubled, with all his family ties and community responding as if he were one of their own; while at the same time he is rejected or challenged by his former girlfriend and by his wife. He walks through his last day almost as if in a daze, and rejects forcibly the formal recognition of his status the local town hall officials wish to confer on him. He plays with his children, makes a last play for his former mistress, he visits his friends and his uncle, all within the frame of the film's given—we could say, its McGuffin—that of a death he never actually encounters.

If the scenes from Dakar are familiar, like a taxi-ride from quartier to quartier, the encounters are defamiliarizing. When he visits his former girlfriend, Nella, who appears to be an elegant modernist artist, we are dropped into this scene, with little background, except for his morning departure from home with the family where his wife Rama calls him a liar and berates him. Here with Nella we see the two create a scene filled with teasing, pursuing and evading, until she makes more serious and exasperated allusions to his wife, and the moment turns disjunctive. His impending death seems no more alienating than this scene where he fails to connect with Nella, and the possibility of not being in the world seems no more pressing than not being with her at that time. The angst remains classical since there is no restoration of intelligibility through his attempt to renew their relationship, and he could still repeat Heidegger's formula: "When I am anxious I am no longer at home in the world. I fail to find the world intelligible" (*Being and Time* 53: 310). His angst is cinematic, as the scene with Nella places him in the location of the alienated lover. We don't see fear or anguish in the scene: he approaches her, she ultimately rejects him, he leaves, and proceeds on to make his way to his uncle where he will rehearse the scene of his death.

The scenes show him alienated, but not face to face with the possibility of his future foreclosed, himself absent from the scene. The scene of life, or the staging of his death, creates a space for time, but that time is enclosed by the opening and closing frames of the film: he lives only within that frame, and within its enclosure experiences alienation, but not solitude or a confrontation with himself where his singularity, "own-ness," (*eigentlichkeit,* also "authenticity") would define his mood and response, would give him definition apart from the people around him. He remains in the fully familiar world of Dakar.

And as he makes the rounds, visiting friends and family, at a crucial point he visits his closest elder, his uncle (Thierno Ndiaye), who happens to be an undertaker. There his uncle subjects him to the treatment the dead receive when being prepared for the *levée du corps*, the final passage to the cemetery. He is given a simulacrum of the washing a corpse receives, down to the soaping and rinsing of the orifices, the cleansing in preparation for being wrapped and carried to the grave. His living body is transformed into a virtual corpse by his uncle, who appears the warmest and wisest of relatives. The figures of Thierno Ndiaye, known for his powerful roles as *Guelwaar*; or le Vieux Samba in *Karmen Gaye*; as himself, in *Ainsi Meurent les Anges*; as the father in *L'Afrance*; other major roles, and this iteration as *l'oncle*, coalesce as his deep voice and commanding air affirm his authority as the wise African elder. Here he has fathered 17 children, with many wives, as Satché, coming to the end of his shortened life, has fathered two small children, leaving a frustrated wife and angry mistress.

Others could die at any time, his uncle tells him, and wouldn't know they have less time left than Satché. But that too is another inauthentic comfort, since Satché hasn't yet come to terms with his own-ness, his own death, his own singularity. That's where the scene of his uncle, the undertaker, laying him out, preliminarily as it were, is so striking. It is as if his uncle were listening to Heidegger, and saying, here, I can give him the experience of what it is like to be dead, or more precisely, to be laid out before his burial. Mor Lam leaped into his grave to keep for himself the savor of his wife's dish[2] and not share it with his neighbors or friends. Satché is prepared to share everything, but in fact can share only virtually what his uncle provides for him, a preparation, a re-enactment, and virtual experience of what the dead man receives at the hands of the undertaker.

As this scene progresses, as the uncle places Satché into a prone position, as he arranges his limbs and picks up each one to rehearse the action of washing it, as he gently inserts his fingers into Satché's nasal orifices and ears, and rubs his eyelids, Satché must lie still and feel what his body will go through 24 hours later. The simulacrum of death is rehearsed. Time becomes non-measured, reduced to a moment without elongation, until the uncle determines it is over, gets up, and bids him farewell.

Film always suggests an interiority with the close-up shot of a face, as if the person is thinking about something related to images we have just seen. As if the world-line[3] of their lives comes to a momentary pause, placed on hold—with digesting and reflecting, and resolution. All that "ownness" to which we have no access, until they come out of the moment and recommence. Here it is as if Satché had experienced his death in substitution, had arisen out of a fake experience into a true aftermath, and then reset the clock for his journey and our engagement.

FIGURE 8.1 Satché, waiting to anticipate death, or the end of the film.

> [The] state-of-mind [mode of disposedness] which can hold open the utter and constant threat to itself arising from Dasein's own most individualized Being, is anxiety. In this state-of-mind, Dasein finds itself face to face with the 'nothing' of the possible impossibility of its existence.
>
> *(Being and Time 53: 310)*

At this moment he is at a cusp between the virtual experience of death and his existential facing of his end. Instead of retreating to an interiority he strides back into the open space of the uncle's compound, where Mecano and Selé are waiting.

FIGURE 8.2 Satché at his uncle's compound

The face-to-face with "nothing" is rebalanced by the reattachment, the rejoining of the world that holds them in its frame. This shot has the tree and red materials in the foreground, his friends seated before him, and the bench in the middle, held in the middle, where he seats himself.

FIGURE 8.3 Empty space of compound

He fills the empty space, the nothingness, and gives everything around it sense, a position in relation to him at the center, and thus a direction for us to follow. His bright red shirt links him to the red in the foreground; his look joins him to his friends. Together they compose a world in which

FIGURE 8.4   Satché fills empty space

he can decide, move, take some reasonable actions, find a sense of belonging physically, as did his uncle when he laid him out. In other words, this presents us with a figure of Dasein[4] in the moment, the instant, before he and as Selé go on their way.

In Heideggerian terms, his death is marked by the conflicting possibilities of authenticity and inauthenticity, of dealing with an experience that everyone can anticipate, that is common to all, that is treated conventionally, as in his uncle's cleansing and wrapping of the body, etc.; or in confronting it personally, individually, as something that is his alone, his "own," his singular experience that will be shut off from himself and others, like the black frame, at the moment when it comes. He is with others who continually evoke his impending death, a "wrapping" up of his life, of all his meaningful relations with the people who most mattered to him in his life; and he is alone, as in the moment of his wakening at the beginning of the day, and his final interior moment in bed at night.

Death is encountered in our lives by anticipation and projection, by accepting the hazardous circumstances that have "thrown" us into existence, into a world where we can see the possibilities for action where we can integrate ourselves into its material substance. But also, a world that confirms our alienation, our angst or anxiety:

Anxiety, at least in the form in which Heidegger is interested, is not directed towards some specific object, but rather opens up the world to me in a certain distinctive way. When I am anxious I am no longer at home in the world. I fail to find the world intelligible. Thus there is an ontological sense (one to do with intelligibility) in which I am not in the world, and the possibility of a world without me (the possibility of my not-Being-in-the-world) is revealed to me. '[The] state-of-mind [mode of disposedness] which can hold open the utter and constant threat to itself arising from Dasein's ownmost individualized Being, is anxiety. In this state-of-mind, Dasein finds itself face to face with the 'nothing' of the possible impossibility of its existence.'

(Being and Time 53: 310) ("Martin Heidegger,"
Stanford Encyclopedia of Philosophy)[5]

If "nothing," still *Tey* emphasizes what Heidegger would find at the heart of inauthenticity in emphasizing the others, the "they" who form the society around Satché from the moment he arises from his bed and opens the door onto the crowd of family members and closest friends, who are there to begin mourning his death while he is still experiencing life. The encounters that follow are not with his image in the mirror, not with the skull of Yorick abreast his grave, not in solitude or isolation. He is never alone for long, if at all.

Heidegger parses two approaches to this moment in terms of expectation and fear of an experience known commonly to all, and thus inauthentic. If it is to be a death he can "own," he must anticipate it. Oddly enough, Heidegger demonstrates this difference in expecting vs anticipating with the example of the taste of a beer!

Inauthenticity in relation to death is also realized in thrownness, through fear, and in projection, through expectation. Fear, as a mode of disposedness, can disclose only particular oncoming events in the world. To fear my own death, then, is once again to treat my death as a case of death. This contrasts with anxiety, the form of disposedness which, as we have seen, discloses my death via the awareness of the possibility of a world in which I am not. The projective analogue to the fear-anxiety distinction is expectation-anticipation. A mundane example might help to illustrate the generic idea. When I expect a beer to taste a certain way, I am waiting for an actual event—a case of that distinctive taste in my mouth—to occur. By contrast, when I anticipate the taste of that beer, one might say that, in a cognitive sense, I actively go out to meet the possibility of that taste. In so doing, I make it mine. Expecting death is thus to wait for a case of death, whereas to anticipate death is to own it.

(Heidegger, Stanford)

Satché is not really situated for us. Despite all the close hugs, fist bounces, and knowing smiles or weeping mothers, he is thrown into the opening scene with no clear past. He is a retournee from America, and that is all. He is actually alone at the beginning; with no clear signs of his own family that will be with him at the end. He is silent in his encounters with most figures, exchanging meaningful glances or physical gestures, but only rarely speaking. That is well since, in fact, Saul Williams is very American. He walks like a Black American, speaks with an American accent, often speaking more slowly than his wife or girlfriend or other interlocutors, and communicates non-verbally conveying physical and vocal qualities that establish a foreignness we must willingly disregard to accept the givens of the plot.[6] This doesn't give him so much an air of alienness as a non-diegetic distance.

This places him on the edges of authentic angst:

> When I am anxious I am no longer at home in the world. I fail to find the world intelligible. Thus there is an ontological sense (one to do with intelligibility) in which I am not in the world, and the possibility of a world without me (the possibility of my not-Being-in-the-world) is revealed to me. '[The] state-of-mind [mode of disposedness] which can hold open the utter and constant threat to itself arising from Dasein's ownmost individualized Being, is anxiety. In this state-of-mind, Dasein finds itself face to face with the 'nothing' of the possible impossibility of its existence.'
>
> *(Being and Time 53: 310) (*"Martin Heidegger," *Stanford Encyclopedia of Philosophy)*

The line between the angst of authenticity and the complacency of inauthenticity can't be read easily in this African context where the meaning of "they," of the "madding crowd" and its "ignoble strife" (Thomas Gray 1751, "Elegy Written in a Country Churchyard"), accords awkwardly with 20th century European notions of alienation and existential angst. Yet this Satché also fits oddly into his homeboy role. His playing at his life, reenacting his death, create a distance.

The intelligibility of his world is gradually revealed to us as the day passes, with him walking from encounter to encounter. He strolls through a Dakar filled with life, as a montage sequence of considerable appeal evokes the striving, dancing, protesting, conflicting moments of insanity and beauty on the streets. He is watching, as if to remember, to carry it on to his last moment, as if not to let go of life. But it is seen from the outside; the "they-ness" of life, life at a distance, life as a collective. It unwinds. His friend Selé catches up with him, they walk home. He has yet to be alone, to face the nothingness of being before him. Being here is accompanied.

Not until the final scene at home, with the day ending, is that face to face with "nothing-ness," with his existential impossibility of being there tomorrow, directly placed before him. Here the cinematic dissolves and continuity/non-continuous editing reshape the experience into a cinematic movement and temporality that suggest the impossible passage of time and life into a new frame.

His time on earth expires, winds down, as he returns home to his wife and children at the end of the day, to find that the movement toward death is like the movement toward the end of a film—the time left is only that which remains on the spool as the final images turn to the black screen that ends all change and movement. Cinematic time, memory, and life merge in the approaching darkness of the final frame.

With the moment that ends the film, and Satché's life, comes an awareness of the time that had been allotted, to him and the film. Before that we only knew where he had come from, and anticipated his movements during the day as continuing, as long as the film continued. The motion of the film, its being shown and lighting up the screen, leads us through a temporality that is invisible until it ends.

Satché ends his day sitting on the chaise longue in his courtyard, his wife next to him, his children now grown up leaving the house, passing outside the gate as their parents call their names. Satché is here between anticipation of a world in which he has another 15 or 20 years to see his children grow, while "in actuality" he is living his last day. He and his wife, played by the same actors, no gray hair etc., are there as though it would have been normal that their day would have ended with the grown-up kids going out and the parents going to bed.

There is no tasting of the beer, only the anticipation. There he is lying in bed with his wife Rama, her back to him, their breathing quiet as sleep descends. He blinks slowly once, the screen goes dark; he opens his eyes, sees Rama's back, the black outline and blue lit surface; then blinks again; opens his eyes; closes his eyes, and it ends.

The Being toward death is twofold: he will stop being in the world, which is re-created in the film around him, ending with Rama and children. His social world from the beginning, evoked in each scene, until the final scene at home, ends. He will also stop seeing the world around him, and as that happens so too do the point-of-view shots which give us that world. He stops the movement and light and vision of the film; he stops the movie; it stops with him. His time coincides with cinematic time through the melding of his eye with the eye of the camera.

The two times are radically different in that regard; but otherwise share the trajectory of the world-line, that is, carry what came before as a past that is still there in the line itself.

The world line anticipates a future with the particle's motion seeming to be endless. Even if motion ends with momentum, there is no end to the photon's motion; the energy or force of gravity always continues its pull on everything, so motion is only over relative to another being. We could say the photon both moves through space, forward, creating time as it moves, and sees itself, experiences itself, each time it encounters another force. The movement is unconscious; the encounter gives it consciousness; and it is limited in its conception of movement and the encounter by its own unique singularity.

But Satché is not alone in bed at the end; or before the end comes. If we see his eyes, in intense close-up

FIGURE 8.5   Satché

it is linked to what he sees, what he saw, what he imagines he will be seeing:

FIGURE 8.6   Rama

His vision of Rama preparing the dinner appears as he seems to be fading, as she begins to appear to him in slow motion, as her gestures become fragmented. Later, as the evening comes on, he is seen—or sees himself— with Rama, both in chaises longues, before their children come out of the house and go out on the town. Their figures are doubled, as if zombies, or fantasies, or shifted by time:

FIGURE 8.7 Satché and Rama

This is not the worldline of the solo particle making its own way through space, its ownness determining the space and time around it. It is closer to the block of time[7] that carries the past, like a collective accumulation of everything the being has encountered and responded to. The future doesn't open up, isn't open, isn't there. The encounters that make the temporality occur can take place only with the other, and it is not now a question of their "they-ness" or inauthenticity imposing a conventional ending on his life. Here Satche's day began and has been nothing but a series of encounters, especially with everyone who was or became part of his life in the past, and who will now end being part of his life.

The particle will enter its black hole. The block moves like the collectivity of beings,[8] some closer, some more distant, but all at play—as in the montage of encounters that followed after the scene at the uncle's compound.

The end of the film brings not only the black screen, but the music announcing the extra-diegetic flow of credits. Then comes the end of all motion associated with the film. The film remains a block of all that happened, and with it the experiences of watching it, also part of the block, like energy encountering another particle's force generated with each viewing.

We remember it, then, carrying it forward in our own cases. But remember especially the end.

Notes

1 To break with the linearity of real numbers and the arrow of time, we turn to imaginary numbers, namely i. If you take the square root of minus one, the answer i does not correspond to real numbers, and for Hawking (1993) gives us a means for constructing the quantum notion of imaginary time: "Imaginary time is a different way to think about the progression of space-time. What we consider real time would be the past, present and future. Imaginary time would be perpendicular to the present (like on a complex plane), allowing for many things to happen at once. Why would we want to sue such an odd concept? It helps with singularities. In them, space time curls in on itself and our known physics breaks down. But with imaginary time, a closed surface (with 3-dimensions) would form instead and would separate from our space time" (Hawking: 81). https://owlcation.com/stem/What-Is-Imaginary-Time

2 The famous tale from Birago Diop's *Contes d'Amadou Koumba*, "L'Os de Mor Lam."

3 The world line anticipates a future with the motion of the particle seeming to be endless. It gives definition to time for a particle as it carries the interactions of the past with its trajectory, and with its motion and direction indicate the path of its future.

4 Dasein, the distinctive mode of being human, linked by Heidegger to Care, for some, the way of life shared by members of a community. https://plato.stanford.edu/entries/heidegger/#toc

5 In "Heidegger," Stanford.

6 Saul Williams on *Aujourd hui*: "This film gave me the level of challenge I really desired. It was just what I needed, headed where I was heading in my idea of performance, which was about ways of communicating without words. For me, words have never been the point. I use words as a tool to say what I feel must be said. But that which I'm trying to say is not only expressed through words, it's through dance and through making love and in so many other ways. So it brings certain kind of balance to work beyond language itself." https://www.imdb.com/name/nm0931654/bio?ref_=nm_ov_bio_sm

7 Two models of time present themselves here. The world-line of a particle that carries all the marks/impressions of its past along the lines of its trajectory—a model that does not include a break from the past, but whose present is ever in motion. The second carries the past with the block of time carved out as it moves "forward": the growing block view in which time is always being created as the past is never discarded.

8 Deleuze uses a similar image of the time-image, borrowing from Bergson.

9

TWO FILMS ABOUT WOMEN WITCHES

Rugano Nyoni, *I Am Not a Witch* (2017); Maia Lekow, Christopher King, *The Letter* (2019)

Kenneth W. Harrow

Part I. *I Am Not a Witch* (2017)

I.

I Am Not a Witch (2017) fits obliquely into the third stage of African cinema that recently has dealt more and more with the elderly, with dying and death, with endings. Obliquely, because this is a film dealing with a child, Shula (Maggie Mulumbwa), who is apparently falsely accused of being a witch at the outset of the film, thus leading us into the world of old women who are the real targets of the accusations.

There is no witchcraft in *I Am Not a Witch*, but rather charlatanry, and even more, a community, not unlike Yaaba's, that believes in *sorciers* and *sorcières*. In this film the setting is Zambia, now renowned for its recent witch hunting episodes—crazes—that have made international headlines.[1] In *I Am Not a* Witch there are witch hunters in the form of one who performs magic to determine whether Shula is a witch. We observe Shula as she is forced to decide who is a thief from among a group of suspects. Nothing in the film places us in a scene where witchcraft could be considered credible by the audience, so the people in the diegesis who affirm the belief are represented as credulous. The film has to deal with the subject more or less as an inside issue, not one being projected for export,[2] in which case it would have been attacked for its politics of representation as sensationalizing.

Terms like credulous and credible do not fit this film particularly well, since the encounter with witchcraft and its belief is depicted in tongue-in-cheek fashion, or worse. *Yaaba* (1989) does not present us with a world

DOI: 10.4324/9781003397595-13

outside that of the village with its structures of belief: it is a world for which a simple notion of the "African" village of the Sahel suffices with no cars or roads to connect it to the city.[3] At the outset of *I Am Not a Witch* we see a tourist bus arrive at a witch village, with the tourists' cameras and guide standing between them and the witches on the other side of a fence. The witches are old women who have painted their faces and put on a silly show for the tourists.

FIGURE 9.1   Old women with painted faces

The narrative point of view indicts the tourists, sympathizes with the old women, but has a meta-dimension that places the scene beyond simple critique. For instance, the sound of Vivaldi's "Four Seasons" accompanies the initial arrival of tourists, and classical music is deployed elsewhere, placing the diegesis in a vaguely intermediary space not inappropriate for Euro-African diaspora sensibilities, as seen in so many films of today. Included here would be films of the Esiri brothers, Jide Akinleminu, Mati Diop, Maimouna Doucouré, Ekwa Msangi, Jessica Beshir, and many more . . . indeed, perhaps this appearing as a dominant trend. For this younger generation the term "diaspora" is no longer relevant. They occupy both North/South terrains as authochthons in a world that has been reconfigured by global forces. The outside is not looking in, it is in, and the old extraverted model has been reconfigured into the invagination of the global/local model.

We follow the life of Shula after she is introduced into the camp, inducted into the covey of old lady witches, as it were, and eventually placed in the home of the overweight government official, Mr. Banda (Henry Phiri), where Banda's witch-mistress/wife Charity (Nancy Murilo) is charged with training Shula how to perform as a witch. There is nothing of the scenes of possession or disorientation that would resemble how witchcraft might be associated with current practices in parts of Zambia or Ghana, where Rugano Nyoni did her research on witch villages.[4] Instead Shula, and the women in the camp, are portrayed as victims, whose acquiescence in any charges is based on their need to survive.

Shula's narrative takes us through a series of episodes in which we see her arbitrarily designating figures as guilty of various crimes, thus marking the drama as an exposé like Arthur Miller's *Crucible*. We see how she and the other witch figures are periodically accused and attacked, but never as though they were anything but victims of misguided accusers, not unlike the souvenirs of naïve tourists who snapped their pictures at the camp. Because they are "government witches," their labor can be sold, and the metaphor for their servile status is the thick ribbon-band attached to their backs, which keeps them in place, laboring at the behest of the government officials who ostensibly profit from this situation. In a sense, the film is a parable for modern day enslavement, with people enslaved to the prejudices toward witches as well as being subservient to powerful social and political figures. To complete this allegorical frame, at the end, Shula cuts the ribbon and flees, only to be brought back dead. With her death, the other witches cut their own ribbons, and are presumably free. The ribbons keep Shula from running away; they are attached to the women accused of witchcraft and forced to work in the fields.

Come, let's sing for Shula

FIGURE 9.2 Old women attached

The highlighting of their visible function imposes a strong allegorical reading on the film, shifting us closer to a critique of realism while edging into satirical polemics, without ever carrying the social critique too far.

Shula is a child, but in the persona of an old woman. Helpless, caught up in an ordinary life where she can't defend herself, and marginalized, she is used by Mr. Banda as would be the case if he were her pimp, and she his property, like Charity, sold to do his bidding. Like Yaaba, she appears without family attachments, without lodging or village. When we first see her, she materializes suddenly on the road, and when she finally is brought to the witches' camp is placed repeatedly in settings that are as open and flat as the savannas of the Sahel. Initially she tries to run away, as she ultimately does at the conclusion. But she is caught, attached to the ribbon-band, and trapped into her role as witch. "Little witch"—this is the term of affection Dramaan used in *Hyènes* for his 17-year-old girlfriend Rama-tou. Banda uses the term "my little witch" over and over as he decides it would be to his profit to have her trained for his purposes. He takes her home, where Charity, his "witch" wife who insists on her respectability, is charged with training her to perform witch functions properly. That includes being able to perform the rain ritual, to identify guilty parties, to do Banda's bidding.

In all this Banda is revealed to be not only a slightly bumbling corrupt government official, who has enriched himself considerably, but the one who appears to be in charge of the use and abuse of the witches, who had been engaged in the maintenance of the witch camp after public accusations had endangered the women's lives, forcing them to take refuge there. Late in the film, as the drought persists despite many rain dances, he is summoned before the traditional ruler who excoriates him for not having successfully compelled Shula to bring rain. This woman ruler, who is seen as arbitrary and distasteful as Banda himself, is also presented as subordinate to a government in whose employ Banda is working.

The plot focuses on Shula, the innocent child, and Banda and his wife, who exploit and deploy Shula as their own instrument, as an unusual and extreme version of child abuse. This is emphasized late in the film when Banda appears on television with Shula and presents her as a genuine witch to the audience. The studio audience made up of a group of young and middle-aged women appears to condemn what they see before their eyes, as Shula is silent while being paraded. Toward the end, the requirement that children be placed in school compels Banda to release her and place her in a school for misfit children, or endangered children, including albinos.[5]

The film functions as though its allegory were imposed by the anachronistic and quirky characters or scenes, particularly those involving Banda or people he interacts with. If we read it throughout in terms of the bumbling Banda or the sympathetic Shula, the film risks having a message that is transparent. But if we read it squint-eyed, à la bell hooks, the characters begin to slide around their functions. For instance, we could ask whether Shula is a witch. As she is obviously presented as an orphan plunked down into an unsympathetic village at the outset, and not taken in by a kind family, as had been the case with Wend Kuuni, the community's culpability becomes the focus. But if her silence and the movement of crimes, money, and exploitation shift around her, her function becomes laid over by that of the old women who provide the community with their "witches." She becomes one of them, and is thus both witch-as-old-woman and witch-as-little-girl, like Ramatou in *Hyènes* who is remembered as Dramaan's "little witch," while also appearing as the old, dangerous woman who destroys him and the past in the end. Once the imperatives of linear temporality tremble, the rigidity of didactic readings begins to give way.

The disjunction between her appearance as helpless little girl and her function as old woman witch enables us to feel sympathy for her, especially when the setting emphasizes her role as a little girl, like at the school or when she cries. More often she is quiet, silenced, and enigmatic, when the events on which witchcraft is blamed descend upon her. An example of her ordinary humanness occurs ironically in the scene at the end of the film with falling rain—rain, which she had been charged magically to bring on. It comes with her death and the mourning of the old women.

FIGURE 9.3 The rain finally falls

The film dances on the edge of the magical, as when she is forced to pick a thief, and arbitrarily chooses Nelson. When they search for evidence, the stolen bag unaccountably is located with him. Similarly, she appears spookily out of nowhere at the beginning, scaring a woman carrying a jug of water, who drops it and cries out that Shula is a witch. And like Dramaan at the end of *Hyènes*, all we see of her is the shroud in which she is wrapped, as if her features, her solid identity, had disappeared.

Her role as little girl/old woman witch is imposed on her, and we work to dismiss that injustice in order to return her to her proper position as poor little girl. But witch films offer impropriety by sarcastic, satirical representations, not just of injustice, but of the class or caste positions that impose their injustice on the helpless: the powerful government, the traditional ruler, even the anger of the crowd ready to beat her or to kill Nelson as a thief. He was found to be guilty because he was fingered by the witch, and because Banda required that set-up to work. Crime and magic are thus intertwined.

To get to where the old people[6] are placed in this scenario, we have to turn our attention away from Banda, away from Shula the child, and focus more on the ones whose minor roles are there because they are old: the old women who are always present in the background, ever there to be called by Shula when she needs help, forming the only home to which Shula can be consigned; the old grandfather who cannot shut off his phone by himself but needs Banda and the guard to remove its battery. He is helpless without them and cannot make his complaint at the court until the phone is silenced. He has almost nothing to say: I was robbed and whoever did it will get his just deserts. He pays Shula back for finding Nelson guilty, and gives Shula a bottle of gin, which she passes on to the ecstatic old women when she returns to the camp.

She brings "lines of credit" to the old women, who can now buy fancy wigs to cover their graying hair, covering the drab hairstyles that go with their roles as farm laborers or stone breakers. They are grandmothers, who threaten Mr. Tembo with death if he dares put Shula back into the fields to work; but they are helpless when she seeks to flee after being forcibly removed from the school, at the behest of the traditional queen ruler who wants her to continue her witchcraft so as to bring rain.

Without the old people, Shula would have to be inserted into the narratives of abused children. But as a witch—an old woman—she can't be easily slotted into the positions of either trafficked victim, exploited field or sex laborer, or discarded grandparent whose claims on property or family members might inconvenience those seeking to come into their own as heads of families. The old represent both a threat, like a witch, and a victim, no longer strong enough to assert their positions of rule and authority. They are weakened, discarded, and also a sight to behold, which is why tourists are brought to their camp for photo ops. And as they play the right roles in the photo ops, painting their faces as proper witches are expected to do, Shula is taught to do the same.

Where are we to situate this figure of the "old woman Shula"? If this were a film designed to be circulated in a Zambian or Ghanaian circuit, where the issue of witch-hunts and witch camps has become dramatic, it would fail to arouse the necessary indignation because of its off-kilter framing and characterization. If it were to be shown at the film festivals, where in fact it was successful in gleaning significant awards, its engaged perspective would accord with an audience whose sympathies for "poor" Africans, be they photogenic children or abused old women, could be assumed—and also critiqued as pandering to Euro-centric views. But it lies between these locales since whatever audience aroused by the issue of witch killings in Africa, be it in Zambia or in London, would find this film's appeal meaningful.

Her death plays on both registers, insider and outsider, young and old figure, as well—as is appropriate for her. The death of the child is tragic, and mourned as such at the end. The death of the old woman is inevitable, mourned as the common fate for our mothers, sad but not tragic.

There are two turning points, but a number of episodes, that prefigure the change in her status that results in her death. When she is first taken into the camp, the grandmothers welcome her and give her a home. When she is placed in the fields, as if a grandmother whose labor was to be exploited like theirs, again they responded forcibly—with one grandmother threatening Mr. Tembo with death if he continued to place Shula in the field.

But when she was taken into Baba Banda's home, and trained by his partner-wife to function as a witch, she becomes dependent on Ms. Banda. That confidence is broken when Ms. Banda stops to buy gin in a store and is attacked by a crowd as a witch. The attack matches other earlier attacks, such as that of Nelson who says Shula will be stoned to death as a witch when he is proven innocent. An unidentified man sees her in the bus, and seeks to attack her, only to be stopped by Banda. She is instructed to bring rain for a white farmer, but by then has lost her confidence and can't perform. Following that, the appearance on television results in failures when the stage audience looks stony-eyed at Banda when he makes his claims about her being a witch. There is then a telephone caller who attacks Banda for child abuse in keeping her from school.

These scenes reject the social role into which she had been thrust as witch, and insist that she is, instead, a child, and as such she has no real support, no real family, and is seen as suffering the abuse and exploitation of children. The TV program announcer asks rhetorically, what if she is just a child? The women's looks in the audience convey the displeasure with Banda. Originally when brought to the witches' camp she was asked to choose whether to be a witch or a goat. Goats are eaten. Witches were like the old women she saw, and so the next morning she said she chose to be a witch. Now that that was becoming difficult due to the Banda's crude exploitation, we see her compelled to return to the camp, back with the tourists and the Vivaldi music that had accompanied her initial arrival.

At the camp she takes up residence inside a large clown head structure, living pitifully by herself.

FIGURE 9.4 Shula's Clownhead home

The tourists come to photograph the witches, who look back at them, unsmiling. When they come to the clown's head, the guide calls out to her. She appears sad to the tourists so they propose taking a picture together. She doesn't answer. In the next scene she attempts to lock Banda out of the bus in which they are travelling. Her days as his little witch are coming to an end.

The transformation is completed when she is withdrawn from the Bandas and placed in the school. For the first time she is seen as a child, amid other children. No one asks her to perform as a witch, and she finally appears happy. It lasts only a brief time. The traditional queen ruler discovers she has been placed in school, instead of doing the serious work of performing a rain dance.

Her death begins when she is yanked by the ribbon on her back out of school and, following the demands of the traditional queen ruler, compelled to undertake a rain dance in the midst of the drought. Her end comes quickly. She is dragged by the sorcerer to a dry field and commanded to perform a rain dance. She performs, shaking her body, her hands, her face set against the blue clouds with wisps of white clouds. Her movements are accompanied by a relatively discordant set of notes played on a cello or violin, distant in every way from the "African rain dance" she performs.

She appears to be in a field covered by the dry stalks of a crop, perhaps corn, that has failed. She takes up pieces and ties them around her waist, on her head. The elderly women see her, and as they come to fetch her, she urinates on herself and passes out. They pick her up and carry her off.

In the reddish hues of the darkness that night, the women call out to her and ask her why she is upset. She says, I should have chosen to be a goat. They say, no, if you had chosen to be a goat, they will kill and eat you for supper. She gets up in the dark, unwinds her ribbon and gathers it up.

The next scene shows the two boys, helpers for Banda, carrying a wrapped body in an oxcart out to the dry field. The old women come to collect her from the field and mourn over her body. As they form a circle to sing their dirge, the rain begins. A mist whitens the screen as the women sit in a circle under the steady rain. After, the truck that had transported them and their ribbons appears with the poles and their ribbon spools. The women are no longer attached. The truck appears alone on a plain.

FIGURE 9.5 Truck alone on plain

II.

Kentridge's project of undoing time's linear Arrow of Time in his installations and writings might be seen as working in contrast to the endings of *Hyènes* (1992) and *I Am Not a Witch* (2017). There is no sense of a return to the past at the end of *I Am Not a Witch*. Rather, another double movement is suggested. Shula dies, her freedom is bought at the expense of her life, there is no future opening, her full life story is recounted and brought to an end. But as the image of the truck at the end suggests, the old women, falsely accused of being witches and put to work as slaves to the government authority, are no longer tied, attached, enslaved. The bands that blow in the breeze are a symbol for their freedom, bought at the expense of Shula's death.

As a figure in this drama Shula is not just a child, unjustly bound and exploited, she is also a witch, an old woman, meeting a death that completes the witch's fate as much as it completed the fate of Yaaba. Her story can now be told because she, it, has been wrapped up at the end, mourned over, and buried. We close the book on Banda, and on the witches' camps. We open the Wikipedia accounts of other such camps in Ghana and Zambia, which Nyoni choses to place before our eyes to contemplate and decide what appropriate action must be taken. We stand very much inside the worlding of a knowledge that decides and judges. We globalize Shula and her story; we world her film, and like the tourists take our pictures home to show to others. Or, if we are not supposed to be those tourists of truth, we take the same pictures home to Dakar where we emulate the same globalized worlding and close the constituted world on her case.

If Shula is an old woman, that is harder to do. Impossible, since her death would no longer be instructive, any more than was Yaaba's, or Ramatou's for that matter, and we would have to press for a temporality, with its measure of a reversal of time that undoes the metronomes of common space and rational measure. Shula becomes closer to the other Ramatou, whom Dramaan came to visit at the end: the little witch, still the little witch, a little witch with whom he had had a daughter, who had left, who returned, and who was both old and prosthetically constituted, and yet the same as before. Time's refusal, cheating the causality that would make sense of her as an agent of globalization, but opening the space for two other old women who seemed to be able to refuse the conventional ending of the witch.

The first is the grandmother in *The Letter*, and the latter in our last chapter, the unforgettable Mantoa from *This Is Not a Burial, It Is a Resurrection*.

Part II: *The Letter* (2019), Maia Lekow, and Christopher King

I.

Margaret Kamango was in her nineties when this film was shot, and shortly after its completion she passed away.[7] She was accused of being a witch by members of her own family: her stepsons (sons of her husband, and thus her sons as she raised them); their relatives; family members concerned about mishaps, lack of pregnancies, illnesses. The context for this exposé, as reported on the radio, on the TV, and as shown in newspaper headlines, in the film, was a wave of episodes in which elderly Kenyans were being accused of witchcraft. Most significantly, the accusations were made by adult children impatient to receive the inheritance of land held by their aging parents or relatives. In some instances, the witch-parents were consigned to a witches camp, at times after suffering deadly attacks. One older man had a deep machete wound on his head. As in *I Am Not a Witch* (2017), these witches were presented as pathetic and victims.

The accusers had on their side the exorcists, in this case an evangelical preacher who brought with him an entourage who travelled to the witch-grandmother's home to undertake a cleansing. All of this is recorded in the film, with most scenes vectored through the point of view of Margaret's grandson Kalisa, whom she had raised. He indicates his confusion between the seriousness with which he takes the charges from his uncle and, implicitly, father, and his sympathy for his grandmother. Eventually, when the exorcist preacher arrives, he sits with his grandmother and aunts, rather than to move over to the side of the exorcist and his male relatives. His choice is reinforced by the filmmakers, Maia Lekow and Christopher King, who shoot the events during the exorcism from the grandmother's part of the compound, away from the evangelical preacher.

In the end, after the predictions of the exorcist preacher about spiritual events to follow the ritual, nothing happens to her, none of the dire predictions or blessings come about. She jubilates, but the split in the family is not shown to have been healed. She remains an old woman, and as the post-exhibition notes of worldfilmreviews.us indicate, she died shortly after the film was completed. It was released at the IDFA Festival on 19 November 2019.[8]

She conjured death, in order that the teleology of the film could be affirmed: the witch did not die from the exorcist's imprecations, she survived. Her life was a study in persistence, and her age imposed the frame for an ending, like that of the old people, men and women, accused of witchcraft in Gothoma camp.[9]

So time for her was based on her lasting through the trial, in the present moment of the film's diegesis. In the film, we mostly access Ma Kamango through her grandson. In that regard, she is like Yaaba, rarely seen except when with Bila.[10] There are few moments in *The Letter* where Kalisa and his grandmother do not appear close. Once in Mombasa we see him apart from her, performing a children's puppet show. But otherwise he is either travelling home or is with her in Kilifi. At another time, in his uncle's house, he raises the question of the witchcraft: they are in the neighboring houses of the compound. Mostly Kalisa appears with her or is discussing this issue.

Similarly, there is the exceptional scene in *The Letter* when Grandma Kamango appears without her grandson Kalisa. It is after she falls and breaks her hip. We see her in the hospital, cared for by one of the aunts. A few months later Kalisa returns home to see her and apologizes for not coming to her. She complains about his absence, and he says the hospital in Nairobi was a long way from Mombasa. Gradually she recovers, first with the help of a wheelchair, then with a walker, a cane, and finally on her two feet. Shortly after her return from Mombasa, relatives begin the exorcism, and once again Kalisa accompanies her. This follows the plotline begun at the outset when Kalisa travels home to see her having heard about the accusations against her. At that time she sits on the couch with him and his father, and they converse desultorily about the fact that Kalisa's father doesn't attend regular Sunday services. She is firm and independent, and doesn't hesitate to assert her place as mother chastising her son.

We see her in the fields, hoeing, breaking up the soil, laughing at Kalisa's awkwardness in handling the hoe. She is over 90 in the scene, and still strong enough to do the fieldwork. She tells Kalisa how the land is to be divided, after he asks the delicate question whether she has made a will, and she tells him he is the only one to whom she has spoken about the matter. There is no written will. Later, when the split in the family has hardened over the accusations against her, she tells Kalisa how she had come into the family as the second wife of his grandfather, after the first wife, her sister, died, and how she raised the children. Those same children are now launching accusations against her.

Kalisa feels torn. Unlike *Yaaba* where the lines between right and wrong are drawn fairly clearly, here Kalisa hesitates before rejecting his father and uncle's claims. The sad scene at the witches' camp might be seen as affecting the viewing audience more than Kalisa. When the horrible spectacle of the exorcism is played out, with the two camps seated at opposite ends of the compound ground, Kalisa sits with his grandmother. But when the evangelical preacher asks those who are for Jesus to stand, he announces, I am going to stand, and does so. He doesn't leave to sit with his father and uncle and their families, but stays next to his grandmother. They share the scene, and we are interpellated indirectly through witnessing the questions he has to deal with in relation to his grandmother. They coalesce around the moment where his aunt stands up with her bible, to curse the evangelical exorcists:

FIGURE 9.6 Aunt countering exorcist

The events that surround Margaret's life cannot be separated from her family, from the account that describes how she came into the family, chose to stay, and raised children. We see her, now old, as the grandmother of children she had raised, including not only Kalisa but another grandchild who is marrying. She is a matriarch, but also, strangely, the rejected, disobeyed, disrespected mother. Her life and the time we attach to her is grounded in three features: her family, and the stories they bring to the film about suspicions of her witchcraft; her close relations to her grandson, and his closest relatives, his uncle and father; her work on the family farm, which we see her performing from the outset. At times images of a bird or sunset intercut her actions, and we might well speculate that Chris King, the cinematographer/co-director from South Africa is trying to give us the spectacle of the "African" landscape. But mostly, the sense of time passing that she generates has to do with those three elements: the charges by family members, her relationship to Kalisa, and her working the land.

Time is thus familiar, relative to personal closeness, and eco-natural. The land she has worked, the seeds we see her plant, the growth of the sprouts, and finally the harvest of the grains, all mark the stages of time in the film, and they are always shown through her presence and actions. Her bare feet, creviced with lines of her walking and working, move to a rhythm we would associate with an old person. Grandmother, Yaaba, Yaye, mother. At her age, time comes in the blocktime model where we are looking back at what filled it.[11]

all my age-mates have passed, I'm the only one left, only God knows why

FIGURE 9.7 Time marked on the land and grandmother's memory

The exorcism functions to focus the events from the outset at the trial by fire she is forced to endure. Two camps set at odds with each other, an enmity building since she replaced her sister as her husband John's wife. And after the exorcism, we move quickly to the conclusion, which is seen in her jubilation that nothing happened to her. The film ends, after her harvest, with newspaper headlines indicating that other unjust attacks on old people were continuing by members of their families avid to gain control over the family property.

Time is marked differently for Kalisa. It is impossible not to present it as being set within the short span of life anticipated for his old grandmother versus his full life before him, with children at home and work he values. Next to Grandmother Kamango, he appears young. Her infirmities are signs of her age.

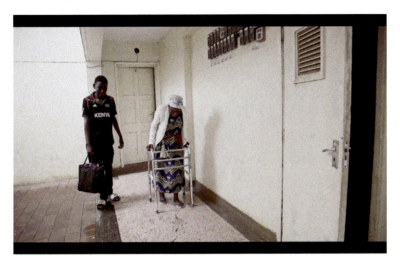

FIGURE 9.8   Grandmother Kamango in her infirmities

His challenge is the need to come to terms with the attacks on the elderly about which he is now learning.

she pretends to be good, but she's killing our children

FIGURE 9.9   Accusation against grandmother

he looked in a mirror, and said it was me who killed the child

FIGURE 9.10   Grandmother's bitter rejoinder

Time for him turns on the reformist agenda of the film: learning about the social ills of witchcraft accusations and exorcisms, becoming a defender of his grandmother. Time for her turns on her larger insertion into the rhythms of nature which are soon to claim her. We see her first, in this mode; followed by Kalisa who learns to connect more closely to the land as she had shown him.

FIGURE 9.11   Grandmother and her field in need of hoeing

FIGURE 9.12   Preparing the land

These two agendas, the social reformist, and the eco-nature framing, create two separate temporalities. The first demands action; the second, work and living within the rhythms of the larger world. As with *Hyènes*, on the one hand the critique of globalized capitalism and its narrow vision is imposed. On the other, the deaths of the old figures put us in touch with a temporality that rides above the immediacy of social demands. The shot of the sunset that follows comes after Kalisa's aunt expresses her doubts about the charges against the grandmother. They are an answer that imposes the temporality of the motions of the sun and the earth, demanding an alternative to the glaring headlines about witch-killings. It isn't a shot of "nature," per se, but of an immutable passage of time where the path, taken for years by the grandmother to her fields, is carved into a space that redefines time with tracks in the worn earth.

FIGURE 9.13   Sunset

II. Death

Margaret Kamango, grandmother to Kalisa, died after the film was completed. We see the time remaining for her to live, in retrospect, going very quickly, as were the major events in her life. Her earlier years are recalled when she was 92, briefly recounted to Kalisa. We pass, via time cuts, from the first scene where he arrives home and talks to her, to the scene where the accusations against her accrued, to the point where the exorcism was held. These are edited so that the passage from one moment in her life to the next is instantaneous. In short, through her we experience the sense of time passing quickly, immediately, as in quantum leaps. We don't experience the rehab time for her to heal from the painful stay in bed after the hip fracture to the use of the walker, the cane, the freedom, and then to the scene in the exorcism. Or back to the fields. We jump through those points like a memory of a series of discrete images that succeed each other rather than flowing into each other like Bergson's notion of time and memory as duration.

Kalisa is young. Time for him is experienced more densely. After he gets word that his grandmother is being accused of witchcraft, he walks us through the steps of returning home, meeting with her, questioning his uncle and father, going to the witch camp and questioning the older residents there, and even returning home to Mombasa to get back to his work. His life is not over or nearly over. He is not facing the prospects of death, burial, and the dissemination of his lands. He has nothing to face like the fates of the elders ensconced in the witches camp to end their days in emptiness.

The relativity of time for these two characters—as for Bila and Yaaba, or for the children in the bunker, in *Hyènes*, who witness Dramaan and Ramatou recalling their youths—is tied into a pattern of relativity that the film recreates, with time passing quickly for the old, slowly for the young. Its meaning emerges from our viewing, our witnessing the passage, our act of viewing corresponding to that of a measuring, as in the physics experiments involving measurements of atoms.

If there were one moment in the film that held the passage of time to its most acute presence, it would be at the exorcism when the grandmother and Kalisa and the aunts are confronted with the force of the evangelical curse:

At that point the aunt could not take any more and felt compelled to act. But before she actually stands, takes her bible, and responds to counter the curse, there is a moment where the act of filming—which we hear the filmmaker remind her co-director to continue with—and the act of viewing are held in tension, like the moment Cheah recounts between experiencing and narrating an event. For the first person narrator, as for the film with its cinematographer hidden from view behind the lens, the experience of what we are seeing and the narration of it coalesces, and is best captured as a still. One woman in a trance of possession, her hands directed toward us,

FIGURE 9.14 Exorcism

toward the grandmother and her grandson and daughters, another woman holding her back; others off to the side not seeing or showing interest in this moment, continuing with their lives as if in another frame. The tension between a still and a motion picture, too, is caught here. We can await the next shot, the next scene, while still feeling the intensity of this moment whose inevitable passing is held as if suspended.

When it is over, the grandmother will return to her life, live out the seven days of the preacher's prediction, and laugh when nothing happens to prove him right. She will return for a space to her life, and then the film will finish, and we will learn of her passing. Kalisa will return to Mombasa; we will attempt to learn more about him, then stop trying. He will presumably go on, long after the film is over, and there will be no end point for his story. The filmmakers too will go on. And eventually this film will have completed its run, and pass into the history and memory of African film. The time for all this to happen will depend upon which trajectory we choose to follow, and it will not be until we put them in relation with each other that something like a sense of the temporality will become visible. But also its limits, as Heidegger has reminded us; we can experience death in anticipation, but not in its actuality.

Notes

1 There are no end of reports on the scandals in Zambia over witch hunting and elderly women being victims of mob attacks, it is perhaps more compelling in thinking about the worlding of this film to place the action closer to the context

of YouTube videos in which we are asked to witness actual victims of witch-craft struggling against their poisonous acts. In this one the sorcerer drives out witches that are hounding a man in his house. Fear, even panic, and violence mark the scene, as if in preparation for some more elaborate footage to constitute the definitive version for the internet audience: https://www.youtube.com/watch?v=xyHjRcAUfkY Accessed August 30 2021.

2 "Introverted" rather than "extroverted," to use Eileen Julien's (2003) terms.

3 Unfairly labeled "calabash" cinema.

4 Kermode, Mark (22 October 2017). "I Am Not a Witch review – magical surrealism". The Observer. Guardian News and Media. Aftab, Kaleem (18 October 2017). "I Am Not a Witch director on the modern persecution of witches in Zambia and Ghana". The Independent.

5 Endangered because of the belief that the use of their body parts can bring the suppliant health or wealth.

6 One might use the more polite designation "elderly," but that would skirt the real impact of the agism that is functioning in this scenario.

7 "Margaret Kamongo (sic) died at the age of 94 in July 2020, but she got to see the film three times." https://worldfilmreviews.us/the-letter/ Accessed September 3, 2021.

8 https://www.imdb.com/title/tt13099242/releaseinfo?ref_=tt_dt_rdat

9 "An ActionAid report on witch camps, published this week, says that more than 70% of residents in Kukuo camp were accused and banished after their husbands died—suggesting that witchcraft allegations are a way of enabling the family to take control of the widow's property." https://www.actionaid.org.uk/doc_lib/ghana_report_single_pages.pdf

   "The camps are a dramatic manifestation of the status of women in Ghana," says Professor Dzodzi Tsikata of the University of Ghana. "Older women" become a target because they are no longer useful to society." https://www.bbc.com/news/magazine-19437130 Accessed September 3, 2021. See the multiple references to the Witches of Gambaga (https://en.wikipedia.org/wiki/Gambaga_Witch_camp), including Npong, Francis (2014). "Witch Camps of Ghana". Utne Reader (Winter): 48–49. Sullivan, Tim (11 January 1998). "A Prison Sometimes a Haven: Ghana's Witch Villages Only Safe Place for Women Accused of Casting Spells." Associated Press. Rocky Mountain News (Denver, CO). Archived from the original on March 29 2015. Accessed November 21 2014 – via HighBeam.

10 In one instance, when Yaaba goes off to see Teryam, she leaves Bila and is seen in the famous long shot walking across the savanna to the river, and then with Teryam to request his help.

11 "Such a theory as this accepts the reality of the present and the past, but holds that the future is simply nothing at all. Nothing has happened to the present by becoming past except that fresh slices of existence have been added to the total history of the world. The past is thus as real as the present. On the other hand, the essence of a present event is, not that it precedes future events, but that there is quite literally *nothing* to which it has the relation of precedence. The sum total of existence is always increasing, and it is this which gives the time-series a sense as well as an order" (Broad 2002, 66–67).

10

THE RESISTANCE OF THE OLD WOMAN

Lemohang Jeremiah Mosese, *This Is Not a Burial, It's a Resurrection* (2019)

Kenneth W. Harrow

Unlike the other versions of Old Woman/Witch-death-time-finishing film, *This Is Not a Burial, It's a Resurrection* (2019) is narrated by a diegetic figure, the lesiba player. The lesiba is an instrument that creates a unique sound with a vibrating string attached to a resonating bowl. The player recounts the story, creating a frame-kernel structure. The frame story opens the film with the lesiba player gradually coming into focus. We are inside a darkened bar setting; men are interposed, drinking, quietly moving about. The lesiba player appears almost like a madman, the lighting and color of the scene generating a sense of unreality as the lesiba's rough tones create an air of relative strangeness. The player is older, weighty in his pronouncements, extraordinary in appearance. An affect of serious and consequential truths unfolds as he begins his story with notes of death.

He begins by talking about the plains of Nasaretha, so-called because of the Christian faith of the villagers. The lesiba player says the people believe that "if you go to the edge of the waters you can still hear the church bells ringing under the water." The audience is then interpellated. As he says, "Take a walk closer to the dam, you will [hear them] for yourself." He continues, "The church bell speaks, tolling beneath, under the waters. In the deep, bells speak when people cannot. . . I saw with my eyes, the dead burying the dead. For this is not a death march, nor a burial, this is a resurrection." The people in the bar appear not to be attending to his narration. He sets the mood, evoking death at the outset: "The genesis, the dead buried their own dead. You, you shall follow in the future. They say in Nasaretha if you put your ear to the ground you can still hear the cries and whispers of those who perished under the flood. Their spirits hallowing from the deep."

DOI: 10.4324/9781003397595-14

A single night became an eternity. They became the departed.

FIGURE 10.1   Lesiba player, *This Is Not a Burial, It's a Resurrection*

When Mantoa, an old woman, appears after this scene, it is in the mountains of Lesotho where the village is located. She is waiting for her son to return for Christmas, as has happened every year. She stands in front of her house, a rondavel, looking across the landscape for him to appear. We learn she has already lost her grandchild and her husband, and lives alone. When his suitcases are delivered to her without him she appears devastated. Nothing stands between her and death.

We have a narrator who brings in death from the outset, while Mantoa waits for it, and when it brings back her son's corpse, she then begins to speak about her own death. The experience of time in each scene becomes marked by her desire to die and be buried. She even arranges for her grave to be dug and designates the lead singer for her funeral dirge. She is tired of life without family; she no longer waits for tomorrow. At one point, she is reprimanded by the village chief for overdoing her keening, as if announcing a death when none had occurred. He tells her that some are calling her a sorceress.

So the first sign of the old woman's story appears with her preoccupation with death, and the second with the Otherness implied by the term sorceress. Toward the end, as the people head out of the village, forced into an exodus by the state's decision to build a dam, she returns against the flow of the crowd, making visible her difference, her refusal to accept.

But on another level she deals with another key feature of time and the old woman's story, and that is the resistance to time's march, to the Arrow of Time. This appears most significantly in the secondary plot line which concerns modernity and progress. Here, as in *Hyènes*, the prospect of progress is treated ironically. The chief says at one point that the word "progress" always causes him pain, and the villagers come to learn how progress will be, again, at their expense. At the end of *Hyènes* we see a site being levelled, presumably the ground on which Colobane had stood. In *This Is Not a Burial,* the leveling takes the form of a flooding that will occur when a dam is built. The village, all the houses, and especially the cemetery will be flooded and lost. And the grave Mantoa sets about having dug, even digging some of it herself so as to be with her ancestors and dead family members, including her husband, child, and grandchild, will be flooded. The villagers are paid, badly, to leave their fields, their homes, and their dead behind them, taking up whatever ancestral bones, belongings, and animals they can, and moving to the capital, where a miserable fate, we learn, will await them.

Dramaan and Ramatou, in *Hyènes*, are conventionally seen as belonging to the Old Order, destined to perish with the transformation into the New Africa brought by the global onset of neoliberalism. We are not far from that situation with Mantoa and Nazaretha, at the opposite end of the continent. Mantoa's son had worked the gold mines, and presumably died there. The monied classes and rulers continue their plans to transform the country to conform to their values, and thus are building dams that dispossess villagers.

This clarifies the meaning of death when introduced by the lesiba player as entailing the dead burying the dead. The dead are both those like Mantoa whose displacement and loss convey the end of life for her; and they are her forebears whose bones lie in the ground.

"The church bell speaks, tolling beneath, under the waters. In the deep, bells speak when people cannot. . . . I saw with my eyes, the dead burying the dead. For this is not a death march, nor a burial, this is a resurrection." The lesiba player continues: "The genesis, the dead buried their own dead. You, you shall follow in the future. They say in Nasaretha if you put your ear to the ground you can still hear the cries and whispers of those who perished under the flood. Their spirits hallowing from the deep."

The hallowing of the spirits extends beyond the immediate family and Mantoa's loss. At one point she explains to the boy, Lasaro, that the plains had been named the Plains of Weeping. There had been a plague and people headed to the city with their ill relatives to seek care, but the ill died en route and had to be buried. Eventually the people grew tired of traveling the distances and settled on the plain where the cemetery had been created. The Plain of Weeping contained the bodies of those who had died in the past. Later, as the villagers were being lobbied by the MP to accept the government's offer of payments and leave for the city, she appealed to them not to abandon their dead. And there the dead, buried in this plain of weeping, extended to those who died in the wars of conquest and resistance. All who died in the Lifawane wars, the Boer Wars, including their Sotho paramount chiefs. All would have to be dug up—the bodies of Lerotholi, Seeiso, Letsi. And everyone who died in wars and in the black plague. The villagers listen and cry out they are not moving. Then the chief tells them, we don't own the land, it is the king's. And with broken tones, tells them they have no choice.

At night Mantoa listens to the obituary notices on the radio. In the day, when she is about, there are always children running, playing, providing speed and motion compared with her slower plodding pace. They rarely speak, except when she tells Lasaro about the history of the name of the Weeping Plain. But when she finally succeeds in convincing the people not to accept the government offers to leave, and they set about plowing, Lasaro stands up and dances in celebration. Then, shockingly, he is shot. His death sets off the villagers' migration. They could not resist. The one who shot him is never seen. Earlier Mantoa's house had been burnt down, and the chief speculates the arsonist was collaborating with the government to drive them out. When the child is killed the villagers lose all hope to continue their resistance. They pack and leave, the fight lost.

As the villagers march out of their village, heading away, Mantoa turns back toward the village where the government's workers are cutting down the trees and preparing for the filling of the reservoir that will flood the cemetery. Mantoa removes her clothes and, her back to us, walks toward them. They warn her not to come any closer, but she continues her naked protest,[1] nudity the only weapon of the Old Woman on the edge of death.

STOP! Don't come any closer!

FIGURE 10.2 Mantoa's naked protest

God leaves their world, she tells the priest. His doubts confront her certainties. Christ's presence is seen in the cross on the wall, the church services, with the white priest and his wife who come to evangelize at the poor village. We are told the story of French missionaries taking 20 years to complete the church, and another ten to confiscate the men's spears and use the metal to make the church bell. Over and over, reminders of Christianity impose themselves on their lives, as in the name Nasaretha, instead of "home." But most of all, the emptiness of the church rhetoric in the face of death is emphasized.

The priest says to Mantoa, times are changing, we cannot withstand the march of time, we have to adapt to change. She looks down, to the side, her pose rejecting what he says. She tells him, "You know what you will see, father? Nothing. You will see nothing, no meaning. there is no meaning to all this. No meaning to my husband's death, to my children's deaths, to my grandchild's death." She pauses, and then throws at him, in his own sorrows, "So it is with your wife's death." She gives him an angry look, and continues, "She will die over and over for the rest of your remaining life. That's grief. Senseless suffering. No meaning to it." Her angst appears in this speech that contrasts with the conventional phrases deployed at the official moments of crisis and death. She is normally reticent, and here when she speaks, it is at a remove from the priest's predictable ministrations. His doubts appear now as grounded in the failures of his church and its teachings to deal with the village life, and especially village death. She strives against the forces destroying their way of life by seeking to perform her own burial, and faces the grave directly, even setting out to dig her own grave. No one can understand this.

She voices her concerns over the flooding of the dam not for the living and their families and homes, but for the dead, whom she wishes to join. She tells the chief the cemetery needs cleaning, that the "modern" plastic bags needed to be picked up, and he responds that they have more important work to do, taking care of the village and the living. But the lesiba player returns the focus again and again to the dead.

The fullest meaning comes when age is confronting death. As she ages, her remaining family will continue to grow older as well, increasing any risk that they will die before she does, as had happened with her son. When the villagers sow their crops, the child Lasaro, who was closest to her, dances in celebration. At her urging the villagers decide to stay. But when a bullet arrives from some unseen source, Lasaro's death is enough to end the villagers' resistance, attesting to the dispossession they had faced all their lives. The new government's modernization plans are the most destructive of all.

The lesiba player intones:

Let the dead bury their own dead. In this house, you shall leave no trace. Bury your existence, lest they say there once lived a sufferer. The soulless march of time has surmounted you. Redeem your days old widow, for the wheel of time has cast you out like an old cloth and turned you into a dung beetle. It's finished. It's finished.

The bleakness of the words cannot convey the powerful effect of his hoarse voice and the rough tonalities of the lesiba, set in the deathly atmosphere of the shabeen. What is finished is not simply life. Indeed, she has the courage to drive the workmen away by working the ultimate Old Woman's weapon, exposing her naked body, her naked genitals, calling up the old powers, as Diabate (2020) writes, to drive them off. The power of pre-Christian spirits' ghostly presence in the graveyard is evoked in her gesture.[2]

With the death of Lasaro, the burial scene enacts a final dirge for the life of the village. The lesiba player warns of the dangers of life ending:

. . . the murderer and arsonist became a coyote that sprawled in the night. They heard rumors. They were surrounded by mortal fear. It was the longest night. A single night became an eternity. They became the departed. The infants clung to their mothers' breasts and refused to grow. Foetuses refused to be born. . . . If that perilous night was not shortened, no one would have survived.[3]

Immediately the following morning the villagers begin their exodus, walking past Mantoa's house. She closes her door and draws her curtains so as not to see them, but in the end has no choice but to join them. The sense of the passing into a deadly modernity is inevitable, until she turns to complete her final gesture of resistance.

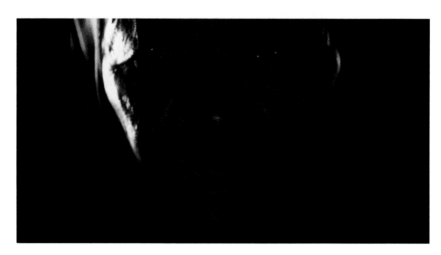

FIGURE 10.3 Mantoa watches villagers departing

The film does not end with that scene. Instead we finish, as with *Yaaba*, with the child who witnesses her sacrifice, and presents the face not for the "burial" but the "resurrection." If it is as such, it is not with the tones of "Abide with Me," as accompanied the earlier village burial of Lasaro. The Christian villagers knew how to carry out a burial. But the resurrection which reached for a transcendence beyond the conventions of the familiar hymns demanded another form, another gesture, which the child who is called ke'moralioamang (daughter of no one) learns to make. The final shot, as in other films with broken children seeing the world in new ways, like *Les 400 Coups*, or *I Am Not a Witch*, is captured in this image of the girl, its caption narrated by the lesiba player: "Many saw death, but ke'moralioamang saw a resurrection":

FIGURE 10.4 Many saw death

II. Death haunts the images: The Gift of Death

FIGURE 10.5   Her mouth was bitter

Four films about old women dying, accused of being witches (*Yaaba* [1989], *I Am Not a Witch* [2017], *The Letter* [2019], *This Is Not a Burial* [2019]), can be seen from another angle if we take the thought from Derrida's *The Gift of Death* that the death in question is a sacrifice. Not a simple sacrifice as in giving a chicken to a god, killing a steer and feeding the poor as Khoudia Lo was charged to do by the *sorcière*. Not a simple fact of dying, as Ramatou in *Hyènes* (1992) tells Dramaan will be their fate, in anticipation of their meeting after that.

Not the dying of the child, the threat of what will happen to Nopoko, if she is not given medicine (in *Yaaba*). Not the death of Grandma Kamango, who plays herself as a nonagenarian, nor that of Fatimata Sanga who played Yaaba and died shortly after the filming was completed, may be counted as a tragedy given their advanced ages. Age advances to death, and the gift of the remaining time shrinks with each passing day. In the biblical accounts Moses was 120 when he died, and wasn't mourned any more than was his brother Aaron (123), or for that matter the ur-father Abraham who was buried at the age of 175, next to his aged wife Sarah (127). These biblical ages are all to be taken, like the actual measured ages of Fatimata

Sanga, or Yaaba, or "grandma," as inauthentic for Dasein, since they are always measured and taken "as if," not *en tant que tel*, as such in and of themselves. And when "as if," they are never a "gift."

It can only be a gift if there is life left in the sacrifice, and by that measure the most generous of the women being sacrificed was Shula, the child whose death freed all the other old women-witches—and whose age, as a child and as an old witch, was not calculable. Further, for the sacrifice to extend beyond its instrumental purpose of saving the land for the people, as Mantoa presumably seeks to do at the end, or even, perversely, Ramatou by making the people of Colobane confront the price of dealing with the spectre of globalization, more than an exchange is needed for the sacrifice to be a gift. An exchange is effected with a finite gift—a life for a life and an eye for an eye. A few sheep for a well. A promise to end the plagues for the liberation of the people. Exchanges, short of gifts, which are not reckonable.

The infinite gift has no measurable reward. As the old women approach the end of their lives, their gifts shift from the calculable value of what their deaths buy to what occurs on the register of death without calculation. At least for Kierkegaard, Abraham's sacrifice of Isaac, the model of the gift of death for Derrida, places his act in conflict with the ethical order. For Derrida (1996) it opposes Abraham to the interests of the family, for whom his act was incomprehensible, and to whom he never spoke about it. For Derrida it becomes an incommunicable act, not because it is so terrifying per se, but because to speak of it would be to place it within the registers of speech, communication, logic, need, and desire. For Abraham it was the action by which his faith and relation to God were marked—a singularity, as Derrida put it. Not a generalizable action, in Kantian ethical terms, but a unique action entirely placed within the scope of Abraham's relationship to Adonai.

The face-to-face encounter of Moses and God, when Moses hid himself in the cleft, comes closest to Derrida's evocation of the approach to the Other, to the other as singular, that Derrida uses to configure the moment when death becomes possible as a gift. The other does not engage in dialogue, does not explain as much as command and give the gifts of mitzvot (i.e., commandments, laws), expecting obedience in return. The list of mitzvot in the Torah is 613, but it might as well be infinite, just as the reward for observance is infinite children; the punishment for apostasy, turning away is infinite pain. The child can't make this into a gift as its life stretches before it. The old woman is never unaware of the time left to her, and even as she laughs about conquering her enemies, as does Grandma Kamango, she can't escape Kalisa's question about what will happen to her lands when she dies; and she admits, she already has a plan, which she explains to him.

Being in the world with her family, she has to care for them as well as herself. She has to assume a responsibility, and for Derrida that is inevitably tied to maintaining the secret of the demonic,[4] that is, the infinitely spiritual source of trembling, what has to remain secret in order to publicly project an ethical demeanor to the world.[5]

Either she is a witch, deserving death, or at the least, to be neutralized by demonic exorcism, or she is one foot from the ancestors, the ones to whom the children should turn for help in overcoming their problems of ill health, infertility, bad luck. Her gift of death can begin only with her being-toward-death, which Heidegger defines as the human intention toward others that is expressed in care, in being-toward authentically rather than in following herd notions and values. For our four African grandmothers, it is hard to tie their immanent deaths and being-toward-others without bringing up the way beliefs in witchcraft shape their relations and encounters. Abraham never faced such charges directly, although twice God intervenes to work sorcery against other rulers who displayed too close attention to Sarah. The mystery and secret, which Derrida asserts are complements to the responsibility that accompanies the gift of death are presented by him as repressed effects of the mysteries, ek-stasies, trances of the times before the rational religious order was effected, or imposed (1996, 3–5). In Africa such times were demonized by the colonial missionaries, whose own repressed demonic orders were never acknowledged. The role of the grandmother-witches was always framed by that Western order of rationality, by the evocation of religion, usually in cemeteries.

Thus, the gift of death comes with the presence of death. *Yaaba* begins with Sana encountering the children in the cemetery. As Nopoko expresses the wish that her dead mother would be with them, Sana tends a grave a few meters off. Sana is placed in her own grave by Noaga toward the end of the film after she dies on the bench outside her house. She had been discovered by Bila and Nopoko when they came to thank her for helping cure Nopoko. Her death is signaled through montage editing, and the return of life to the children is seen in the last shot where they are seen running off to the horizon on the savannah, with no enclosures before them. Their running provides the frame for the old woman's death, as it had marked their initial encounter after the meeting in the cemetery.

Sana does not speak very often. She gestures to Taryam, smiles at Bila, speaks to the boatsman from a distance: her lines of dialogue are few. She appears the model for responsibility, especially as she says nothing in defense of herself, or in justification for the cure she risks her life to bring (her house is being burned down as she is leaving to get the medicine, and yet she still returns with it). She offers the children unconditional care, without the community's approbation. Where originally she had been called a witch by the "inauthentic" figures in the village, who accepted this judgment as an evident truth, she is much closer to the "authentic" figure of care and responsibility envisioned by Heidegger as the one who faces her death, from the outset till the end.

She is the sacrifice, as is Abraham, who has one son he loves and yet is willing to sacrifice. And this is done entirely without Yaaba becoming a knight of faith, a true believer in the Other who doesn't respond. She is realized as the foil to the false marabout/sorcerer who claims he has the powers to determine her status as a witch and has the powers to cure. The children respond to her immediately, without words. Most importantly, as an outcast she is without family, her mother having died in her childbirth, so that her being named by the children Yaaba, grandmother, is transformative, indicative of her acceptance of responsibility in relation to them.

Her death seals that relationship as it appears, ultimately, as a gift. The scenes in the cemetery, the grave at the end, all reinforce the link between responsibility to the Other, care, authenticity, and old age and death.[6] Heidegger's well-known position on death and authenticity is that it is only through being-toward-death that the individual, the person whose being is engaged in this, its existence as Dasein, can establish a position of authenticity, and in doing that entails openness to care. The important distinction he establishes turns on the need to deal with our own death, not death in the abstract, not the death of others which only they can experience, and after which, obviously, nothing about it can be communicated to us. Yaaba's engagement with death, even her willing self-sacrifice on Nopoko's behalf, all place her in a relationship with death that is marked by her own life-story, her having borne accusations of causing her mother's death, as a witch-child; her bearing accusations of having set the house on fire in the village or causing Nopoko's illness. She is not simply a scapegoat, but more importantly the foil to the villagers for whom gossip, common truths, commonly held beliefs, and common accusations betray an inauthenticity that contrasts with the solitude of authentic Dasein in confronting one's own experience of mortality.

This is all the more ironic since the "inauthentic" popular view of the film as not filling the accurate role of a postcolonial artifact misses the point concerning authenticity, in Heideggerian terms—that is, finding a world of being with others, without falling back on the conventional and trite clichéd understandings of world and people.[7] "Africa" is most susceptible to this inauthenticity when seen in the perspective of otherness, just as the other from the African perspective falls equally into the inauthentic. This differs from Heidegger's notion of inauthenticity, which he associates with the group think of the "they-self": "So authenticity is not about being isolated from others, but rather about finding a different way of relating to others such that one is not lost to the they-self" ("Martin Heidegger." Np.)[8]

Again the irony is that the very term "authentic" is used both as a derogatory term when considering trite conventional approaches to Africa, as well as being used as a defensive term to ward off Eurocentric appropriations and constructions of Africa. An "authentic" statue would be constrained by Western museum standards; an authentic film by film festivals devoted to world cinemas.[9] Africa has borne the burden of the term "authenticity" ever since Europeans constructed it as the dark continent on which to write their own "inventions" (Mudimbe 1988).

Death is the central concern, for care and authenticity, or Dasein, and for the story of the old woman-witch. Films like *Blood Diamonds* (2006) or action films that turn on the easy distribution of corpses turn away from the individual's engagement with their own death. My concern here is specifically with the witch's turn to her own death. Most dramatically, as with Ramatou's descending the stairs at the end—her own stairs, her own body, her own mortality. Not the death of figures who constitute "their" deaths. Heidegger's formulation here demonstrates how authenticity is central to the issue:

> In everyday Being-towards-death, the self that figures in the for-the-sake-of-itself structure is not the authentic mine-self, but rather the inauthentic they-self. *In effect, the "they" obscures our awareness of the meaning of our own deaths by de-individualizing death.* As Heidegger explains: in "Dasein's public way of interpreting, it is said that 'one dies', because everyone else and oneself can talk himself into saying that 'in no case is it I myself', for this 'one' is the *'nobody'*" (*Being and Time* 51: 297). In this way, everyday Dasein flees from the meaning of its own death, in a manner determined by the "they". It is in this evasion in the face of death, interpreted as a further way in which Dasein covers up Being, that everyday Dasein's fallen-ness now manifests itself. To be clear: evasion here does not necessarily mean that I refuse outright to acknowledge that I will someday die. After all, as I might say, 'everyone dies'. However, the certainty of death achieved by idle talk of this kind is of the wrong sort.
>
> *(Being and Time* 53: 309) ("Martin Heidegger," *Stanford Encyclopedia of Philosophy*, np, my stress)

The authenticity of care, with being-toward-death, might seem increasingly appropriate for elders whose deaths are approaching, whose lives had mostly passed, whose ties to their children and grandchildren form more and more of the substance of their lives. But every move to place a group into one category immediately entails the potential formulation of its opposite, the old who worry about dying and find it easier and easier to escape into the "idle chatter" (Heidegger) of truths about "passing" that are designed to ease the passage, ease the diversion by seeing the situation as one shared by all, rather than experienced by oneself, one's "own-ness" (Heidegger). Witches are victims of two easy solutions to the problem of old age and property. First, they are the thieves par excellence in their abilities to fly by night and steal into people's homes while they are asleep and steal their souls (Geschiere). And they are equally easily charged with every conceivable illness or ill fortune that befalls their victims, as if stealing their livelihoods and lives. They are the scapegoats for others' misfortunes; or rather, the excuse for others, and as such the ultimate vehicle for others' inauthenticity.

Heidegger focuses on speech to establish the distinction between the authentic and inauthentic, in a way that speaks directly to our question of how the older people can establish their care:

> Nevertheless, we can say this: when care is realized authentically, I experience discourse as *reticence*, as a keeping silent (ignoring the chatter of idle talk) so that I may hear the call of conscience; I experience projection onto guilt as a possible way of Being in which I take responsibility for a lack or a not-Being that is located firmly in my own self (where "taking responsibility for" means recognizing that not-Being is one of *my* essential structures); and I experience thrownness as anxiety[10], a mode of disposedness that, as we have seen, leaves me estranged from the familiar field of intelligibility determined by the "they" and thereby discloses the possibility of my own not-Being. So, reticence, guilt and anxiety all have the effect of extracting Dasein from the ontological clutches of the "they". That is why the unitary structure of reticence-guilt-anxiety characterizes the Being of authentic Dasein.
>
> *("Martin Heidegger")*

Yaaba falls directly into those categories. Almost oddly, since alienation from the community is hardly an African convention, whereas "angst" is a by-word for European existential fiction, especially in the earlier years of the Theatre of the Absurd (e.g. *Der Besuch der Alten Dame*, 1956). But Yaaba, like Ramatou, is hardly given to individual expressions of angst. She is isolated, so her reticence is an inevitable feature of her isolation; her responsibility for her own death must be inferred from her visits to the cemetery, but more particularly from her attempts to save Nopoko over the opposition of the village. Her anguish at being stoned by the vicious boys is written onto her well-known image;

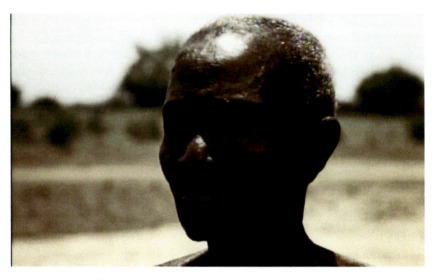

FIGURE 10.6   Yaaba

but her gentle laugh of pleasure at being befriended by Bila is counter-poised against the stoning incident. Although circumstances, not character, can be viewed as accounting for her stance, in the end she will be occupying the same spaces of exclusion as witches expelled, if not killed, by the village. In that regard, she is "thrown" not only into existence, as a feature that authenticity must take into account, but into the existence of the exile—the ultimate threat posed against all the witches, indeed all the elders, all the old woman viewed as no longer productive for the community, as hanging on at the expense of their grown children, as a threat to the existential health of the family or village—the "they."

The witches and their feasts are the threat (Geschiere), and as Ramatou says to the elders of Colobane when they come to ask her to invest in the village and its future, I have bought it all up, all the lands and buildings that matter. Before you ask, be sure you have been invited to the lions' feast. She had been excluded before she became a lion, and now can exclude all those who are not, all those who gather together to take her gifts, her bribes, who pontificate and spout reasons to kill Dramaan in the name of "justice." In Ionesco's *Rhinoceros* (1959) all the people turn into rhinoceroses, into the same kind of beast, sharing the same thoughts and words, turning despite themselves; like the *professeur* in *Hyènes* who feels himself turning into "them." When Ramatou goes down the final steps to her fate, she casts a last look out at sea, in the direction of Gorée. First witches and lions, and then slaves and hyenas.

Shula has to choose between being a witch, which she thought she understood when she was accused and attacked at the beginning, or being a goat. When she arrives at the village of witches, those are her options. In all cases, the witches have no more choice in the affair than do the old people about being old. Inauthentically they are cast into the "they," not free to claim "I am not a witch" when it is death to defy the charges. In the case of Wend Kuuni's mother she and her son are cast out of the village, and when she wanders in the wilderness she is on her own and dies of thirst. He is saved and taken in. The village had cast out; the village took in. The lines between authentic and inauthentic could not be established; and perhaps we could interpret his traumatic inability to speak as a sign of that reticence of the Dasein, with its guilt, its introspection, and especially its angst.

They are old, but reticent, made so by the force that has accounted for their age. In the village of witches they might sing and dance; but when they are being exorcised or stoned, they lose their voices, and no one wants to hear their complaints, much less their problems, their aches, their cries against ingratitude. Their children or grandchildren face different lives, and the young people who return to their elders, the Yaabas, the Grandma Makondas, are the exception. These women face a world the young do not, one they can imagine going on without them. This is the world of witches who descend staircases, who fly off from their ribbon-bands, who fly in the night, not to the certainty of eating the souls of the living but to the uncertainty of the emptiness that emerges only in the night. Heidegger saw angst. I see witches, beings who face the villages that no longer hold them in their hands, if not quite as desperate as albinos cut up for their body parts. Shula is a witch and albino and child cut into pieces, so that the bodies of old women offer the proper way to see her, held like a trapped figure in the tree, toward the end of the film. Heidegger calls this no longer being at home in the world:

> When I am anxious I am no longer at home in the world. I fail to find the world intelligible. Thus there is an ontological sense (one to do with intelligibility) in which I am not in the world, and the possibility of a world without me (the possibility of my not-Being-in-the-world) is revealed to me. "[The] state-of-mind [mode of disposedness] which can hold open the utter and constant threat to itself arising from Dasein's ownmost individualized Being, is anxiety. In this state-of-mind, Dasein finds itself face to face with the "nothing" of the possible impossibility of its existence.
>
> *(Being and Time* 53: 310) ("Martin Heidegger")

There was a time when African films that were thought to play to an audience's desire to see the "real" Africa were dubbed Calabash movies, and *Yaaba* would have been cited as an example. But it is hard to satirize the "Africanness" of Calabash movies[11] when popular images abound on social media. Nigerian films now are willing to go to the limits of the spectacle, and *Calabash* begins with a witchdoctor holding a bowl of magical substances that burst into flames in his hands. It goes from there.

For Derrida the "threshold of responsibility" will emerge before the gaze of the other, "of a person as transcendent other, as an other who looks at me, but who looks without the-subject-who-says-I being able to reach the other, see her, hold her within the reach of my gaze" (1996: 26–27). The threshold appears when Bila hides and Sana laughs and indicates with her chin to Nopoko where he is. He is put off by being betrayed, but both children now emerge before her gaze. She is Other to them at that point; but soon becomes "Yaaba" when he brings her a chicken as a gift. Levinas poses a similar relationship: when I look at a stranger—not someone who has a claim on my indulgence—I must respond to her appeal not to exercise power over her, even kill her, though she be a stranger (*Entre Nous*). If it is a gift to someone in our family, or community, it is attached to obligations, it creates obligations. But death ends obligations, leading to the parceling out of land. But if my responsibility is built on care (*sorge*), the interactions are marked by incommensurability between the figures seeing each other, responding to each other. The response transgresses the imposed conventions, rules, order, by virtue of the gift, and of the unstated, the mystery or secret to which all authentic appeals are related. This leads Derrida to this lapidary conclusion: "The exercise of responsibility seems to leave no choice but this one, however uncomfortable it be, of paradox, heresy, and secrecy" (29). Exceeding the inauthenticity of order runs the risk, always, of the Yaabas being expelled. Paradox, heresy, and secrecy are the byways of witchery, and following that path, away from a Christianity, or any dogmatic religious practice, he claims it runs the risk of "conversion and apostasy: there is no responsibility without a dissident and inventive rupture with respect to tradition, authority, orthodoxy, or doctrine" (29).

Perhaps of all the witches that face this accusation the most interesting might be Shula, who is, as we see her, just a girl, whose apostasy is, in fact, from her role and training as witch. The crisis of faith that marks *This Is Not a Burial* is bizarrely inverted in *I Am Not a Witch*, where being a witch is presented as not hidden (they are openly marked by the ribbon-bands) and discredited, as the accusers are seen as not credible, are ridiculed. If they are discredited at the end, they never achieve Dasein, never know the angst of the witch, the authenticity of the sacrifice, or the care that it brings. Most of all that Dasein is only a limit to be approached asymptotically, as if an approximation to a truth. We never descend to the depths with Ramatou at the end; never see how Shula or Yaaba die. Mantoa ends with her defiance of the workers who warn her not to approach. The witches' carnival is invisible to ordinary eyes; the sacrifice must remain hidden.

Notes

1 Naminata Diabate, *Naked Agency: Genital Cursing and Biopolitics in Africa* (2020).
2 Diabate's description of the deployment of this power is quite nuanced, and works well to describe Mantoa as both a figure of power and helplessness: ""This formulation of openness (that marks nakedness) as both enabling and disallowing moves beyond the bifurcated logic of victimhood versus sovereignty to suggest that women's agency, especially in relation to naked bodies used collectively, is ever unfolding and empowering yet precarious" (128).
3 This dark note matches the ending of *Hyènes* where instead of coyotes on the prowl it is hyenas who mark the end of life before the devastating onset of modernity.
4 "Borrowed from Late Latin *daemonicus,* borrowed from Greek *daemonikós,* from *daimon-, daímōn* 'superhuman power, spirit intermediate between gods and humans.'"
https://www.merriam-webster.com/dictionary/demonic
5 Derrida has an extended discussion of Jan Patočka's concepts of "enthusiasm" or the "demonic." The demonic is marked by the esoteric, the secret or the sacred (*The Gift of Death*).
6 "Since one cannot experience one's own death, it seems that the kind of phenomenological analysis that has hitherto driven the argument of *Being and Time* breaks down, right at the crucial moment. One possible response to this worry, canvassed explicitly by Heidegger, is to suggest that Dasein understands death through experiencing the death of others. However, the sense in which we experience the death of others falls short of what is needed. We mourn departed others and miss their presence in the world. But that is to experience Being-with them as dead, which is a mode of our continued existence. As Heidegger explains:

> 'The greater the phenomenal appropriateness with which we take the no-longer-Dasein of the deceased, the more plainly is it shown that in such Being-with the dead, the authentic Being-come-to-an-end of the deceased is precisely the sort of thing which we do *not* experience. Death does indeed reveal itself as a loss, but a loss such as is experienced by those who remain. In suffering this loss, however, we have no way of access to the loss-of-Being as such which the dying man 'suffers'. The dying of Others is not something which we experience in a genuine sense; at most we are always just 'there alongside'.'" (*Being and Time* 47: 282) Cited in "Martin Heidegger" *Stanford Encyclopedia of Philosophy*, (https://plato.stanford.edu/entries/heidegger/#Dea)

7 The Stanford Encyclopedia of Philosophy has a lengthy entrée on Heidegger's notion of authenticity.
"As one might expect, Heidegger argues that Being-towards-death not only has the three-dimensional character of care, but is realized in authentic and inauthentic modes. Let's begin with the authentic mode. . . . Given the analysis of death as a possibility, the authentic form of projection in the case of death

is anticipation. Indeed Heidegger often uses the term anticipation in a narrow way, simply to mean being aware of death as a possibility. But death is disclosed authentically not only in projection (the first dimension of care) but also in thrownness (the second dimension)["having-been-thrown-intro-the-world" "Martin Heidegger"]. The key phenomenon here is the mode of disposedness that Heidegger calls *anxiety*. Anxiety, at least in the form in which Heidegger is interested, is not directed towards some specific object, but rather opens up the world to me in a certain distinctive way. When I am anxious I am no longer at home in the world. I fail to find the world intelligible. Thus there is an ontological sense (one to do with intelligibility) in which I am not in the world, and the possibility of a world without me (the possibility of my not-Being-in-the-world) is revealed to me. "[The] state-of-mind [mode of disposedness] which can hold open the utter and constant threat to itself arising from Dasein's ownmost individualized Being, is anxiety. In this state-of-mind, Dasein finds itself face to face with the 'nothing' of the possible impossibility of its existence." (*Being and Time* 53: 310) ("Martin Heidegger," *Stanford Encyclopedia of Philosophy*, np)

"Inauthenticity in relation to death is also realized in thrownness, through *fear*, and in projection, through *expectation*. Fear, as a mode of disposedness, can disclose only particular oncoming events *in* the world. To fear my own death, then, is once again to treat my death as a case of death. This contrasts with anxiety, the form of disposedness which, as we have seen, discloses my death via the awareness of the possibility of a world in which I am not. The projective analogue to the fear-anxiety distinction is expectation-anticipation. A mundane example might help to illustrate the generic idea. When I expect a beer to taste a certain way, I am waiting for an actual event—a case of that distinctive taste in my mouth—to occur. By contrast, when I anticipate the taste of that beer, one might say that, in a cognitive sense, I actively go out to meet the possibility of that taste. In so doing, I make it mine. Expecting death is thus to wait for a case of death, whereas to anticipate death is to own it.

[Heidegger also] suggests that discourse has inauthentic modes, for instance when it is manifested as idle talk; and in yet other sections we find the claim that fallen-ness has an authentic manifestation called a *moment-of-vision* (e.g., *Being and Time* 68: 401). Regarding the general relations between discourse, fallen-ness and authenticity, then, the conceptual landscape is not entirely clear." ("Martin Heidegger," *Stanford Encyclopedia of Philosophy*, np)

8 In contrast to Heidegger's negative take on "they-ness" one might cite ubuntu, often evoked as the positive relations afforded by the community, or even the grounding of being in community.

9 Cf. Olivier Barlet on this issue, in *Africultures*:

"The need for an African critique
I try to reinforce reflection on films, in order to contribute to educating the public. As chief editor of the journal *African Screen*, I attach importance to a journalist's cultural background. A Tunisian will explain *Halfaouine* (Ferid Boughedir) better than someone else: he or she will be more likely to get to the essential. I am thus wary of Western critics due to the divide between social reality cinema in Africa and the prevailing psychological cinema in the West. One group's criteria cannot be applied to the other. Since 1986, African films such as *Yeelen* have been represented as « happy syntheses », as Ferid Boughedir put it. Souleymane Cissé was in the process of opening a hitherto unexplored path. Yet, the European critics analyzed the film at

face value (magical or mystical) and gave an image that influenced the other filmmakers. The Europeans, who didn't understand the content, showered praise on the film seeing it as an escapist, exotic film. If an African critique really existed, both the audience and the filmmakers would benefit in terms of reflection and depth of understanding. Word of mouth is more effective than articles in the newspapers which are not always read: if a film speaks about them, the audience adheres. African critics can only intervene once the film has been shown in Europe: the articles written by the European critics remain decisive. A real African critique is a void that needs filling, therefore, on the same level as exploitation, distribution, etc.: a critique which does not start out from the same reading of the image as in Europe, but which thinks about how the filmmakers can be close to their public and take inspiration from their culture."
   http://africultures.com/interview-with-clement-tapsoba-by-olivier-bar-let-5276/ Accessed September 14, 2021.

10 "Throwness" "As Dasein, I ineluctably find myself in a world that matters to me in some way or another. This is what Heidegger calls *thrownness* (*Gewor-fenheit*), a having-been-thrown into the world. 'Disposedness' is Kisiel's (2002) translation of *Befindlichkeit*, a term rendered somewhat infelicitously by Mac-quarrie and Robinson as 'state-of-mind'. Disposedness is the receptiveness (the just finding things mattering to one) of Dasein, which explains why Richardson (1963) renders *Befindlichkeit* as 'already-having-found-oneself-there-ness'." ("Martin Heidegger," *Stanford Encyclopedia of Philosophy*, np)
11 See my article "Manthia Diawara's Waves and the Problem of the Authentic." (Dec. 2015) *African Studies Review* 58, no. 3: 13–30.

CONCLUSION

An Opera of This World (2017), Manthia Diawara: The Encounter with the Other Face-to-Face

Kenneth W. Harrow

> Levinas's descriptions show that 'in the beginning was the human relation'. The primacy of relation explains why it is that human beings are interested in the questions of ethics at all. But for that reason, Levinas has made interpretative choices. To situate first philosophy in the face-to-face encounter is to choose to begin philosophy not with the world, not with God, but with what will be argued to be the prime condition for human communication.
>
> (Levinas, 2019)

We can think of the face-to-face as the encounter. In cinema there are various manners of constructing a face-to-face. Literally there is the one person seeing or meeting another, and the camera can echo the encounter with alternating shots of each, constructing the scene of dialogue, the shot reverse-shot, where the camera is not announcing its presence. One could use a stationary camera as well, or place the camera in a bizarre location, or have it move, as though someone were observing the two figures in dialogue, in which case we have the face-to-face and a third party.

I like to think of this encounter as also engendered when one scene follows another, leading to montage editing, and genres that purport to create meaning, as in Eisenstein's films, in Russian montage cinema. We can abstract the juxtaposition of any two scenes as encounters, with resulting narratives, constructed as in documentaries intended to convey a message, or an encounter like that seen when a camera has us made aware of the face-to-face.

DOI: 10.4324/9781003397595-15

Levinas's "face-to-face" has a primeval dimension to it: "the core element of intersubjective life: the other person addresses me, calls to me. He does not even have to utter words in order for me to *feel* the summons implicit in his approach." Most importantly, "Beyond any other philosophical concerns, the fundamental intuition of Levinas's philosophy is the *non-reciprocal relation of responsibility*"[1](my stress).[2]

The weirdest part of Levinas's conception of this encounter is the recognition by the other than I am capable of harming that person, of killing that other person. From this recognition comes a commandant, thou shalt not kill. I recognize in the face of the other my responsibility to respond to their appeal not to harm them. The appeal of the face engenders the recognition of something in that face that calls to me as a person, not as a thing.

The relevance of this approach to the question of immigration is obvious, and it compels us to read Manthia Diawara's *An Opera of The World* (2017) in terms of such encounters, including most notably that of the audience with the images and characters. It speaks directly to our times when the crisis of migration has become central to postcolonial concerns. Aside from the political consequences that have rewritten the political landscape, there is the concern with representing the issues. My interest here is the specificity of the face-to-face, not simply a willingness to accept others who are different. Not simply a rationale for immigration based on crude calculations of profiting from the aspirations or desperation of others, the myriad stories behind the figure of the refugee. My interest first is in recognizing the face-to-face as the fundamental basis for being, what Levinas calls the human being. The interaction is what cinema can evoke.

We can complement the work of the camera in establishing the face-to-face relationship, the encounter, with a broader notion provided by physics, both special relativity and quantum mechanics. From the former we have the notion that any measurements of time and space must be considered in relative terms, that is, that no "event"—no physical entity—exists in a location in time and space by itself. Simply, whether on a macro or micro level, we are always in some degree of interaction with what surrounds us.

The quantum physicist Karen Barad (2007) uses the term "inter-act," which basically holds that the elements of force and matter in the universe are always in interaction with each other. Some of those interactions are at too great a distance, and involve too weak forces to substantially, measurably, or perceptually affect the elements in interaction. But the basic concept remains: everything in the universe is in interaction.[3] This is one of the fundamental principles of physics. It can be expressed in strange ways, as with entanglement where the notions of locality and distance leave us at a loss to explain how two particles appear to be in sync at distances that are too great for actions in sync to be possible.

However, it isn't simply double-slit experiments that matter for us since we can say all of life is marked by interactions, by the experience of "entr-action." The observation of the experimenter intra-acts/enters into acts, with the process of taking a measurement. For the situation of a science lab, the entire configuration consists of experimenter who sets up the experiment and measures the results and the equipment—all of which function as an apparatus. The results of the experiment are a function of the relationships of the entire apparatus, not unlike the cinematic apparatus that also entails an action of recording and then projecting an image onto a screen. This is seen by a viewer and marked at a moment in time in such a way as to generate a "result" that can be read only by taking into account all that went into the creation of the image and the reaction of the viewer. In physics the uncertainty principle affirms that no observation can be made without interactions that affect what is being measured; in cinema no film can exist, i.e. as an audience experience, without the latter entering into the interaction, just as the filmmaker must do with the apparatus in both the broad ideological and narrow technical sense. The internal images of the diegesis interact, as does the frame, and the viewing level. We return to the penetration/entr'acte of each level with the other, leaving us with concepts like Derrida's invagination or supplement as inevitably forming part of the experience.

The interlinking of the parts of the apparatus as entr'acte would not be the case if the viewer/experimenter were separate from the set-up for the experiment and the screen on which the result appears. The result must be seen and recorded, the devices subject to the experimenter's adjustments; and oddly enough, the interference of the experimenter in setting up and then viewing the results functions as if it were part of the experiment. In cinema we'd signal the self-reflection of the viewer as integral to whatever meaning the image would record or convey; as if the same apparatus that "sees" and records the real event is already enmeshed in the event, the reading of its appearance, and its meaning (Harrow 2022: 71–2).

What appears fundamental to us when we encounter objects located in time and space is their physical, material presence, which we imagine we can record by measuring with clocks and mechanical devices. In fact, we can always do this in a classical sense, giving us a cinema not unlike what Deleuze identifies as one of movement-images, or a story and characters whose actions and meanings function as if determined by rational forces or motives. It is tied together cogently. This ignores what the Deleuzean time-images insist upon, which is the need to take cognizance not of how a implies b, but how we are observing this while it happens, and how our observation makes central the issue of time rather than motion. Deleuze evokes this beautifully in his image of the crystal.[4] We can call time that moves forward linearly Classical; but we can call time-images Relational, susceptible to leaps that answer to forces that we continually disrupt in the process of observing and measuring them.

The uncertainty is more than post-modern; it is fundamental to the nature of our existence. At the quantum level, according to Carlo Rovelli, time is not a variable in the equations that provide us with basic information concerning the fundamental level of what exists, but is generated by the interactions of particles or waves. From cogito ergo sum we pass to: we interact and therefore we are.

What Levinas enables us to do is to project the need to understand the other, to arrive at our preliminary attempts to provide meaning, by turning to the interactions, and specifically those that entail the vis-à-vis of human encounters. Film gives us the face. Diawara records the encounters because he repeatedly strives to place in relationship with each other the meeting of those faces with ours—we who see them due to the work of the camera, aware of that work, of its being set before us, of its presence, of the implied cameraman, director, and *metteur-en-scène*, with a subject to be confronted, and most of all, so as to impose an implicit call and a response to each image. Every single shot of this film calls out, from the past to the present, to the moment of singularity when the call, falling within our horizon, imposes the expectation of a meeting, a response. What works for the film apparatus has a counterpart with the apparatus of quantum mechanics: the observer is implicated in what they see, just as Barad had put it, we are part of the world in its differential becoming (2007).

Which encounters, and within what frames, does *An Opera of The World* privilege?

I will signal some of the key ones to try to highlight the principle on which this study of contemporary African cinema is based, namely, that the directions undertaken by African filmmakers, especially since the onset of the digital age of the long 1990s down to the present, have been uneasily set in tension with that massive dominant force in cinema studies dubbed World Cinema. The same mechanisms that have marked globalization, under the impress of neoliberal capitalism, rather than African nation building and its collaborative ventures in engagé cinema, are now presenting themselves to the film industry in Africa. The result is that some of the pressures to commercialize are now succeeding in marking places for African films on networks like Amazon or Netflix, with all the strictures their algorithms imply. But more, many more films made by independent auteurs are being made and are availing themselves of less widely viewed companies, like Kino Lorber, Icarus, or ArtMattan Productions/ADIFF. Dozens of smaller independent production companies come online when new films are made. Finally, film festivals always provide some distribution for independent films. None of this is permanent; even the Edinburgh Film Festival had to fold this year (2022), and great opportunities for viewing African cinema sections of major festivals, like Toronto's Planet Africa, have ended. Where once FESPACO ruled for decades in the world of African Cinema, along with Carthage, now we have Durban and Zanzibar's film festivals competing, often with a wider range of African films.

The question I wish to address at this point is how we are to frame the encounters we will signal in *An Opera of The World*, so as to suggest alternative possibilities to those likely to arise in the World Cinema approaches. How we would think about these moments in a film made by a well-known filmmaker and scholar, one who has engaged us with his work on many aspects of African culture, to its housing, Negritude, cinema, and thought, to broad questions of Africanness as viewed in the personal essay-films (and importantly, in his bio-book writings also framed about his own experiences) of Diawara (*We Won't Budge: An African Exile in the World*, 2003; *In Search of Africa*, 1998).

Consider his earliest major film, *Rouch in Reverse* (1995), coming after his first documentary on Sembène (*Sembène: the Making of African Cinema*, 1994). In *Rouch*, Diawara playfully reverses the roles of ethnographer and informant. Rouch plays along, bringing Diawara into his home, and laying out the basic keys to his notion of cinéma verité along with the central function of editing. It is all made enjoyable as Diawara avoids challenging Rouch on his approach in *Les Maîtres fous* (1955), Rouch's most contested film. The shocking images of trancing Haukas—with whom Rouch saw his own camerawork as similarly being guided by trances, and his voiceover commentary as consonant with the images, that is, without prejudgments, was received in France by African intellectuals as an embarrassment. It posed the larger question of framing, where Rouch's narrow notion of truth in unprearranged shots leaves out the question of the World into which a film enters and is seen, its horizon of expectations. Diawara believed the audience of his film could catch the subtlety of his own congenial position in engaging Rouch without criticizing him for avoiding controversy. It is that unforgettable voice of Diawara that always brings us back to his control over the narrative and images.

In *Opera*, Diawara quickly draws us into a similar relationship with major European/American figures, notably Alexander Kluge who responds to Diawara's questions about high culture—opera—and how it might be regarded in Africa. As Kluge opines on the basic nature of 18th Century opera, and how it might be viewed as reflecting African sensibilities, Diawara is seen as smilingly approving his and Richard Sennet's words, which some viewers found disconcerting. What is occluded in that reaction is Diawara's staging of the interviews, inevitably forcing them into the montage relationship with the clips of the immigrants in the water, the opera, and then subsequent evocations of such flights in the past when it was to the south that European Jews fled.[5] Their musings follow the establishing scenes where the centering of Diawara's role is seen.

Diawara clarifies his goal in juxtaposing voices with scenes from the opera, reaching for Glissant's "chaos opera":

In making the film, I made Édouard Glissant's concept of 'Chaos-Opera' my own, in order to create relationships between Bintou Were, a Sahel Opera and all the human migrations that took place before it, during, or after. *An Opera of the World* is therefore conceived as a 'Chaos-Opera', an encounter between words, music and dance, attempting to make a sense of human migrations and the new cultures born out of them. In the film, I use the views of experts whom I call 'Prompters': these include a poet/philosopher (Glissant); historians, sociologists, filmmakers and creative writers (Alexander Kluge, Nicole Lapierre, Fatou Diome and Richard Sennett); and a journalist and activist for refugees (Agnès Matrahji). Together, they help me to structure and move my story forward, and to show that throughout human history such movements (migrations and emigrations) have often resulted in the creation of new and dynamic humanities, rather than negative and fearful cultural asymmetries.(1)

The notion of 'Chaos-Opera' is Glissant's way of breaking boundaries and revealing relationships between things, no matter how great their differences, and how distant they are from one another, in space and in time. For our purpose here, 'Chaos-Opera' is an opera that brings to light the subterranean relationships and connections between all human migrations, whether they are induced by wars, dictatorships, famines, or simply the search for new adventures and opportunities, regardless of when they take place in history, or where they issue from: Africa, Europe, Asia or the Americas.(1) [6]

The opening shot of the ocean is soon pierced by the familiar, ever shocking spectacle of people wearing life jackets in the water, at risk of drowning, and also being hauled on board rescue ships. On land we see a body bag being carried off. The scene then cuts to Bamako, with its *mise-en-scène* giving shots of people in the streets, walking over the bridge, women crossing the scene as they sing, coming to the constructions used for the staging. At every point where a setting is proposed we are open to the challenge of seeing the rehearsal for departures and dangers.

The opera performance in Bamako opens with voices singing in one of the many African languages used in Koulsy Lamko and Wassis Diop's libretto. The solemn scene and music stage a funeral with a bier being transported, and then ladders being carried, presumably by refugees whose attempts to scale the walls of the fortresses (Melilla, Ceuta) speak for themselves.

FIGURE 11.1 Ladders being carried to scale walls

As these images of the actors/singers flow forward, the African score shifts to Monteverdi's baroque aria "Arianna's Lament." Simultaneously the camera pulls back to reveal the darkened backs of the audience, highlighting the act of performance, and as this is a film, reflecting the gaze back onto our own position as viewers of those watching the scene. The reflecting carries over directly to the questions about the montage: the intellectual montage that will reside in images placed in juxtaposition so as to propose and query: what audience, what perspective, what world are we asked to enter into? The links are established by montage, and we next cut to Diawara himself, on Lesbos, addressing the spectator as a familiar figure who introduces himself, and invites us to accompany him on his journey. Then the encounter with Alexander Kluge and Richard Sennett, with whom Diawara, and we, view the footage of the *Opera of the World*. The encounters with thinkers and writers, discussing the issue of immigration. The encounter with the opera itself. And the encounter with footage showing migrants from the past set over against those of the present.

Diawara stages all the encounters, all these interpellations, so that even if the staging involves only one person, we are interpellated. A Syrian man cries out, O Sea, look what has become of us, and we feel the call in our depth of being. We are asked, pleaded with: let us in! Diawara is always present in staging the encounter with the past, with the familiar fate of Walter Benjamin and Hannah Arendt, with the tattooed numbers, and those faces looking out at us, all those faces, re-presented to us via Diawara's slow drawl and direct call to be compassionate.

FIGURE 11.2 Immigrant children's faces

Bintou Were is all our daughters, her dead child no less ours than Morrison's Beloved. The ethical call for responsibility when we see him or her looking at us must emerge along the lines of what Diawara has always found in the past when he had become a Black American, looking back on his friends and former life in Mali, or Guinea. The past catches back up with him when his conversation with Kluge turns to Kluge's own moving account of his great-great-great French Protestant grandparents having fled to Germany, seeking asylum. The face-to-face is stretched far beyond the individual perception of the Other standing alone in their looking back on their interlocutor, to those multitudes fleeing across borders in desperation, carrying us into those fleeing when Nazis drove millions of refugees south, attempting to reach Marseilles or Portugal, to board vessels headed west across the Atlantic. And in Chaos-Opera form, Diawara cuts back to the moments where he is discussing opera or migration with Kruge and Sennett, or elsewhere with Diome.

In each of the faces we are viewing, including those of the "prompters," including Diawara himself, we have to distill out the ethics of the face-to-face so as to recognize Levinas's underlying call of responsibility in the moment of seeing the face looking at us, and asking, without us knowing who they are, in any sense whatever, not to cause them harm. This should take three efforts: first, to see ourselves as those being seen, not as invisible unseen audience members; to see ourselves as sharing a presence for those temporally removed from us, but still caught back up in the encounter in all its iterations, as in the crystal image; to see ourselves in the act of seeing a face in performance as in the camera's eye, then and now, no matter how distant, as still responsible for the ethical demand not to cause harm to the other. Each side of the shot-reverse-shot says, I am here, and becomes religious in the sense Levinas meant when he described that as the foundational moment for an infinity given in its affect.

As we watch the scene of the funeral unfold at the beginning of the opera, the camera pulls back to reveal the back of Kluge's head as he and Manthia are watching the images on a screen. Manthia has asked about completing Lamko's previously voiced claim that operatic style spectacles often form part of the everyday life in Africa, as when people as a chorus carry out tasks like marching to the sacred woods for some ritual purpose. Kluge takes up the thought to historicize European opera, so that we perceive the issue as evoking the emotional pull of people crossing the borders then and now. Opera enables us to express what we cannot normally say in ordinary life, so it becomes a vehicle for the people's inner feelings. It descends from the heights of elite culture with which it is associated today to the "plebian" levels which were at its origins. Its traces are what are intercalated into all the scenes of the film which return us to the question, who are the refugees, where do they want to go, or, as refugees, why are we/they risking our lives and leaving home?

The music from the opera, the vocal composition from Lamko and Monteverdi, the scenes of emigration and the recollections of past attempts, intersect emotionally. If it is chaos, it comes together as opera, with Lamko's libretto providing the overlay of action and voices: the common people seeking to leave, the calls of the traditional griot to resist, the deceptive arguments of the coyotes luring the young men to follow, after paying. All this reaches a culmination when the young Bintou loses the baby she is carrying while attempting to climb the ladder that would enable her to cross into Melilla. Her loss crosses with Arianne who pleads with Theseus.

Kruge evokes the mixed German French features of the Arianne aria, concluding that he himself is also like the chorus of those who had come before, from his father's side and mother's side, just as Diawara too was the result of a chorus of ancestors. Each is comfortably evoked so that we might see the comparison as harmonizing the work of the cultures, the operas, so that the opposition of high and low cultures, plebians and aristocrats, doesn't come in the way of cultural encounters. However, the backdrop of the opening shots of refugees in the water, and funerals, brings chaos to that harmonious view of operas. We are continually called to reach for that bridge, that border, as the interview with Fatou Diome reveals how she too serendipitously chanced upon opera in Strassbourg and happened to find the appeal.

Arianne's cries to Theseus set the stage for the drama of emigration and its losses:

> Oh Theseus, oh my Theseus,
> if you knew, oh God,
> if you only knew
> how much poor Arianna
> is frightened,
> perhaps, overcome with remorse,
> you would return your prow shorewards again.
> But with the serene winds
> you sail on happily, while I remain here weeping.[7]

In a compelling scene that highlight the contradictions in the call for emigration we see a Syrian man whose cries to the waves are filled with heartbreak: "Oh sea, look what has become of us, please don't send your

FIGURE 11.3 A Syrian man's lament

sinister waves against us." The backdrop is filled with signs of people having drowned. As he sings, we see a camera recording his gestures, and understand the lament is being recorded.

We are channeled in our thinking about emigration by the world horizon we have constructed, and the cinema that interpellates us, inevitably joining its emotions to our orientation. I am thinking of the *passeurs* or smugglers, as Diawara called them—coyotes, in the Americas—who profit from helping emigrants reach the North. On the one hand, the figure of the tall young *passeur* in the Opera—self-assured, dominating the stage— becomes joined to the original images of the children on the shores, or people drowned, rescued, bedraggled, and always on the march, striving to get past the barriers or borders. And of course this echoes the encouragements of the griots, seen increasingly as corrupt, urging young people to be courageous and basically go for the golden eggs in European capitals, go north, so as to be able to send money home.

On the other hand, beyond the lament of the Syrian man, lies the issue of who controls the horizon, who even has the right to opine over the decisions of the emigrants. In one moment we call them refugees, not immigrants, and run the range of technical definitions that would require them to be endangered at home; on the other hand, we reluctantly acknowledge the economic side to the emigration. Wars in Sudan or Syria or Afghanistan; economic disasters in Nicuaragua or Venezuela or the Sahel. The more these causes are parsed by Western NGOs, the more the agency of the emigrant becomes disregarded, which is precisely James Ferguson's (2006) point about African people's own right to determine what form of modernity to seek for their own lives.

When we return to the power of the opera, the conflicting views on whether to leave for the north or not is overlaid with the story of Bintou Were herself, a young woman impregnated by several men, and now determined to get to Europe so her child will be born there and have European citizenship. Her power in confronting this world with its griots, young warriors, and corrupt smugglers is conveyed in her stance, which she takes when the smuggler tells the youth they need him to get past the obstacles en route to "Bordeaux, Paris, Nantes."

As her anger boils over in recounting her abuse at the hands of the arrogant men, and as her determination to leave confounds their attempts to control her, we can find a model for her daring the patriarchy, challenging the old men and leaving home in Sembène's equally, or even more daring early novelette, *Vehi Ciosane* (1966). There it was a young girl whose father impregnated her. The village imam and elders supported the father, so the young girl rebelled and left for Dakar on her own. That adds an additional layer of complexity to Bintou Were's choice to accuse the men and then leave, pregnant, defiant, and courageous.

FIGURE 11.4 Bintou Were confronts a smuggler

There is a climactic scene, where they arrive at the perimeter walls of Melilla, and Bintou scales the walls only to have the smuggler pull out the ladder from under her. She loses the baby. The tragedy is compounded, becomes opera. We see Bintou Were caught on the ladder like a Jesus figure, her shadow projected onto the wall as in Kentridge's shadow theatre, powerfully suspended in space.

FIGURE 11.5 Bintou suspended on a ladder

Conclusion

"My hosts gave me the opportunity to become what I am today, a professor in a prestigious university." As he walks along the shore, the detritus from the boat-people littering the littoral, Manthia Diawara picks up an empty plastic bottle, and walks us back to the opening shot of the sea, the voice of Arianne's aria filling the spaces with the images of the surface. He has given back what he could, the gift, as Derrida would have put it, that is offered not in repayment but rather as a mournful intonation pleading to be heard, again.

FIGURE 11.6   Diawara along the shore

Diawara frames his goals beautifully in terms of Glissant's call for us to retain our capacity to tremble before the Other:

> I wanted to achieve two goals in making *An Opera of the World*. Firstly, to be faithful to the spirit of the original Bintou Were, a Sahel Opera. I wanted to show that it is a visionary work of art, which tests our commitment to such concepts as human rights, hospitality, empathy and human dignity. As Glissant would put it, we are increasingly in danger of losing our capacity to tremble with the trembling of others, the migrants.[8]

Nothing in world cinema will work quite as this film does in gentle terms to remember the hospitality that was offered to us before, like that offered to Aeneas by Dido, and to return again to its sweet and painful notes in the present. World cinema has another "world" before its eyes. Diawara looks to the African opera for a place where the dialogue between worlds is to begin.

Epilogue

In his brilliant installation piece on this same theme as *Opera*, John Akomfrah intercalates images of the sea with this transcript that conveys all the drama of Arianne's call to Theseus, and of Bintou Were's loss:

> VITO (NIGERIAN REFUGEE): Inside the net there was big, big fish.
> *[Music and waves continue]*
> I can't really explain.
> *[rippling water; wind chimes]*
> If anyone fall inside they would eat us because those fish were very big.
> *[Clock ticking]*
> *[Music and rippling water resume]*
> The waves, it can even move a house, the waves.
> *[Music and rippling water continue]*
> *[Radio static]*
> PAUL KENYON (BBC NEWSCASTER): There were 27 of them on board. None had been to sea before. They come from all across the continent, traveling northwards to the coast.
> *[Waves crashing]*
> VITO (NIGERIAN REFUGEE): I shout, "Jesus save me. Jesus save me."
> *[Clock ticking; water rippling and crashing]*
> PAUL KENYON (BBC NEWSCASTER): Numbers reported dead or missing here this year are the highest ever: nearly 500. Last month, on one day, 14 dead bodies were found floating in the sea.
> *[Wind and waves]*
> VITO (NIGERIAN REFUGEE): Jesus save me. Jesus save me.
> *[Echoey music with wind and waves]*
> PAUL KENYON (BBC NEWSCASTER): They clambered onto one of these: the tuna cage. Exhausted, unable to swim, stranded. The migrants' boats started taking on water. The people traffickers told them that the crossing would take less than an hour. The pilot swam back to shore. They headed off on what was to become one of the most dramatic survival stories from this year's crossings.[9]

Notes

1 Here are the basics from Levinas on the face-to-face: "To understand the other is to speak to him" (1998: 6).

"[T]he person with whom I am in relation, I call being, but in calling him *being*, I call upon him . . . . in understanding this being, I simultaneously tell him my understanding . . ." (7)

"Man is the only being I cannot meet without my expressing this meeting itself to him . . . . In every attitude toward the human being there is a greeting—even if it is the refusal of a greeting . . . ." (7)

"This bond with the other which is not reducible to the representation of the other, but to his invocation, and in which invocation is not preceded by an understanding, I call *religion*. The essence of discourse is prayer. What distinguishes thought directed toward a thing from a bond with a person is that in the latter case a vocative is uttered: what is named is at the same time what is called.

. . . If the word religion is, however, to indicate that the relation between men, irreducible to understanding, is by that fact distanced from the exercise of power, but in human faces joins the Infinite—I accept that ethical resonance of the word and all those Kantian reverberations" (8).

2 https://plato.stanford.edu/entries/levinas/

3 The entr'acte is the moment without which no encounter would be possible.

Although these experiments, these moments of viewing, appear scientific, repeatable, and thus universal, they are marked at their core by an undecidability that destabilizes attempts to portray the results as universal. They are like that measurement of time by the universal clock that has become more and more accurate, all the while recording a moment whose time is a function of whether it is recorded by a clock within one frame or within another. The parts of the apparatus are linked, an entr'acte, which would not be the case if the viewer/experimenter were separate from the set-up for the experiment and the screen on which the result appears. Yet the result must be seen and recorded, the devices subject to the experimenter's adjustments; and oddly enough, the interference of the experimenter in setting up and then viewing the results functions as if it were part of the experiment. In cinema we'd signal the self-reflection of the viewer as integral to whatever meaning the image would record or convey; as if the same apparatus that "sees" and records the real event is already enmeshed in the event, the reading of its appearance, and its meaning. Phenomena and noumena are broached, and between the two lies a space we can call "entre" through which all acts of an encounter also generate a durée that becomes performative, an "acte" (Harrow 2022: 71–2).

4 "The crystal-image, which forms the cornerstone of Deleuze's time-image, is a shot that fuses the pastness of the recorded event with the presentness of its viewing. The crystal-image is the indivisible unity of the virtual image and the actual image. The virtual image is subjective, in the past, and recollected. The virtual image as 'pure recollection' exists outside of consciousness, in time. It is always somewhere in the temporal past, but still alive and ready to be 'recalled' by an actual image. The actual image is objective, in the present, and perceived. The crystal-image always lives at the limit of an indiscernible actual and virtual image.

With the crystal-image, Deleuze assigns a form of temporality that accounts for the "present/pastness" of the film image. The crystal-image shapes time as a constant two-way mirror that splits the present into two heterogeneous directions, "one of which is launched towards the future while the other falls into the past. Time consists of this split, and it is . . . time, that we see in the crystal" (Cinema 2, 81). https://offscreen.com/view/bergson2

5   Although Jews tried to emigrate to any country that would take them, the usual route followed by German and French refugees was first south to France, often Paris, and then to Marseilles. The Resistance coordinated flights and placements when they could, when visas could be obtained. As channels of flight in France closed down with the Petain government's collaboration, many sought refuge in Spain, and from there to Portugal where some ships were still carrying refugees overseas.

6   https://maumaus.org/resources/Maumaus_An-Opera-of-the-World_Manthia_Diawara_text.pdf

7   https://www.girolamo.de/single/g11005E.html

8   https://maumaus.org/resources/Maumaus_An-Opera-of-the-World_Manthia_Diawara_text.pdf

9   https://mcachicago.org/Exhibitions/2019/Water-After-All/Transcripts

FILMS CITED

Primary Films in This Study

Anyaene, Chineze. *Ije: The Journey*. 2010.
Bouchareb, Rachid. *Little Senegal*. 2000.
Denis, Claire. *Chocolat*. 1988.
Diawara, Manthia. *An Opera of the World*. 2017.
Dosunmu, Andrew. *Mother of George*. 2013.
Gomis, Alain. *Tey*. 2012.
Haroun, Mahamat-Saleh. *Sotigui Kouyaté, A Modern Griot*. 1995.
Kelani, Tunde. *Dazzling Mirage*. 2014.
Kelani, Tunde. *Ti Oluwa Ni Ile*. 1993.
Lekow, Maia and Christopher King. *The Letter*. 2019.
Loreau, Dominique. *Les Noms n'habitent nulle part*. 1994.
Mosese, Lemohang Jeremiah. *This Is Not a Burial. It's a Resurrection*. 2019.
Nyoni, Rugano. *I Am Not a Witch*. 2017.
Rapu, Chris, Kenneth Nnuebe. *Living in Bondage*. 1992.

Secondary Films

Abbeyquaye, Ernest. *A Mother's Revenge*. 1994.
Afolayan, Kunle. *The Figurine/Araromire*. 2009.
Afolayan, Kunle. *Phone Swap*. 2012.
Agu, Francis. *Jezebel*. 1994.
Alassane, Moustapha. *FVVA: Femme, Villa, Voiture, Argent*. 1972.
Amadi Okoroafor, Andy. *Relentless*. 2010.
Antonioni, Michelangelo. *Passenger*. 1975.
Arase, Frank. *Beyonce, the President's Daughter*. 2006.
Bahrani, Ramin. *Goodbye Solo*. 2008.

Bekolo, Jean-Pierre. *Aristotle's Plot*. 1996.

Bekolo, Jean-Pierre. *Les Choses et les mots de Mudimbe*. 2015.

Bekolo, Jean-Pierre. *Quartier Mozart*. 1992.

Borgeaud, Pierre-Yves. *Return to Gorée*. 2007.

De Sica, Vittorio. *Miracle in Milan*. 1951.

Denis, Claire. *354 Rhums*. 2008.

Denis, Claire. *Beau Travail*. 1999.

Denis, Claire. *Les Salauds*. 2013.

Denis, Claire. *Trouble Every Day*. 2001.

Denis, Claire. *White Material*. 2009.

Diawara, Manthia. *Rouch in Reverse*. 1995.

Diawara, Manthia. *Sembène: the Making of African Cinema*. 1994.

Diop, Alice. *Nous*. 2021.

Diop, Mati. *Atlantiques*. 2019.

Djadjam, Mostefa. *Frontières*. 2001.

Doucouré, Maïmouna. *Mignonnes*. 2020.

Duparc, Henri. *Bal Poussière*. 1989.

Fellini, Federico. *8 ½*. 1963.

Frears, Stephen. *Dirty Pretty Things*. 2002.

Gaye, Dyana. *Des Etoiles*. 2013.

Gerima, Haile. *Sankofa*. 1993.

Gilou, Thomas. *Black Mic Mac*. 1986.

Gitai, Amos *Golem, Spirit of Exile*. 1992.

Godard, Jean Luc. *Weekend*. 1967.

Godard, Jean Luc. *Pierrot le fou*. 1965.

Gomes, Flora. *The Blue Eyes of Yonta*. 1992.

Gomis, Alain. *L'Afrance*. 2001.

Gyang, Kenneth. *Oloture*. 2019.

Gyang, Kenneth. *Confusion Na Wa*. 2013.

Haroun, Mahamat-Saleh. *Bye Bye Africa*. 1999.

Haroun, Mahamat-Saleh. *Lingue*. 2021.

Haroun, Mahamat-Saleh. *Grigris*. 2013.

Jarmusch, Jim. *Down by Law*. 1986.

Kaboré, Gaston. *Zan Boko*. 1988.

Kelani, Tunde. *Abena*. 2006.

Kelani, Tunde. *Arugba*. 2009.

Kelani, Tunde. *Thunderbolt: Magun*. 2001.

Kelani, Tunde. *Arugba*. 2008.

Kelani, Tunde. *MAAMi*. 2011.

Kelani, Tunde. *Saworoide*. 1999.

Kelani, Tunde. *The Campus Queen*. 2004.

Kellou, Dorothee-Myrien. *In Mansourah You Separated Us*. 2019.

Kouyaté, Dani. *Keita: L'héritage du griot*. 1995.

Kouyaté, Dani. *Sia, le rêve du python*. 2001.

Linklater, Richard. *Before Sunrise* (1995)

Loreau, Dominique. *Divine Carcasse*. 1998.

Mambéty, Djibril Diop. *Badou Boy*. 1970.

Mambéty, Djibril Diop. *Hyènes*. 1992.

Mambéty, Djibril Diop. *Touk Bouki.* 1973.

Marker, Chris. *Sans Soleil.* 1983.

Masya, Mbithi *Kati Kati.* 2016.

Minh-ha, Trinh T. *Reassemblage.* 1983.

Ngangura, Mweze. *La Vie est belle.* 1987.

Oriahi, Daniel. *Taxi Driver: Oko Ashewo.* 2015.

Ouédraogo, Idrissa. *Yaaba.* 1989.

Parks, Gordon. *Shaft.* 1971.

Parks, Jr. Gordon. *Superfly.* 1972.

Peebles, Melvin Van. *Sweet Sweetback's Baadasssss Song.* 1971.

Ramaka, Joseph. *Karmen Gei.* 2001.

Ray, Satrajit. *Pather Panchali.* 1955.

Reed, Carol. *The Third Man.* 1949.

Renais, Alain, Chris Marker and Ghislain Cloquet. *Les Statues meurent aussi.* 1953.

Renais, Alain. *Hiroshima Mon Amour.* 1959.

Rouch, Jean. *Cocorico M. Poulet.* 1974.

Rouch, Jean. *Les maîtres fous.* 1955.

Safo, Socrate. *Ghost Tears.* 1992.

Safo, Socrate, *Step Dad.* 1994.

Schlesinger, John. *Midnight Cowboy.* 1969.

Scorsese, Martin. *Taxi Driver.* 1976.

Sembène Ousmane. *Borom Sarret.* 1963.

Sembène Ousmane. *Faat Kine.* 2001.

Sembène Ousmane. *Moolaadé.* 2004.

Sembène Ousmane. *Guelwaar.* 1992.

Sembène Ousmane. *Xala.* 1975.

Sembène Ousmane. *Camp de Thiaroye.* 1988.

Sene Absa, Moussa. *Ainsi Meurent les anges.* 2001.

Sissako, Abderrahmane. *Bamako.* 2006.

Sissako, Abderrahmane. *Heremakono.* 2002.

Sissako, Abderrahmane. *La vie sur terre.* 1998.

Sissako, Abderrahmane. *Sissoko Rostov-Luanda.* 1998.

Sissoko, Cheick Oumar. *La Genèse.* 1999.

Tabio, Juan Carlos. *The Elephant and the Bicycle.* 1994.

Teno, Jean-Marie. *Afrique, je te plumeria.* 1992.

Teno, Jean-Marie. *Chef.* 1999.

Truffaut, François. *Day for Night.* 1973.

Wenders, Wim. *Paris, Texas.* 1984.

Wenders, Wim. *Wings of Desire.* 1987.

Wenders, Wim. *Tokyo-Ga.* 1985.

Wenders, Wim. *In Weite Ferne, so nah [So Far, So Near].* 1993.

Zwick, Edward. *Blood Diamond.* 2006.

WORKS CITED

Abani, Chris. 2004. *Graceland*. NY: Farrar, Strauss, and Giroux.

Achebe, Chinua. (1958) 1972. *Things Fall Apart*. London: Heinemann.

Adejunmobi, Moradewun. 2007. "Nigerian Video Film As Minor Transnational Practice." *Postcolonial Text* 3, no. 2: 1–16.

Adejunmobi, Moradewun. 2014. "Evolving Nollywood Templates for Minor Transnational Film." *Black Camera* 5, no. 2 (Spring): 74–94.

Adesokan, Akin. 2001. *Postcolonial Artists and Global Aesthetics*. Bloomington: Indiana UP.

Aftab, Kaleem. 2017. "I Am Not a Witch director on the Modern Persecution of Witches in Zambia and Ghana." *The Independent*, October 18. https://www.independent.co.uk/arts-entertainment/films/features/i-am-not-a-witch-rungano-nyoni-a8007081.html Accessed December 26, 2022.

Aig-Umoukhuede, Frank. (1955) 1963. "One Wife Be for One Man." In *The Penguin Book of Modern African Poetry*, edited by Gerald Moore. Harmondsworth: Penguin.

"Ainsi Meurent les Anges." *California Newsreel*. https://newsreel.org/video/AINSI-MEURENT-LES-ANGES Accessed 26 December, 2022.

Akomfrah, John. *Vertigo Sea*. https://mcachicago.org/Exhibitions/2019/Water-After-All/Transcripts Accessed 26 December, 2022.

Andrews, Dudley. 2004. "An Atlas of World Cinema." *Journal of Cinema and Media* 45, no. 2 (Fall): 9–23.

Appadurai, Arjun. 1996. *Modernity At Large: Cultural Dimensions Of Globalization*. Minneapolis: University of Minnesota Press.

Arendt, Hannah. 1958. *The Human Condition*. Chicago: The University of Chicago Press.

"Arianna's Lament, Monteverdi." https://www.girolamo.de/single/g11005E.html Accessed 26 December, 2022.

Ashliman, D. L. "The Disobedient Daughter Who Married a Skull." https://sites.pitt.edu/~dash/skull.html Accessed 26 December, 2022.

Asiegbu, Johnson. 1984. *Nigeria and its British Invaders*. New York: Nok.

Bach, Daniel, Yann Lebeau and Kunle Awumo. 2001. *Nigeria during the Abacha years, 1993–1998: the domestic and international politics of democratization: the proceedings of a conference held in Bordeaux, France at the Centre d'étude d'Afrique noire, 1996*. Ibadan, Nigeria: IFRA/CEAN.

Bagayogo, Shaka. 1989. "Places and Power Theory in the Mande World: Today and in the Past." Cah. Sci. Hum 25, no. 4: 445–460.

Barad, Karen. 2007. *Meeting the Universe Halfway: Quantum Physics and Entanglement of Matter and Meaning*. Durham, NC: Duke University Press.

Barlet, Olivier. 2017. "Section Five: FESPACO 2017: A Discredited Festival." *Black Camera* 9, no. 1 (Fall): 307–322.

Barlet, Olivier. 1996. "Interview with Clement Tapsoba." *Africultures*, March. http://africultures.com/interview-with-clement-tapsoba-by-olivier-barlet-5276/ Accessed September 14, 2021.

Bayart, Jean-François. 1989. *L'État en Afrique: La Politique du Ventre*. Paris: Fayard. http://africasacountry.com/'2014/05/the-politics-of-the-belly/. Translated in 1993: *The State in Africa: The Politics of the Belly*. London and NY: Longman.

Bayart, Jean-François. 2007. *Global Subjects*. Translated by Andrew Brown. Cambridge: Polity Press.

Bebey, Francis. "Paroles dAgatha." https://greatsong.net/PAROLES-FRANCIS-BEBEY,AGATHA,102678357.html Accessed 26 December, 2022.

Bhabha, Homi. 1994. *The Location of Culture*. NY: Routledge.

Bird, Charles S. and Martha B. Kendell. 1980. "The Mande Hero: Text and Context," in *Explorations in African Systems of Thought*, edited by Ivan Karp, Charles S. Bird, 13–26. Indiana University Press. Reprinted as Ivan Karp and Charles S. Bird, eds. 1987. *Explorations in African Systems of Thought*. Smithsonian Institution Press.

Bjornson, Richard. 1977. *The Picaresque Hero in European Fiction*. Madison, WI: University of Wisconsin Press.

Brennan, Louis. 2018. "How Netflix Expanded to 190 Countries in 7 years." *Harvard Business Review*, 12 October. https://hbr.org/2018/10/how-netflix-expanded-to-190-countries-in-7-years Accessed 8 February, 2023.

Broad, C. D. 2002. *Scientific Thought*. London: Routledge.

Brooks, Peter. 1995. *The Melodramatic Imagination*. New Haven: Yale University Press.

Burridge, Kenelm. 1969. *New Heaven, New Earth: A study of Millenarian Activities*. London: Basil Blackwell.

Butler, Judith and Athena Athanasiou. 2013. *Dispossession*. Cambridge, New York: Polity.

Carland, John M. 1985. *The Colonial Office and Nigeria*. Basingstoke, UK: Macmillan.

Chakrabarty, Dipesh. 2003. *Habitations of Modernity: Essays in the Wake of Subaltern Studies*. Chicago: University of Chicago Press.

Chatterjee, Partha. 1997. *Our Modernity*. Dakar: Codesria.

Cheah, Pheng. 2016. *What Is a World?* Durham, NC: Duke University Press.

"Chocolat (clown)." https://en.wikipedia.org/wiki/Chocolat_(clown) Accessed 26 December, 2022.

Comaroff, Jean and John Comaroff. 2000. "Millennial Capitalism: First Thoughts on a Second Coming." *Popular Culture* 12, no. 2: 291–343. Republished in *Millennial Capitalism and the Culture of Neoliberalism.* Durham and London: Duke University Press, 2001.

Comaroff, Jean and John Comaroff. 2001. *Millennial Capitalism: First Thoughts on a Second Coming.* Durham: Duke University Press.

Comaroff, Jean, and John Comaroff. 1993. *Modernity and Its Malcontents.* Chicago: University of Chicago Press.

Cooper, Frederick. 1977. *Plantation Slavery on the East Coast of Africa.* New Haven and London: Yale University Press.

Cooper, Frederick. 1980. *From Slaves to Squatters. Plantation Labour and Agriculture in Zanzibar and Coastal Kenya: 1890–1925.* New Haven and London: Yale University Press.

Curry-Machado, Jonathan, ed. 2013. *Global Histories, Imperial Commodities, Local Interactions.* Cambridge Imperial and Post-Colonial Studies, Palgrave Macmillan.

Dayrell, Elphinstone. 1910. *Folk Stories from Southern Nigeria, West Africa*, no. 8. London: Longmans, Green, and Co.

Deleuze, Gilles. 1989. *Cinema 2: The Time Image.* London: Athlone.

"Demonic." https://www.merriam-webster.com/dictionary/demonic Accessed 26 December, 2022.

Derrida, Jacques. 1982. "Différance," in *Margins of Philosophy*, translated by Alan Bass, 3–27. Chicago: University of Chicago Press.

Derrida, Jacques. 1994. *Spectres of Marx.* Derrida, Jacques. London: Routledge.

Derrida, Jacques. 1996. *The Gift of Death.* Chicago: University of Chicago Press.

Derrida, Jacques. 1980. "The Law of Genre." *Critical Inquiry* 7, no. 1 (Autumn): 55–81.

Diabate, Naminata. 2020. *Naked Agency: Genital Cursing and Biopolitics in Africa*, Duke University Press.

Diawara, Manthia. 1998. *In Search of Africa.* Cambridge: Harvard University Press.

Diawara, Manthia. 2003. *We Won't Budge: An African Exile in the World.* New York: Basic Civitas Books.

Diawara, Manthia. 2010. *African Film: New Forms of Aesthetics and Politics.* Munich, New York: Prestel.

Diawara, Manthia. "An Opera of the World." https://maumaus.org/resources/Maumaus_An-Opera-of-the-World_Manthia_Diawara_text.pdf. Accessed 26 December, 2022.

Dima, Vlad. 2017. *Sonic Space in Djibril Diop Mambety's Films.* Bloomington: Indiana University Press.

Dima, Vlad. 2022. *Meaning-Less-Ness in Postcolonial Cinema.* MSU Press.

Dima, Vlad. 2012. "Aural Narrative Planes In Djibril Diop Mambety's Films." *Journal of Film and Video* 64, no. 3 (Fall): 38–52.

Diop, Birago. 1961. "L'Os de Mor Lass." *Contes d'Amadou Koumba.* Paris: Présence Africaine.

Diop, Birago. 1978. *La Plume raboutée*. Paris: Présence Africaine.

Diop, Birago. "Les Souffles." In Senghor, Léopold Sédar, ed. *Anthologie de la nouvelle poésie nègre et malgache*. Paris: Présence Africaine, 1948.

Diop, David. 1956. "Afrique mon Afrique." *Coups de Pilon*. Paris: Présence Africaine.

Dirks, Tim. *The History of Film: the 1980s*. https://www.filmsite.org/80sintro.html

Djando, Dominique. "Footit et Chocolat." http://www.circopedia.org/Foottit_%26_Chocolat. Accessed Dec 26, 2022.

"Domionique Loreau." http://www.dominiqueloreau.be/ Accessed Dec 26 December, 2022.

"Dominique Loreau." *Cinergie.be*. https://www.cinergie.be/personne/loreau-dominique Accessed Dec. 26, 2022

Dovey, Lindiwe. 2015. *Curating Africa in the Age of Film Festivals*. New York, London: Palgrave Macmillan.

Drabinski, John E. 2019. "Sites of relation and 'Tout-Monde." *Angelaki*, 24:3: 157–172.

Durovicova, Natasa and Kathleen Newman, eds. 2010. *World Cinemas, Transnational* Perspectives. New York and Abingdon: Routledge.

"DVD-Video." https://en.wikipedia.org/wiki/DVD-Video. Accessed Dec. 26, 2022.

"Epave." http://www.wordreference.com/fren/epave. Accessed Dec. 26, 2022.

Fabian, Johannes. 1983. *Time and the Other: How Anthropology Makes Its Object*. New York: Columbia University Press.

Falola, Toyin and Heaton, Michael. 2008. *A History of Nigeria*. Cambridge: Cambridge UP.

Fanon, Franz. (1952) 1967. *Black Skin, White Masks*. NY: Grove Press.

Fanon, Franz. 1961. Wretched of the Earth. New York: Grove Press.

Ferguson, James. 1999. *Expectations of Modernity: Myths and Meanings of Urban Life on The Zambian Copperbelt*. Berkeley: University of California Press.

Ferguson, James. 2006. *Global Shadows: Africa in the Neoliberal World Order*. Durham and London: Duke University Press.

Fisiy, Cyprian F. and Peter Geschiere. 2002. "Witchcraft, development and paranoia in Cameroon: interactions between popular, academic and state discourse." In *Magical Interpretations, Material Realities: Modernity, Witchcraft, and the Occult in Postcolonial Africa*, edited by Henrietta L. Moore and Todd Sanders.

Francis, Jaekel. 1997. *History of Nigerian Railway: Opening the Nation to sea air and road transportation*. Safari Books.

Freeman, Liam and Seb Emina. 2018. "Why Lagos Is West Africa's Capital of Culture." *British Vogue*, October 30. https://www.vogue.co.uk/article/why-lagos-is-west-africas-capital-of-culture?fbclid=IwAR2j9pO2-7IbL7doI1fSdg_AeSqcvkrGbLhGINwQzUDxjl06GsoYsN8d4Yc Accessed 26 December, 2022.

Galt, Rosalind and Karl Schooner. 2010. *Global Art Cinema*. Oxford: Oxford University Press.

"Gambaga Witch Camp" (https://en.wikipedia.org/wiki/Gambaga_Witch_camp) Accessed 26 December, 2022.

Garritano, Carmela. 2013. *African Video Movies and Global Desires: A Ghanaian History*. Athens, OH: Ohio University Press.

Gaudet, Marcia. 1992. "Bouki, The Hyena, in Louisiana and African Tales." *The Journal of American Folklore* 105, no. 415 (Winter): 66–72.

Geschiere, Peter. 2009. *The Perils of Belonging: Autochthony, Citizenship and Exclusion in Africa and Europe.* Chicago: University of Chicago Press.

Geschiere, Peter. 2013. *Witchcraft, Intimacy, and Trust: Africa in Comparison.* Chicago: U Chicago Press.

"Ghana Witch Camps: Witches Live in Exile." 2012. *BBC News*, September 1. https://www.bbc.com/news/magazine-19437130 Accessed September 3, 2021.

Gikandi, Simon. 2001. "Cultural Translation and the African Self: A (Post)colonial Case Study." *Interventions* 3, no. 3, 355–375.

Gikandi, Simon. 1996. *Maps of Englishness: Writing Identity in the Culture of Colonialism.* New York: Columbia University Press.

Gikandi, Simon. 2011. *Slavery and the Culture of Taste.* New York: Columbia University Press.

Green-Simms, Lindsey. 2017. *Postcolonial Automobility: Cars, Cultural Production, and Global Mobility in West Africa.* Minneapolis: University of Minneapolis Press.

Grinker, Roy R, Stephen C. Lubkemann, and Christopher B. Steiner. 2010. *Perspectives on Africa: A Reader in Culture, History, and Representation.* Chichester, West Sussex: Wiley-Blackwell.

"Growing Block Universe." https://en.wikipedia.org/wiki/Growing_block_uni verse Accessed 26 December, 2022.

Gugler, Josef. 2010. "African Films in the Classroom." *African Studies Review* 53, no. 3: 1–17.

Guneratne, Anthony and Wimal Dissanayake, eds. 2003. *Rethinking Third Cinema.* London: Routledge.

Gustaffson, Henrik. 2014. "Points of Flight, Lines of Fracture: Claire Denis's Uncanny Landscape." In *The Films of Claire Denis: Intimacy on the Border*, edited by Marjorie Vecchio. New York: Palgrave Macmillan.

Guttman, Cynthia. (2001), "Sotigui Kouyaté : The wise man of the stage." UNESCO Courier (October), pp. 47–51. https://unesdoc.unesco.org/ark:/48223/pf0000123798

Haley, Alex. 1976. *Roots.* New York: Doubleday.

Hardt, Michael and Antonio Negri. 2001. *Empire.* Cambridge: Harvard UP.

Harrow Kenneth. 2007. *African Cinema: From the Political to the Postmodern.* Bloomington, IN: Indiana University Press.

Harrow, Kenneth W. 2015. "Manthia Diawara's Waves and the Problem of the Authentic." *African Studies Review* 58, no. 3 (December): 13–30.

Harrow, Kenneth W. 2022. *Space and Time in African Cinema and Cine-scapes.* London and NY: Routledge University Press.

Harvey, David. 1989. *The Condition of Postmodernity.* Oxford: Blackwell.

Harvey, David. 1996. *Justice, Nature, & the Geography of Difference.* Oxford: Blackwell.

Hawking, Stephen. 1993. *Black Holes and Baby Universes.* New York: Bantam Publishing.

Haynes, Jonathan. (1997) 2000. *Nigerian Video Films.* Athens: Ohio Univ., Center for Internat. Studies.

Haynes, Jonathan. 2016. *Nollywood: The Creation of Nigerian Film Genres*. Chicago: Chicago University Press.

Heidegger, Martin. (1927) 1962. *Being and Time*, translated by J. Macquarrie and E. Robinson. Oxford: Basil Blackwell.

"Heidegger, Martin." Stanford Encyclopedia of Philosophy. (Stanford: References to *Being and Time* refers to Macquarrie and Robinson English translation.) https://plato.stanford.edu/entries/heidegger/#toc Accessed 28 May 2022.

Hjort, Mette. "On the Plurality of Cinematic Transnationalism." In *World Cinemas, Transnational Perspectives*, edited by Natasa Durovicova and Kathleen Newman. New York and Abingdon: Routledge.

Hochschild, Adam. 1998. *King Leopold's Ghost: A Story of Greed, Terror, and Heroism in Colonial Africa*. Boston: Houghton Mifflin.

Hoffmann, Claudia. 2010. *Subaltern Migrancy And Transnational Locality: The Undocumented African Immigrant In International Cinema*. Dissertation, the University Of Florida. https://ufdcimages.uflib.ufl.edu/UF/E0/04/19/89/00001/hoffmann_c_pdf.txt Accessed 26 December, 2022

Jansen, Jan. 1996. "Kinship as Political Discourse: The Representation of Harmony and Change in Mande." *Younger Brother in Mande: Kinship and Politics in West Africa* (1–7) https://www.cambridge.org/core/journals/history-in-africa/article/abs/polities-and-political-discourse-was-mande-already-a-segmentary-society-in-the-middle-ages/D3F558EFE7CF2378C98E702ABAB22FF9

Julien, Eileen. 2003. "The Extroverted African Novel." *Il romanzo*: 5. Milano: Einaudi; and Franco Moretti, ed. *The Novel*. Vol. 2. Princeton, NJ: Princeton University Press, 2006: 667–698. Reprinted: "The Extroverted African Novel, Revisited: African Novels at Home, In the World." *Journal of African Cultural Studies* 30, no. 3 (2018, 24 May): 371–381.

Kelani, Tunde. "My Challenges, Successes, Life as a Filmmaker—Tunde Kelani." *Nigeria.com*. https://www.nigeriafilms.com/movie-news/91-directors-producers-report/11314-my-challenges-life-successes-as-a-film-maker-tunde-kelani. Also see https://www.thenigerianvoice.com/thread/41186/55306/1 Accessed 17 December, 2017.

Kelley, Leonard. 2022. "What Is Imaginary Time? *Owlocation*, October 31. https://owlcation.com/stem/What-Is-Imaginary-Time Accessed 26 December, 2022.

Kentridge, William. 2014. *Six Drawing Lessons*. Cambridge: Harvard University Press.

"Kenya - The Letter." 2020. *World Film Reviews*, 28 December. https://worldfilm-reviews.us/the-letter/ Accessed September 3, 2021.

Kenyatta, Jomo. (1938) 2015. *Facing Mount Kenya: The Traditional Life of the Gikuyu*. Nairobi: Kenway Publications.

Kermode, Mark. 2017. "I Am Not a Witch review – magical surrealism." *Guardian News and Media* (October 22). https://www.theguardian.com/film/2017/oct/22/i-am-not-a-witch-review-magical-surrealism-margaret-mulubwa-run gano-nyoni Accessed December 25, 2022.

Klein, Martin A. 1998. *Slavery and Colonial Rule in French West Africa*. New York and England: Cambridge University Press.

Larkin, Brian. 2008. *Signal and Noise: Media, Infrastructure, and Urban Culture in Nigeria*. Durham: Duke University Press.

Lensu, Suvi. 2016. "Filming Home, Plurality of Identity, Belonging and Homing in Transnational African Cinema." *Nokoko* 5: 1–33.

Levinas, Emmanuel. (2006) 2019. https://plato.stanford.edu/entries/levinas/ Accessed 26 December, 2022.

Lévinas, Emmanuel. 1998. *Entre Nous: On Thinking-of-the-Other*. New York: Columbia University Press.

Lewis, Peter. 1996. "From Prebendalism to Predation: The Political Economy of Decline in Nigeria." *The Journal of Modern African Studies* 34, no. 1: 79–103.

Lewis, Peter. 2007. *Growing Apart: Oil, Politics, and Economic Change in Indonesia and Nigeria*. Ann Arbor: University of Michigan Press.

Lewis, Peter. 2008. *From Prebendalism to Predation: the Political Economy of Decline in Nigeria*. Cambridge: Cambridge University Press.

Lobato, Ramon. 2012. *Shadow Economies of Cinema: Mapping Informal Film Distribution*. London: BFI, Palgrave Macmillan.

Macy, Harry. "Before the Five-Borough City: The Old Cities, Towns, and Villages that Camer Together to Form 'Greater New York.'" https://www.newyork familyhistory.org/blog/five-borough-city-old-cities-towns-and-villages-came-together-form-greater-new-york Accessed February 8, 2023.

Marisa Parham. 2009. *Haunting and Displacement in African American Literature and Culture*. Routledge.

Marks, Laura. 1999. *The Skin of the Film*. Massachusetts: Blackwell.

Mbembe, Achille. 2001. *On the Postcolony*. Berkeley, CA: University of California Press. (Originally *De la postcolonie. Essai sur l'imagination politique dans l'Afrique contemporaine*. Paris, Karthala, 2000.)

Mbembe, Achille. 2017. *Critique of Black Reason*. Translated by Laurent Dubois. Durham: Duke University Press.

Meyer, Birgit. 1998. "The Power of Money: Politics, Occult Forces, and Pentacostalism in Ghana." *African Studies Review* 41, no. 2 (December): 15–37.

Mitra, Ritu. 2015. "Palimpsests of Trauma: Excavating Memories in Qurratulain Hyder." *States Of Affect: Trauma in Partition/Post-Partition South Asia*. Dissertation, Michigan State University.

Moore, Henrietta L. and Todd Sanders, eds. 2002. *Magical Interpretations, Material Realities: Modernity, Witchcraft, and the Occult in Postcolonial Africa*. London: Routledge.

Moorman, Marissa. "*The Politics of the Belly*." In https://africasacountry.com/2014/05/the-politics-of-the-belly.

Morris, Meaghan, Siu Leung Li, and Stephen Chin, eds. 2005. *Hong Kong Connections: Transnational Imagination in Action Cinema*. Durham: Duke University Press.

Morris, Meaghan. 2004. "Transnational Imagination in African Cinema: Hong Kong and the Making of a Global Popular Culture." *Inter-Asia Cultural Studies* 5, no. 2: 181–99.

"Market in Lagos." https://upload.wikimedia.org/wikipedia/commons/e/ec/Market_in_Lagos%2C_Nigeria.jpg Accessed December 26, 2022

Mudimbe, V. Y. 1988. *The Invention of Africa: Gnosis, Philosophy and the Order of Knowledge*, Indiana University Press.

"Mulberry Street NYC" https://en.wikipedia.org/wiki/File:Mulberry_Street_NYC_c1900_LOC_3g04637u_edit.jpg Accessed December 26, 2022.

Murphy, John. 2004. "Senegal Slave House's past questioned", *The Seattle Times*, July 17. Accessed June 16, 2009.

Nancy, Jean-Luc. 2014. "Interview with Claire Denis." In *The Films of Claire Denis: Intimacy on the Border*, edited by Marjorie Vecchio. New York: Palgrave Macmillan.

"Netflix Chairman and Co-CEO Reed Hastings on resubscribing for success." 2022. *CEO: North America*. https://ceo-na.com/executive-interviews/netflix-chairman-and-co-ceo-reed-hastings-on-resubscribing-for-success/ Accessed February 8, 2023.

Newell, Sasha. 2012. *The Modernity Bluff: Crime, Consumption, and Citizenship in Côte d'Ivoire*. Chicago: U Chicago Press.

Ndalianis, Angela. 2004. *Neo-Baroque Aesthetics and Contemporary Entertainment*. Cambridge: MIT Press.

Noiriel, Gérard. 2016. *Chocolat, la véritable histoire de l'homme sans nom Paris*. Bayard Culture.

Nora, Pierre. 1984. *Les Lieux de mémoire*. Paris: Gallimard.

Nora, Pierre. 1989. "Between Memory and History: Les Lieux de Mémoire." *Representations* 26 (Spring): 7–24. https://www.jstor.org/stable/2928520?seq=1#page_scan_tab_contents Accessed 26 December, 2022.

Npong, Francis. 2014. "Witch Camps of Ghana." Utne Reader (Winter): 48–49.

Nsehe, Mfonobong. 2011. "The Most Expensive Neighborhood in Nigeria." *Forbes* (May 4). http://www.forbes.com/sites/mfonobongnsehe/2011/05/04/the-most-expensive-neighborhood-in-nigeria/ Accessed April 16, 2015.

Nyamnjoh, Francis B. 2011. "Bushfalling: Negotiation of Identity and Belonging in Fiction and Ethnography." *American Ethnologist* 38, no. 4 (11 November): 701–713.

Oyono, Ferdinand. 1956. *Une vie de boy*. Paris: Juilliard.

Panzacchi, Cornelia. 1994. "The Livelihoods of Traditional Griots in Modern Senegal." *Africa* 64, no. 2: 190–210.

Pellegin, Arthur. 2014, May 27. "Qui Etait Paul Marty." http://rol-benzaken.centerblog.net/185.html. Accessed February 8, 2023.

"Philip D. Curtin." https://military-history.fandom.com/wiki/Philip_D._Curtin. See Murphy, John. "Senegal Slave House's past questioned", The Seattle Times, July 17, 2004. Accessed June 16, 2009.

Piot, Charles. 1999. *Remotely Global: Village Modernity in West Africa*. Chicago: University of Chicago Press.

Popescu, Monica. 2020. *At Penpoint*. Durham: Duke University Press.

Prince, Stephen. 2007. *American Cinema of the 1980s: Themes and Variations*. New Brunswick: Rutgers University Press.

"Rectificatif." Le Temps, no. 17676 (1909, November 19): 3. Cited in https://fr.wikipedia.org/wiki/Chocolat_(clown)#cite_note-Le_Temps_(1909d)-43

Reid, Mark. 1993. *Redefining Black Film*. Berkeley: University of California Press.

Rodney, Walter. 1989. *How Europe Underdeveloped Africa*. Nairobi: East African Educational Publishers.

Rovelli, Carlo. 2018. *The Order of Time*. New York: Riverhead Books.

Ruelle, Catherine and Reine Berthelot. "Sotigui Kouyaté raconté par son épouse Esther Marty-Kouyaté." http://lavoixdugriot.blogspot.com/2011/12/sotigui-kouyate-raconte-par-son-epouse.html Accessed December 17, 2022.

Sanders, Diane. 2001. "Chocolat." *Senses of Cinema* (November). http://sensesof cinema.com/2001/cteq/chocolat-2/ Accessed December 26, 2022.

"Saul Williams Biography." *IMDB*. https://www.imdb.com/name/nm0931654/bio?ref_=nm_ov_bio_sm Accessed December 26, 2022.

Sembène Ousmane. 1966. *Vehi Ciosane ou la blanche Genèse suivi du Mandat.* Présence Africaine.

Sene, Cheikh. 2022. "La Maison des esclaves de Goree: à l'intersection entre histoire, mémoires et émotions." *African Studies Review* 65, no. 2 (June): 354–371.

Senghor, Léopold Sédar, ed. 1948. *Anthologie de la nouvelle poésie nègre et malgache.* Paris: Présence Africaine.

Senghor, Leopold. 1975. "Harlem." In *The Negritude Poets: An Anthology of Translations from the French*, edited by Ellen Conroy Kennedy. New York: Thunder's Mouth Press.

"Si vous étiez une pâtisserie, laquelle seriez vous ? Et pourquoi ? (Faites moi rire !)" *Quora.* https://fr.quora.com/Si-vous-%C3%A9tiez-une-p%C3%A2tisserie-laq uelle-seriez-vous-Et-pourquoi-Faites-moi-rire Accessed December 26, 2022.

Simms-Greene, Lindsey. 2017. *Postcolonial Automobility: Car Culture in west Africa.* Minneapolis and London: University of Minnesota Press.

Simone, A. M. 2004. *For the City yet to Come: Changing African Life in Four Cities.* Durham: Duke University Press.

Simone, AbdouMaliq. 2001. "Ways of Seeing: Beyond the New Nativism." *African Studies Review* 44, no. 2 (September): 15–41. https://www.african.cam.ac.uk/images/files/articles/simone Accessed December 26, 2022.

Soyinka, Wole. 1975 (premiered 2002). *Death and the King's Horseman.* New York: Norton.

Stam, Robert. "Beyond Third Cinema: The Aesthetics of Hybridity." In *Rethinking Third Cinema*, edited by Anthony Guneratne and Wimal Dissanayake. London: Routledge.

Sullivan, Tim. 1998. "A Prison Sometimes a Haven: Ghana's Witch Villages Only Safe Place for Women Accused of Casting Spells." Associated Press. Rocky Mountain News (Denver, CO), 11 January. Archived from the original on 29 March 2015. Retrieved 21 November, 2014 – via HighBeam.

Swindell, Ken. 1994. "The Commercial Development of the North: Company and Government Relations, 1900–1906", *Paideuma* 40: 149–162.

"Technology of the New York City Subway" https://en.wikipedia.org/wiki/Tech nology_of_the_New_York_City_Subway Accessed December 26, 2022.

Todd, Andrew. 2010, May 2. "Sotigui Kouyate Obituary." https://www.theguard ian.com/stage/2010/may/02/sotigui-kouyate-obituary

Tompkins, Jane. 1977. "Reviewed Works: *The Melodramatic Imagination: Balzac, Henry James, Melodrama and the Mode of Excess,* by Peter Brooks; *Language and Knowledge in the Late Novels of Henry James,* by Ruth Bernard Yeazell." *Modern Fiction Studies* 23, no. 2 (Summer): 262–264.

Totaro, Donato. 1999. "Gilles Deleuze's Bersonian Film Project: Part 2." *Offscreen* (March). https://offscreen.com/view/bergson2 Accessed December 26, 2022.

"Tunde Kelani Launches Online TV Channel." *Asiri Magazine.* http://asirimaga zine.com/en/tunde-kelani-launches-online-tv-channel/ Accessed December 21, 2017.

Umez, Bedford Nwabueze. 2005. *Your Excellency.* Otsego, Michigan: Pagefree.

Vecchio, Marjorie. 2014. *The Films of Claire Denis: Intimacy on the Border.* New York: Palgrave Macmillian.

Wallerstein, Emmanuel. 1979. *The Capitalist World-Economy.* Cambridge: Cambridge University Press.

Wallerstein, Emmanuel. 2004. *World Systems Analysis.* Duke University Press.

Weheliye, Alexander. 2014. *Habeas Viscus.* Duke University Press.

Whitaker, Kati. 2012, 30 August. "Hundreds of Women Trapped in Ghana's 'Witch Camps." https://www.telegraph.co.uk/news/worldnews/africaandindian ocean/ghana/9509493/Hundreds-of-women-trapped-in-Ghanas-witch-camps. htmlTelegraph.co.uk.

"World Line." https://en.wikipedia.org/wiki/World_line Accessed December 26, 2022.

Wright, Michelle. 2015. *Physics of Blackness: Beyond the Middle Passage Epistemology.* Minneapolis: University of Minnesota Press.

Young, Crawford. 1994. *The African Colonial State in Comparative Perspective.* New Haven: Yale University Press.

Žižek, Slavoj, ed. 1992. *Everything You Always Wanted to Know about Lacan (But Were Afraid to Ask Hitchcock).* London and New York: Verso.

Žižek, Slavoj. 1999. *The Žižek Reader.* Edited by Elizabeth Wright and Edmond Wright. Maiden, Massachusetts: Blackwell.

Žižek, Slavoj. 1998 (1991). *Looking Awry.* Cambridge, MA, and London: MIT Press.

INDEX